The Portable Anaïs Nin

☙ THE PORTABLE ANAÏS NIN ❧

Compiled, introduced, and annotated by

Benjamin Franklin V

SKY BLUE PRESS
San Antonio, Texas

Published by:
Sky Blue Press
San Antonio, Texas

ISBN: 0-9774851-8-8
ISBN13: 978-0-9774851-8-5

Cover photo: Soichi Sunami

Library of Congress Cataloging-in-Publication Data

Nin, Anaïs, 1903-1977.
  [Selections. 2011]
  The portable Anais Nin / by Anais Nin ; compiled, introduced, and annotated by Benjamin Franklin V.
    p. cm.
ISBN 978-0-9774851-8-5 (pbk. : alk. paper)
I. Franklin, Benjamin, 1939- II. Title.
PS3527.I865A6 2011
 818'.52--dc22

                         2011017361

Second printing, 2015.

As always, to Jo, Abigail, Rebecca, Elizabeth, and Louisa

◌ৈ TABLE OF CONTENTS ⹂

❧ PREFACE ❧

The compelling reason behind the production of this book was noted some fifteen years ago by Gunther Stuhlmann, Anaïs Nin's literary agent and collaborator in the editing and publication of her famous diaries. Stuhlmann proposed a book that would, as he put it, "introduce a new generation of readers to *the writer* Anaïs Nin rather than to the 'personality' which has been distorted and denigrated in recent years... I visualize a handy volume which creates an overall view of the many facets of Nin's work and ideas by *drawing on her actual writing*." In other words, he imagined a sort of "autobiography" that included diary excerpts, critical writing, fiction, and other forms of Nin's writing organized in a way that would reveal her life as a *writer*. Stuhlmann's proposal was typed up, placed in a folder, and filed away under the title *The Portable Anaïs Nin*. Illness resulted in his untimely death in 2002, and the proposal remained unseen for several years.

A few years ago, Stuhlmann's wife, Barbara, found the folder and sent it to us, believing that it contained the seed of a valuable book. The late Rupert Pole, the Trustee of The Anaïs Nin Trust, backed the idea of a new anthology. Benjamin Franklin V, who has been at the forefront of Nin study for more than four decades, was the catalyst who made this book a reality. His selections and annotations fulfill and perhaps even surpass Stuhlmann's vision.

Franklin's philosophy of chronologically arranging diary passages, works of fiction, critical essays, and interviews *in their entirety* has resulted in a multi-layered book. On one level, there are representative excerpts from the best of Nin's writing; on another, there is a clear view of her growth as a writer, one whose life experiences and relationships recorded in her diary evolved into her fiction and overall writing theory; finally, readers new to Anaïs Nin will be enabled to make informed choices when further exploring her work.

The Portable Anaïs Nin, as Stuhlmann envisioned, is "an invitation to an engaging literary adventure trip, which could, and should, gain an entirely new audience for Anaïs Nin's work."

Paul Herron
Sky Blue Press

⊂ঽ INTRODUCTION ৩০

Anaïs Nin was never more popular than in the early and mid 1970s. After decades as an all-but-ignored fiction writer, she gained acclaim with the publication of the first volume of her diary in 1966. As more volumes appeared, her recognition increased, both because of the nature of the books and because their publication more-or-less coincided with the rise of second-wave feminism. Many readers viewed Nin as an idol, as the ultimate woman, as one who apparently succeeded in a man's world on her own terms. She lectured at colleges and universities, where her books were taught; was interviewed frequently; corresponded voluminously; wrote blurbs for and introductions to other writers' books. She received scholarly attention through articles and monographs. Her fame spread: her books were published in England, and elsewhere in translation. In 1973, the publisher of Nin's fiction, the Swallow Press in Chicago, acknowledged Nin's reputation by publishing *Anaïs Nin Reader*, which contains selections from Nin's published writings. By then, all the fiction Nin intended for publication had been published, as had her criticism; four volumes of the diary were in print. From this material, the editor of the *Reader*, Philip K. Jason, a major Nin scholar, made judicious selections. Since the publication of his book, however, the number of Nin titles has approximately doubled, with eleven new volumes of the diary and two books of erotica being most important. Now, the time seems right for another sampling of Nin's work, not only because of the existence of this new material or because almost forty years have passed since the publication of Jason's book, but also to encourage a reconsideration of Nin's writing, which no longer attracts the dedicated readership it did in 1973.

In 1914, at age eleven, Nin began keeping a diary as a letter to her father, who had abandoned the family; she continued it for the remainder of her life. From this enormous document, Harcourt ultimately published fifteen volumes, the first two in conjunction with the Denver publisher Alan Swallow. All are represented here by selections that present a complete event or scene. In these excerpts, Nin writes about family members, friends, analysis, sex, abortion, music, dancing, writing, and death, among other topics.

The diary occasionally presents two versions of events. This is so because sensitive material omitted from the first two volumes (1966, 1967) is included in the posthumously published diaries covering the years 1931-1939, books presented as "unexpurgated." These later books (*Henry and June* [1986], *Incest* [1992], *Fire* [1995], *Nearer the Moon* [1996] and *Mirages* [2013]) were published specifically to present the previously withheld material. For episodes published in substantially different forms, I use the "unexpurgated" versions. For example, I include a selection about Nin and June Miller (dated January 1932) from *Henry and June*, which mentions Nin's husband, Hugh Guiler, and her cousin, Eduardo Sánchez, instead of similar material (dated 31 December 1931) from *The Diary of Anaïs Nin, 1931-1934*, which does not refer to them.

The word "unexpurgated" suggests completeness, openness, frankness. Indeed, the four volumes of the diary so identified include graphic descriptions of the author's relationships, most notably with Henry Miller and Nin's father. Forthright though these revelations seem, they might not be as complete or accurate as "unexpurgated" implies. This possibility exists because, as biographer Deirdre Bair notes, in 1920 Nin "began a lifelong pattern: as she wrote new [diary entries], she constantly revised the old." Bair also observes that in the 1940s, Nin rewrote all the diaries, an action that constituted her "first consistent and complete reinvention of her past."[1] This is not to say, though, that the diaries—expurgated or unexpurgated—are untrue either in their general depictions of events or emotionally. Rewriting need not alter basic truths.

Two principles governed the selecting of fiction for this book: I wanted entire works or complete sections of books rather than a few pages from here and there, and I desired pieces that represent Nin at or near what I think is her best. *The House of Incest*, her first book of fiction, is, in my judgment, her most accomplished one, so I include it. How to represent Nin's erotica, written in the early 1940s but not published during Nin's lifetime? Because some of the diary selections included here have strong sexual content and I do not wish to overemphasize this aspect of Nin's work, I reproduce one of the shortest erotic stories, "Manuel." From the non-erotic short fiction, I include "Houseboat," the initial story in *Under a Glass Bell*, not only because of its position in the book, but also because it continues the theme of *House of Incest*, which is a major theme in her fiction generally: the impulse to live apart from reality leads to a living death and therefore must be resisted.[2] Inspired by the author's experiences on a houseboat on the Seine, the story illustrates Nin's use of diary material as a source for fiction. After "Lillian and Djuna" appeared in *This Hunger* (1945) and *Ladders to Fire* (1946), Nin changed its title to "This Hunger" when she published the second book in *Cities of the Interior* (1959). I include "This Hunger" because it is the first part of Nin's initial novel (*Ladders to Fire*) and because it primarily concerns Lillian, on whom Nin focuses at the end of *Seduction of the Minotaur* (1961), which concludes Nin's continuous novel.[3] Lillian frames the whole. Like

"Lillian and Djuna"/"This Hunger," "Stella" appeared in *This Hunger* and *Ladders to Fire* (as the first part) before being repositioned. In 1961, Nin placed it in *Winter of Artifice*, where it remains. I intend "Stella" to serve as an example of a Nin novella.

Nin wrote non-fiction prose of a critical nature. Her two earliest mature publications focus on D. H. Lawrence: a 1930 article in *Canadian Forum*, where she uses the pseudonym Melisendra, and *D. H. Lawrence: An Unprofessional Study* (1932). Later, she addressed issues relating to the writing of fiction in the essays *Realism and Reality* (1946) and *On Writing* (1947) and discussed contemporary authors in *The Novel of the Future* (1968). Here, I represent this aspect of Nin's writing with the two essays published in the mid 1940s because they express, succinctly, her literary attitudes at the beginning of her career as a novelist.

During the last decade of her life, Nin was interviewed many times, and interviews were published in such places as *Mademoiselle*, *Vogue*, *The Los Angeles Times*, *The San Francisco Chronicle*, and *Chicago Review*. Wendy M. DuBow collected some of them in *Conversations with Anaïs Nin* (1994). Nin's comments about writing make the interview included here, conducted by Duane Schneider and absent from DuBow's book, particularly valuable.

Before each selection, I provide its *Context* or indicate its subject. Following almost every non-fiction selection, I identify people, publications, and artistic works to which Nin refers. Treating such information in a paragraph avoids the cumbersomeness of using many footnotes in short selections. Also with the non-fiction, I translate words, phrases, and sentences that are written in languages other than English, with the exception of those commonly understood and, usually, those for which Nin's texts provide translations. In my comments about the non-fiction, I include diacritical markings when called for (as with Joaquín), though—believing in the sanctity of the text—I do not add diacritics to Nin's texts (Joaquin).

I use the text of the last American edition of works published during the author's lifetime because it presumably represents Nin's final textual preferences.[4] Two selections, the prologue to *Ladders to Fire* (1963) and the preface to *Under a Glass Bell* (1968), were published only in England. I use the 1968 version of the latter because while it was edited for inclusion in the collection published by Penguin in 1978, I cannot determine if Nin, who died in 1977, made the changes. With works published posthumously, I use the first editions.

In his *Reader*, Jason provides a section of Nin's fiction and another of non-fiction. With a few exceptions, I arrange the contents of this book chronologically, regardless of genre, from a 1915 diary entry about Nin's parents to one about death (1975-1976). (Dates Nin gives to diary entries might not always be accurate.) Such an arrangement permits the charting of Nin's interests and attitudes, themes and techniques, from age twelve to her early seventies. The exceptions are these: with "Manuel," I add two comments Nin composed about writing erotica, one from near the end of her life; with "Houseboat," I provide Nin's statements from 1944 and 1968 about *Under a Glass Bell*, of which "Houseboat" became a part; with "This Hunger," I include Nin's 1946 and 1963 prologues to *Ladders to Fire*, as well as the 1974 preface to *Cities of the Interior*, because they deal with Nin's continuous novel, which "This Hunger" introduces.

With pleasure, I acknowledge the assistance of Marilee Birchfield, Karen Brown, Mary Bull, Paul J. Cammarata, John Carter, Gerri C. Corson, Jo Cottingham, Judith T. Dent, Melinda Droulia, Amy Edwards, Jeanne M. Garane, Joshua B. Garris, Rebecca B. Gettys, Betty J. Glass, Lauren Glover, Donald J. Greiner, Paul Herron, Craig Keeney, Thomas A. Marcil, Patti J. Marinelli, Adrian Massey, Anthony D. McKissick, Lucille P. Mould, Francess Murray, Robert W. Newcomb, Scott Phinney, Duane Schneider, Matt Steinmetz, Barbara Stuhlmann, Jacquelyn K. Sundstrand, René Tanner, Sharon Verba, Virginia Weathers, Judy Wilson, Andrea Wright, and the Anaïs Nin Trust.

Benjamin Franklin V
University of South Carolina

Notes

1 Deirdre Bair, *Anaïs Nin: A Biography* (New York: Putnam's, 1995), 76, 279.

2 For vague, unconvincing reasons, Gunther Stuhlmann, Nin's agent, rearranged the contents of *Under a Glass Bell* in 1995, despite Nin's long-held belief that her sequence of stories was as she desired it. At the time of this writing, 2010, Stuhlmann's arrangement of the stories, which places "The Labyrinth" first, remains in print with Swallow Press/Ohio University Press. For a discussion of the positioning of stories in Nin's collection, see Benjamin Franklin V, "Noli Me Tangere: The Structure of Anaïs Nin's *Under a Glass Bell*," *Studies in Short Fiction* 34 (Fall 1997): 459-79. "Houseboat" is the only work present in both Jason's *Reader* and this book; although the earlier volume includes excerpts from *House of Incest*, the prose poem is published here in complete form.

3 Nin's continuous novel includes *Ladders to Fire* (1946), *Children of the Albatross* (1947), *The Four-Chambered Heart* (1950), *A Spy in the House of Love* (1954), and *Seduction of the Minotaur* (1961). The final novel was originally *Solar Barque* (1958), the text of which Nin expanded and titled *Seduction of the Minotaur*. She published the novels in one volume as *Cities of the Interior* in 1959, with *Solar Barque* as the last novel, and again in 1974, with *Seduction of the Minotaur* replacing *Solar Barque*.

4 To identify various editions of Nin's books published during the author's lifetime, see Franklin, *Anaïs Nin Character Dictionary and Index to Diary Excerpts* (Troy, MI: Sky Blue Press, 2009), 62-65.

❧ BIOGRAPHICAL SKETCHES ❧

In order to avoid redundancy in the paragraphs following selections from Nin's non-fiction, I characterize here all the people and three places mentioned multiple times in it and in my comments about it. At the appropriate places, I identify people mentioned only once.

René Allendy (1889-1942) was a psychoanalyst who treated Nin, Hugh Guiler, and Eduardo Sánchez. He and Nin had an affair.

Antonin Artaud (1896-1948), a French writer and surrealist, is perhaps best known for his concept of the theater of cruelty; an actor, he performed in the films *Napoléon* (1927) and *La Passion de Jeanne d'Arc* (1928).

Clichy is a suburb of Paris.

Lawrence Durrell (1912-1990) moved to Paris from Corfu to be with Henry Miller, an author he admired; they and Nin referred to themselves as "the three musqueteers." Durrell is probably best known as the author of *The Alexandria Quartet*, which is comprised of *Justine* (1957), *Balthazar* (1958), *Mountolive* (1958), and *Clea* (1960).

John Erskine (1879-1951) taught literature at Columbia University, where Hugh Guiler was one of his students; his many books include *The Private Life of Helen of Troy* (1925).

Oliver Evans (1915-1981) wrote the first scholarly book about Nin, *Anaïs Nin* (1968).

Manuel de Falla (1876-1946) was a Spanish composer who taught Joaquín Nin-Culmell. *El Amor Brujo* (1915) is one of his notable compositions.

Michael Fraenkel (1896-1957), born in Lithuania, wrote about death in such works as *Bastard Death* (1936) and *Death Is not Enough* (1962). He helped establish the Carrefour Press and Siana Editions, both in Paris.

Enrique Granados (1867-1916) was a Spanish composer and pianist who established the Catalan tradition of piano playing, founded the Granados Academy in Barcelona, and influenced Manuel de Falla. As a composer, he is best known for his suite *Goyescas* (1911).

Eugene Graves, a college friend of Hugh Guiler, impressed Nin with his intelligence.

Hugh (Hugo) Guiler (1898-1985), a banker, was married to Nin from 1923 until her death in 1977. As Ian Hugo, he was a filmmaker (Nin performs in some of his films) and engraver (his engravings appear in several of Nin's books).

Helba Huara, a dancer from Peru, appeared in the musical revue *A Night in Spain* in New York (1927). She was the mother of the painter Elsa Henriquez (1926-) and the wife of Gonzalo Moré, Nin's lover.

James Joyce (1892-1941), author of *A Portrait of the Artist as a Young Man* (1916), *Ulysses* (1922), and *Finnegan's Wake* (1939), was one of the major modern novelists.

D. H. Lawrence (1885-1930), British novelist, influenced Nin and was the subject of her first book. Among his novels are *Women in Love* (1921) and *Lady Chatterley's Lover* (1928).

Louveciennes is the Paris suburb where, in the 1930s, Nin lived with her husband, mother, and younger brother.

Richard F. Maynard (1875-1964) was a sculptor and portraitist who used Nin as a subject.

Barbara Miller (1919-1986) was the daughter of Henry Miller and Beatrice Miller.

Beatrice Sylvas Wickens Miller (1892-1984) was the first wife of Henry Miller.

Henry Miller (1891-1980) was an aspiring novelist when Nin met him in Paris. She details their affair in *Henry and June* (1986), which was made into a movie in 1990. She wrote the preface to and financed the publication of *Tropic of Cancer* (1934), Miller's first novel; he dedicated his second one, *Black Spring* (1936), to her.

June Mansfield Miller (1902-1979) was the second wife of Henry Miller; she and Nin were attracted to each other to the degree that they fondled each other and kissed.

Gonzalo Moré (1897-1966) was a Peruvian Marxist who met Nin in Paris and became her lover. He was married to Helba Huara. To him, Nin dedicated *Under a Glass Bell and Other Stories* (1948).

Joaquín (Father, Papa) Nin (1879-1949), composer and pianist, was the father of Nin and two sons. In 1933, he and his daughter had an affair, mainly in Valescure, France.

María Luísa (Maruca) Rodríguez de Nin was a childhood friend of Nin; she studied piano with Joaquín Nin and married him, becoming his second wife and Anaïs Nin's step-mother.

Rosa (Maman, Mother) Culmell de Nin (1871-1954) was the mother of Nin and two sons. Deserted by her husband, Joaquín Nin, she took her children to the United States in 1914.

Thorvald Nin (1905-1991), the older of Nin's brothers, became a businessman.

Joaquín Nin-Culmell (1908-2004), the younger of Nin's brothers, adopted the name Nin-Culmell to distinguish himself from his father. He became a pianist, composer, and teacher.

Alfred Perlès (1897-1991) was the roommate of Henry Miller; they worked as proofreaders at the Paris edition of the *Chicago Tribune.*

Marcel Proust (1871-1922) wrote the revolutionary and influential novel *À la recherche du temps perdu* (*In Search of Lost Time*) (1913-1927).

Samuel Putnam (1892-1950) edited the *New Review* in 1931 and 1932, first in Paris and then in Mirmande, France. He wrote *Paris Was Our Mistress: Memoirs of a Lost & Found Generation* (1947) and translated *Don Quixote* (1949).

Otto Rank (1884-1939) was Nin's second psychoanalyst and the second with whom she had an affair.

Richmond Hill (Queens), New York, is where Nin lived with her mother and brothers from 1919 until her 1923 marriage to Hugh Guiler.

Eduardo Sánchez (1904-1990) was a cousin of Nin for whom she had deep feelings, including erotic ones, despite his homosexuality.

George Sand was the nom de plume of Amantine Aurore Lucile Dupin (1804-1876), a voluminous French writer (*La Mare au diable* [1846] and many other novels) and rebel who is perhaps best known for her romantic affairs.

Gunther Stuhlmann (1927-2002), Nin's literary agent for many years, helped her edit her diary.

Alan Swallow (1915-1966) began publishing Nin's books in 1961. In time, he published all her available fiction, in addition to *D. H. Lawrence: An Unprofessional Study* (1964) and, with Harcourt, Brace & World, the first two volumes of *The Diary of Anaïs Nin* (1966, 1967).

Princess Natasha Troubetskoia was a Russian painter in Paris for whom Nin sat and whose apartment Nin sometimes used for assignations.

Mark Twain was the nom de plume of Samuel Langhorne Clemens (1835-1910), author of classic stories and novels, including "The Celebrated Jumping Frog of Calaveras County" (1865) and *Adventures of Huckleberry Finn* (1884).

Edmund Wilson (1895-1972), possibly the major twentieth-century American man of letters, reviewed Nin's *Under a Glass Bell*, *This Hunger*, and *Ladders to Fire* in *The New Yorker*. He and Nin had a brief affair that was unrelated to their professional relationship.

Émile Zola (1840-1902) was a French author whose many books include the naturalistic novel *Nana* (1880).

ℭ *LINOTTE* ℬ

(22 September-[?] October 1915)
On Maman and Papa

Context

Following the 1913 desertion of his family by Joaquín Nin, Rosa Culmell de Nin moved with their children to the apartment of his parents in Barcelona. The next year, she took the children to New York. In July 1914, eleven-year-old Anaïs Nin wrote her first diary entry. Fourteen months later, she reflected on her parents and her love for them, as well as on the nature of marriage generally and the horrors of divorce. Divorce papers were delivered to her mother in 1924. Nin's comments about marriage assume significance in the *Context* of her marriage to Hugh Guiler.

◆ ◆ ◆ ◆

September 22, 1915. I am sitting on the grass with my eyes half-closed, thinking of Papa, of the war. I have been reliving my life from the earliest days I can remember. Then, as in a dream, I saw myself grown up. Writing stories, with Papa and Maman nearby, it seemed as though I saw the sea in front of me. The waves rocked me gently as I described my impressions to Papa and Maman. Suddenly I arose and it seemed to me I said, How I love you, Papa and Maman. And I heard a murmured answer, Together. But the wind rose, the trees bent, and among the whirlwinds of dead leaves, I saw the sky suddenly darken. Then a sharp pain went through me. The leaves were my dream, a gust of wind. Reality swept them up and carried them far, far away so that I shall never see them and the blue sky of my dreams became the dark sky of the truth, yes, the truth. Papa wasn't with me. Why? It seemed as though I wept inside and I held my head in my hand. My mind could hardly resist the tempest that assailed it. Yes, and among the angry waves an everlasting Why? kept repeating. Why? Why? I tell myself there is a simple reason. Papa's work keeps him in Paris. He doesn't come here because he has nothing to do here. He is waiting for us in Paris. My heart leaped and said, No, no, but didn't say why. One day I shall know why. But my heart, which is never wrong, said no to that natural response.

October [?]. I am in Central Park. It is a beautiful day, but since I started school the sun is less bright. With little cries of distress, the birds huddle before the first winter wind. The trees lose their leaves and the yellow leaves soar into space and whirl in every direction before fleeing on a last gust of wind. People who go for a walk hurry back home immediately with their hands in their pockets, saying, It is cold today, I have to put on my big coat, the winter comes too early. Yes, especially for me, winter has come too early. The wind has carried away all my dreams, those that I believed were real. A veil has been torn away from my heart and again I must say, Papa won't come. Why not? Today I think I have the answer, and this mournful phrase constantly runs through my head and wounds me: Papa is angry with Maman. Suddenly, various pictures come to my unhappy mind. Papa was severe, and often Maman tried to intervene. They have two different personalities, they weren't meant for each other and that has separated them. That and a thousand things that I didn't understand now are clear to me. And I forgive Maman for having led us along so as not to spoil our childhood. But now, little by little, with God's help, I have come to understand; the truth is more painful, more terrible, and more so since I was not prepared for it. The trip to Spain to visit Grandmother was a partial separation. That rekindles a hope in me of seeing Papa and Maman together again before I leave this unjust world.

Could the parting be my fault? Must I go on living as a witness to the separation of the two people that I love most in the world? Oh, my confidant, what it costs me to admit that! To tell the truth, if I haven't opened your pages for a long time, it was because I knew I had to make this painful confession. My mind was asleep, I didn't want to see it, and today, yes, in spite of myself... It's too much, too much! God has struck me in my weakest spot. He has struck those I love. I bless Him, may His will be done, but I still have my diary and I can pour out my sorrow. A mother's caress cannot console my broken heart. I need the union of the two.

Right now, I envy the poor man with no coat, no food, but let our family and our home be as solid as a rock, made by God's hand, that nothing can dissolve or break apart! Such families are fortunate, but unfortunate are those that the world can separate.

People want to renounce God's commandments, they want to improve on them, and what is the result? What has become of the sacred union of man and woman? A violent union seen as a game of dolls, a doll marriage that can be broken whenever they please, as in a game. The name of this disgrace is divorce. How can the tree be cut off from its roots? The tree, the leaves will die. One cannot live without the other. How then can one separate two lives that are interwoven, two who have shared the same breath? The two will perish miserably without happiness, like the tree without its root. Modern marriage has become like everything else these days, madness, frivolity, ostentation and the intoxication of eternal youth, and the result is, old, young, and middle-aged are all children, thoughtless people, guided only by their natural impulses, the passion God has given us, not so that we may give in to it, but that we may earn the promised reward by subduing it and going counter to it.

But it isn't just the parents who are made unhappy by divorce. What happens to the children? Shall I finally be one of those children? What a terrible uncertainty. Oh, no, it is bad enough that Papa and Maman should be angry, but who says it must come to divorce? I can't think of it without trembling. I imagine my hurt, and if it should happen, I know I would no longer have the strength to smile, and I could say, of all the bad things in the world, divorce is the worst.

One day I will know whether what I have written today is true. But please God may that day never come and may our family never die, that is, never be shattered!

Now I am calmer. I have reread these last pages and I think that if, one day when I am gone, someone reads them (with an indiscretion that I forgive in advance), he will say, The child must have read that somewhere, to write about divorce as she does. No. In spite of my age, I know life and I can judge people at first glance. I have one example as my measuring stick and that is my ideas, my impressions, if you prefer. Try to find a book these days that speaks ill of divorce.

Notes

Text: *Linotte: The Early Diary of Anaïs Nin, 1914-1920*, translated by Jean L. Sherman (New York: Harcourt Brace Jovanovich, 1978), 84-86.

Papa is Joaquín Nin; Maman is Rosa Culmell de Nin; Grandmother is Angela Castellanos de Nin, the mother of Joaquín Nin; "my confidant" is Nin's diary.

␣ *EARLY DIARY 2* ␣

Context

Here, Nin details early impressions of Hugh Guiler. They met in Richmond Hill in March 1921 and were married in Havana two years later.

◆ ◆ ◆ ◆

July 17, 1921. Yesterday I watched the road for hours, expecting Hugo, but he did not pass, and when the evening came I sat on the porch thinking of him while Mother, Belica and her friend Mr. Hernandez talked, and suddenly I heard him calling me from the garden. He had come with a friend, Mr. Hazin, to invite me to the moving pictures. Thus again we almost forgot where we were and whispered. Hugo made me laugh often, I who thought myself so hopelessly serious. And there we sat in the open air, under the sky, very far away from the story of troubles, hatred and profane love unfolding before us, although now and then Hugo would pretend to be ashamed and sit tense and rigid and silent, trying to appear interested in the story—in vain. You see, we ourselves were building up a story much more to our liking, the story of our friendship, which seems to grow every minute we are together, and those minutes are scarce indeed, but we make the most of them. Later, Hugo accepted refreshments, and we offered him among other things a piece of chocolate cake which I had made. I gave him Musset's poems to read and my notebooks with extracts from my readings, and I returned regretfully Erskine's *Essays*. I do believe that it is time for me to describe Hugo as well as I can so that you may know as much of him as I do; and not so much by being with him do I know him, as by *intuition*.

Hugo is very tall, of slight build and perfect symmetry. My first impression of him, the night of his dance, was that he possessed the ease and grace belonging to the gentleman, mingled with great simplicity and frankness, the touchstone of his character, I was afterward to find out. His face is oval, the oval of the idealist and the dreamer; his features very regular and clearly defined. All his strength lies in his broad forehead, in his intelligent, clear and expressive eyes. His lips are delicate and sensitive, but firmly, resolutely controlled. The nostrils are delicately chiseled, tender, mobile, but the chin is strong and firm. This ensemble is characteristic of his nature—that mixture of strength and decision with feeling and depth and tenderness. I see goodness, sincerity and genuineness in his smile, which is open, frank and simple. I see kindness and understanding and delicacy in his eyes, and concentrated thought and wisdom are stamped on his forehead.

And not a gesture that is not spontaneous and natural, not a word that does not come from the heart. Outwardly he is all manliness, splendid, resolute. Inwardly he has the poet's wondrous fancies, balanced judgment, clear perceptions, practicability and wisdom. And then, as far as I can see, unselfishness, not a trace of egoism or conceit. His flashes of humor, his quiet optimism and yet keen understanding of the pathetic, his confidence and trust in people, his love of nature and music and poetry, his idealism, make of Hugo's character a thing incredibly harmonious and complete.

I can compare him with no one. Eduardo was my equal; he was younger and not half as strong and firm of purpose. Although it seems strange that I should say this, that I should think Hugo greater and finer than all my friends when in reality I have seen little of him. I seem to have known Hugo a long time, although I never dreamed of one who could possess at once all the best and finest qualities and those I most prize.

This morning Hugo telephoned to arrange a game of tennis with Thorvald next Saturday, then he asked for me and told me he did not think he would see me today, as the Parkers had company. I asked him if he had read a little of my notebook.

"I read it all."

"Did you like many things in it?"

"I liked *everything.*"

"Even my own criticisms?"

And he answered, "They were the best of all."

It seems, too, that we may go out during the week, and later Hugo wants me to meet his best friend, Eugene Graves, who loves what we love, and perhaps more devotedly, because he does not share his heart with other things; he is fond of solitude, of the hermit's life, and is said to be unsociable, according to the standards of the world. Hugo believes him a genius.

Oh, that the world were filled with friends like these! And yet the very rarity of reasonable conversation, of spiritual relationships, makes them dearer and sweeter when they come to us. One of my fondest dreams is to find myself someday in a home with a husband and children, and with friends with whom one can share the love of books and music, talented, intellectual friends, not gossipers, vain women and idle men, social butterflies expecting to be amused, unable to think or to speak their thoughts and whose purpose in life is to fill the hour, caring not a whit whether they are accomplishing *something*, helping someone, embellishing the world or serving humanity. Here I have spoken of two kinds of people, those I admire, those I abhor. And I know that I am in the right; I know that my choice is made forever, that I will remain unchanged through the years—for this worship of mine for the things of the mind is rooted within my very nature.

Evening. I have come to the end of another volume. My last words to each one are usually of thoughts that come to me as I look back. But tonight my heart holds naught but thankfulness—as it did once before, upon musing on all the good that comes to me.

Above all things, my thoughts are with Hugo, and I am thankful that he has come into my life. It is an Ideal that has come to life, a breathing, living dream, and it all happened because I believed, trusted and hoped.

Notes

Text: *The Early Diary of Anaïs Nin, Volume Two, 1920-1923* (New York: Harcourt Brace Jovanovich, 1982), 244-46.

Hugo is Hugh Guiler. Mother is Rosa Culmell de Nin. Belica is Belica Tallet, a friend of Nin. I cannot identify Mr. Hernandez or Mr. Hazin. The French novelist, poet, and playwright Alfred de Musset (1810-1857) is perhaps best known for *La Confession d'un enfant du siècle* (1835), a fictionalized account of his affair with George Sand. Volumes of John Erskine's essays include The *Kinds of Poetry* (1920) and *The Moral Obligation to Be Intelligent* (1921). Eduardo is Eduardo Sánchez; Thorvald is Thorvald Nin. The Parkers are the family of Guiler's mother.

⚝ *EARLY DIARY 3* ⚝

(19 January 1925)
Early marital crisis

Context

When National City Bank transferred Hugh Guiler from New York to Paris, he and Nin moved there in December 1924. Writing a month later, Nin reflects on her first marital crisis, precipitated by fearing, in New York, that her husband's American colleagues would somehow compromise Guiler's basic character when the spouses were apart. Married fewer than two years, Nin remains fearful when confronted with a similar situation in Paris. She wants Guiler to remain pure, unlike her father, whom she found morally corrupt when with him a few weeks earlier.

◆ ◆ ◆ ◆

January 19, 1925. My Love and I have passed through the first crisis of our marriage—passed triumphantly. But forever after I shall never be at rest—the fear has come too close to me, and I am a fatalist. I trust him, I believe him, but I mistrust and dread influences beyond him, the world. The very beginning of it (I promised then to write of it) was in New York. Hugh was invited out, for the first time without me, by S. from the bank, to a party of men. It was when we were in the rented room on 75th Street. I was, in reality as well as mentally, completely alone that night. I went to bed and tried to read. The minutes were maddeningly long. At eight o'clock I noted that he would be sitting down to the dinner. At nine o'clock, that he must be finished... Then my agony began, for I did not know what he was to do afterwards, and I was fearful and horribly jealous, jealous of those men, whom I knew to be so inferior to Hugh, so unlike him, so hateful, jealous of what they might teach him, what they might show him—fearful that he would return to me sullied, changed, even if vaguely, by an experience I had no share in. My imagination was working with all its usual fire and wildness. I cried bitterly, I paced the room, I wrote about other things, those furthest from my thoughts. Twice during the evening the telephone rang, but I was too terrified by my physical loneliness to answer it. At ten o'clock he came. He was more loving than he had ever been. He told me he had missed me, that he had not enjoyed himself at all, and had telephoned me twice. Finally, it seemed that he had even left them to do whatever they pleased, to come back to me. I was happy. I loved him more. I almost forgot all about the incident and our love continued untroubled by doubt and fear.

But now in Paris, I have to face a stranger thing. Hugh's work entails more sociability, and C., one of the men with whom it is important to maintain friendliness, is among the most detestable I have met in that respect. He invites Hugh to extravagant lunches, urges him to belong to clubs, and finally, on Sunday, he invited us both to a tea to meet his wife.

The tea took place in a luxurious hotel. Besides his wife, a small, pretty woman, we met a painter and his wife—a most curious combination of Breton and Hindu, who entertained us continuously with her untiring egoism, so that by the end of the afternoon I knew her life, her feelings, her soul, her ambitions—everything. During the one moment that she left us, to call up a friend, C.'s wife turned to me and we had a curious talk. Her husband never comes home to lunch and seldom to dinner. He is out continuously without her.

"And what do you do meanwhile?" I asked, profoundly troubled.

"I go out, too," she answered me, without the least satisfaction; rather, I thought, very sadly. This, with a few lingering, reproachful glances at her husband, who was talking with the painter, showed me her unhappiness. She asked me about Hugh and was surprised when I told her how seldom he stayed away for lunch—and the two times he did were because of her husband. Instantly she feared for my happiness. She warned me unselfishly not to let C. put ideas into Hugh's head, not to let Hugh fall into a terrible habit. While we were talking, the painter was inviting C. and Hugh to come and visit his studio. Hugh naively never doubted that I was included, but I, with premonition, managed to whisper to him: "Dear, I do not think he means me to come."

The surprise on Hugh's face made my heart leap. He turned to C. and asked him jokingly if "the wives are in on this." C. seriously said, "No, indeed, there I draw the line."

I shivered with a new feeling of iciness, as if I had received a mortal wound. The tea was over. Hugh and I went out into the fog and jumped on a shadowy bus, and we talked. He did not realize that the apparently meaningless initiation called for an important decision. I did, with a surer instinct than his. I told him that, if he accepted this, he would accept everything. C. would see that Hugh was willing to go out without me, and before he realized it, he would be floating down the selfsame stream.

I was fighting, like the most primitive woman, for the life of our love, for his purity, for our ideals of unity and loyalty, fighting to keep him from everything that a man like C. stands for, and I fought with every wile and trick and arm in my possession. I triumphed. I kept him—but I lost peace and security. I am tormented now by new fears, alarmed by new dangers. There is not a moment that I do not think: He is mine today, but tomorrow?... I want to grow accustomed to the thought of losing him someday, because I am too fatalistic to believe that we can always be as happy together as we are now. I want to face the very worst ways of losing him—to men, to their coarser companionship, to drink or to another woman. How horrible these things sound, how monstrous—how unlike Hugh, with his clear eyes, the goodness and kindness which emanates from him, Hugh with his loyal smile, his deep love.

My love for him is tyrannical because it is ideal, because I love his soul, his thoughts, because I could no more bear the sullying of his body than of his mind. I want not only his love but his ideal self preserved, stainless.

It is with the same puritanical soul that I look on my father as egotistical, untrue to the very core. He lies to me so much, in order to create a certain effect on me, in order to be for me something which he is not in reality, that I cannot love him. He is at heart cold and moved only by what affects him directly—his happiness and his comfort. I fear for the happiness of the Little Lady—she must be selfless and wonderfully devoted. Of course, she is his disciple, in piano as well as in life, and believes all he is. And yet, she is so true herself.

I wait for circumstances to separate us. I am cowardly in front of him. I do not want to hurt him, and yet all I can say to him, if I ever do say it, is: "I do not want to see you anymore because I do not love you and I am not interested in you."

Hugh, who is so good, cannot understand that I detest in Father things which I have spent my life destroying in myself. He cannot see that Father's traits were in my blood, that I knew them deeply, that I willfully and consciously crushed them out of my character. And what a struggle I endured.

Now when I see him, the embodiment of falsity, of selfishness, the depths of which I have sounded, I see him more clearly than anyone else could. He poses, he affects weariness, affection, he lies whenever he can glorify himself, he boasts of his charity; with false modesty he pretends to look down on his work. With him I am unhappy. The atmosphere is false, vicious and, in a subtle way, degrading. He is everything I struggled not to be. I feel him laughing at Hugh's candor. I know what he would think of Richard M., of Johnnie, of Eugene, even. In some way he would not respect the *sacredness* of my life—and there are many things which, with all his intelligence, he will never understand.

I think Mother was right when she begged us, illogically enough, not to see Father.

"You are too *good*, too *good*, Thorvald, Hugh and you, to *understand why*!" She was explaining with her *feelings*, her *instincts*, and at the time Thorvald, Hugh and I were not impressed because we wanted a logical explanation. But I think I realize now what she felt—the abyss between his ideals and ours— the bottomless abyss which it is useless to try and span.

It is with a mother's illogical relief that I saw Thorvald go away. I felt that away from Father he was secure. I am glad that I am left alone with the Problem. Alone, yes, because not even Hugh can understand my instinctive dislike, and I would not want him to understand.

Notes

Text: *The Early Diary of Anaïs Nin, Volume Three, 1923-1927* (San Diego: Harcourt Brace Jovanovich, 1983), 92-95.

Hugh is Hugh Guiler. "Little Lady" is María Luísa (Maruca) Rodríguez de Nin. Richard M. is Richard F. Maynard; Johnnie is John Guiler (b. ca. 1901), brother of Hugh. Eugene is Eugene Graves. Mother is Rosa Culmell de Nin; Father is Joaquín Nin. Thorvald is Thorvald Nin.

such a cerebral..." And I, such an "imaginative..." that my conception of what the moment *should* be, what it would seem to him afterward, in retrospect, and to me, crushes me.

Little by little, I came out of all these states: physical ecstasy, mental turmoil, sadness, and joy. John being away for two days, I talked to him only here, and dreamed. The senses grew calm, and my head clear.

I have only a painful, profound, absolute need of seeing him again once before he goes to New York. I know now the whole thing will mean more to me than to him, because I am made that way, because I am a bottomless well, full of echoes and re-echoes, unsoundable.

It was Thursday evening at Mother's, for the playing of Joaquin's Trio, that he finally felt attracted. The week before, we had had a long talk. He knew then what I didn't know, that he wanted to kiss me. Thursday night I apparently looked better than usual. I was aglow with the excitement of my "theatre engagement." Our eyes met during the music with an alarmingly personal brilliance; we didn't know what the other was thinking, but, whatever it was, it was for no one else in the room.

I felt his excitement Friday. We had only talked an hour. I had an engagement. I put on my jade-green cape and gave him his copy of *Uncle Sam*; he was standing up and watching me. I went to the desk to get my key, feeling nervous and upset. When he walked toward me I knew instantly what was going to happen. His grip on my shoulders was very strong. I had my back turned to him at the moment; he turned me toward him and bent over me. All I had was a blind surging up of all my being to him, a desire to drink, to absorb him. His tongue in my mouth seemed like his very own flesh penetrating me. It was a long kiss—strong, possessive, absolute. And that was all that counted—the rest, his words, mine, his reluctance to go away, my calling up to break my engagement, the other hour and a half we spent together, were misty and unsatisfactory. I couldn't tell whether he was talking about indifferent things to cover a feeling or because the feeling was gone. I was surprised because when I called up about my engagement, he said, "I'm glad to see you have trouble with the telephone too—I was always afraid it was due to my bad French." A plain little sentence. But wasn't I saying them too, to cover the turmoil. Silly things. Things I didn't mean. And I was annoyed because my hands were ice-cold; he had never seen this happen to anyone and he teased me about it, and I showed him how they grew warm again when we talked about philosophy!

He should not have stayed so long. I wanted to be alone, to gather myself up and all my poor scattered feelings. And what depression afterward—

always, after small excitements, after music, dinners, evenings out, talk, and doubly so after that afternoon—a terrible depression. A bad night—fitful, dreamful, and a sudden realization that Thursday night I had *dreamed* that John kissed me, dreamed all that did happen. Visible signs of a strange destiny overpowering me. Yet I want to be wise, rational, and John would be the first to laugh at all this, if I told him.

The next morning, Saturday, I was restless, moving endlessly about the house, making desperate efforts to write a coherent letter to Lorraine [Maynard]. When the telephone rang my heart gave such a jump that I couldn't answer it at first. When I did, in a deep voice, John asked if we could play tennis with him Sunday morning.

Today on the tennis court, though, I couldn't rest from thoughts of John for a second. But with my racket in hand, hitting hard balls, smelling the flowers, and being burned by the blessed sun, I felt very courageous and very strong and very woman and shouted defiantly to my great man: "Oh, I'll get over your kiss."

I know how insincere I am, because if he came in this minute and said again what I *didn't believe* the other day, "I love Lilith and *you*, too," in a tone that would convince me, I wouldn't try any more to cure myself, but would make a permanent place in my life for it.

May 21. I am so conscious of the wonder of life that when Lorraine writes me a letter in which regret and inertia show clearly, I take an hour off to write her a long comforting letter, trying not only to inject my own enthusiasm into her but to communicate to her my own life, so as to carry her up in it— though I can't tell her what is really happening, because it would break up her ideal world. And in the end I tell her, so she won't be sad, that she carries the most precious of all worlds within herself in her writing, because now I know *this is true*. All the madness and turmoil of these last days disappeared last night after I had written. I kept only the most supernatural ecstasy and sense of enrichment. In John, the kiss might be dissolved by other incidents, but I possess it now until I die, buried deep within me, fixed, imprisoned; and I can live it over again as often as I desire.

May 23. He came while I was out this afternoon, and I went out because I couldn't face the possible disappointment of his not coming; we had made no appointment. But it was his first day back from Bordeaux.

In the taxi, driving home at a furious pace, nearly met annihilation, and for a second I *desired* it. Because I am always afraid when I have reached a peak of life, of its being the highest and the last.

May 25. Formal dinner given by John for some of his friends at Laperouse. When he offered his arm to me, he pressed mine hard and I responded. I who had come all in white, in a quiet mood outwardly, felt my restraint broken and madness again holding me. At the table he drank to me directly. After dinner, which seemed interminable, he insisted on being taken home by us though there was no room in the car. I realized suddenly he was burning up, as I was. I would have liked to feel his forehead, his heart.

In his apartment, we talked; he read to us from *The Sleeping Beauty*. Pauline and Graham were falling asleep. Hugh and I prepared to leave. "I'll go with you," said John. Pauline left the room angrily. It was half past twelve. In the car, on the way over, John pressed my knee in his hand. I sat close to him. I could feel his excitement and he, mine. We came up to the apartment. I opened the door to the balcony and suggested we sit there. There was a full moon. We put the lights out.

Hugh went to the kitchen to get something to drink. John and I stood there, facing each other, tendue par un désir affolant [taut with mad desire]. Yet we had to sit there, talking, only looking at each other, and twice I thought that in front of Hugh he would kiss me as he did the other night, and that all my life would explode. Looking at me, into me, he said he had not slept for several nights. I had a desperate desire to be tender to him, to soothe him, to be his. His fever and mine were melting into one another in spite of all barriers.

At half past two, as he stood by the door, ready to go, his eyes devoured me again, and I almost screamed: "I'll come with you." The pain of seeing him going away alone was intolerable. He wanted me. So did Hugh want me. I almost went crazy when we started to undress and he said softly: "I loved you tonight, little Pussy."

For the first time, I didn't babble, as I always do, about all my thoughts, which amuses Hugh, who smiles, assents, shakes his head, while he undresses. He was surprised and said, "Did you catch cold on the balcony?" John! John!

Evening. After the kiss, John teased me about Lilith. "Do you still like her?" he asked.

"Of course," I answered truthfully enough. It does not hurt me that we talk about her; that she is his great love. She is the woman for him, so much older, wiser, braver, and more *humorous*. She has more to give him. I am only his little love—just more than a flirt, and for a few days. He will return entirely to Lilith now, and to flirtations with the many women who propose to him after reading his novels. His life is really overcrowded with love.

May 27. This morning when the doorbell rang, I knew it was he. I knew, too, that he wanted to say an ordinary good-bye and that he thought we could escape the feeling of the other night. He walked from the door through the hallway into the parlor; I closed the door. The maid was out. We stood for a minute facing each other. I wore a red-and-white sheer chiffon dress without sleeves. It was very hot but my body was as always cool. I had been doing my accounts—had put away the fever of thought. He had been terribly busy with the details of his trip. We were facing each other in the brilliant morning, clearheaded, self-possessed, for only a second. Even now I can't understand the all-sweeping force of that impulse which again drew us together, in spite of terrible obstacles, in spite of Lilith and of Hugh, and of all our ideas and dreams. He drew me to the divan, and we kissed, kissed, kissed, profoundly, desperately, hungrily.

"This isn't fair," murmured John, "but so lovely, so lovely." His hands caressed all of my body, sought my breasts, and my most secret, most sensitive part. "I want to kiss your breasts—go and put something else on. I want to see them—I don't want to tear this dress."

I stood up. Something he had written came to my mind, about our right to see the body we love. I took my Spanish shawl to my room and came back to him wrapped in it alone. He carried me to the divan and stretched himself next to me. He kissed me, caressed me, penetrated my legs, was bathed in the moisture of my desire, but could not penetrate me entirely. He was powerless. He murmured plaintively, "I love you too much—I have thought too much about this, and now I think of Hugh. I love *you, you,* all of you, your mind, your unique self."

"I understand," I said. "It really all happened the other night. This is not the moment, not the mood. Don't be sad, don't be sad."

"Forgive me." All our strength had gone into dreams! "Lovely one—how beautiful your body is. Stand up; let me look at you."

I stood up and opened my shawl.

"The body of a dancer, Anaïs—what a precious gift you've made me, letting me see you."

When I came back, dressed, he was standing by the window.

"You are not sad?" I asked.

"It was our destiny, Anaïs—perhaps it was better so. At first I hated myself for being unable to pay tribute to a beautiful lady, but you are not only *that*, to me, today. But now I am a little bit glad because of Hugh—though I want you. Oh, I want you, and someday I'm going to possess you entirely."

We sat on the couch—he held me close. He fondled my breasts, which he found incredibly sensitive to his touch, hard-tipped, quivering.

"Lovely breasts. You are like a little faun—so sensitive, so little, so fine, darling little pagan." And, because I looked disappointed, "This is a compliment, you know."

"A faun is not a woman," I said.

"You are both" (kissing the *woman*). "You know I came this morning just to see you, not to make love to you, which is in a way, a higher compliment. But I couldn't help myself."

After a while: "You won't hate Lilith, because she thinks so much of you."

"No, I can't dislike her. She makes you happy. She is really the woman for you."

"It is absolutely true that I love her and you."

And a little later, "You won't experiment with love any more?"

"I couldn't play now, or endure anything mediocre after you."

"That is a wonderful thing for you to say, Anaïs."

I asked him, "What did you think after that first kiss?"

"I didn't think at all—it was lovely. I just wanted another." It is strange. I wasn't hurt at his powerlessness. I felt his love surging up, surrounding me, in spite of the fact that it was not consummated. We were both happy for the *others*, though frank enough to laugh at our *technical* faithfulness, and John said it was unbelievable we could be happy merely because we didn't surrender entirely physically and yet so entirely in every other way.

"Neither one of us was cut out for the life of a Don Juan. We *feel*, we *think*, our passions."

After many more kisses we said good-bye.

Last night, *the* last night, he took us out to dinner and to dance. He was alternately sad and flippant. I was dazed. When we danced he showed me again the most intense desire and a love of my body. He spoke beautifully to me while Hugh and Pauline danced. "I really paid you the highest compliment the other day, Anaïs. You didn't rouse the rake to a forgetfulness of your wonder—yet ever since, I have been haunted by your beauty, your lovely, unbelievable, sensitive body, so much your *own*, like your mind and your face. I didn't realize until now what a miracle individuality is—such as yours—little faun, little faun with the sensitive breasts—how I have thought of them—I must be careful not to describe them. Oh, Anaïs, you are going to make many men bad. You have the power."

After a while we couldn't stand dancing together any more. One more desperate embrace of all our selves, and we parted really. This morning at the station it was only a pale, sad, domestic scene, far removed from the true separation. He surprised everybody, however, by showing his sadness. His sister Rhoda said, "Extraordinary to see John have regrets. He is always looking *forward*, enthusiastic about what he leaves but also about what he is going to meet."

I didn't lose my courage until afterward—alone. I realized then how much I had given, how much I had received, and I felt a déchirement [rending] which his absence of a few months would not explain, but my secret feeling is that we are separated for good and that Lilith will keep him now, and that I must remember I belong to Hugh.

I began even the day John came so near to possessing me to make up to Hugh by an increase of devotion, of energy in the creation of our life together. I built up a new conception of his own value and of what I must do for him. I couldn't understand John worrying about *me*. I don't care about myself. I *love* all the pain and all the struggle that comes to me. But Hugh is now my Religion, my God, the end of my life. I must give him more than I have taken away from him. John has genius and power; Hugh has a mystical quality which appears only in the greatest poets. I am going to inspire him and then free him of me, whenever he wants. All this could be destroyed in a minute if I broke his faith in me, since I am his *religion*, his all. I won't break this faith; I'll even bring *lies* upon myself, into my life. They won't do me any harm. My lies are here—this book will be sealed. I have sifted everything; only beauty remains. Everything human, weak that happens to me will not remain so. I take, even from John, only what is finest. The white heat. In such a white heat, you can mold anything. And on myself, above all, I work with merciless fingers. These fingers are soft and tender only for others.

If Hugh knew today what I am, he would crumble. If I learned today that Hugh is what I am, has done what I have, I would *understand*. My happiness would crumble but not my understanding or my pity; and not my love of life.

I discovered the qualities that are missing from John's writing: tenderness, pity, a tragic sense of life—the knowledge of the poets. He told me Monday how his heartaches were always covered by facetiousness—that he was never wittier than when he was suffering. He always *shakes* off sorrow by humor, like the French, refuses to let it penetrate him, to let it make too long an impress. Partly "pudeur" [reserve], partly stoicism, partly an intellectual fear of sentiment.

He, so eager to possess all precious experiences, actually rejects the most profound of them all.

With me he must have suffered; I made him doubt himself, his philosophy, his love. Lilith is a triumphant, liberated, happy woman. I am the faun, little and wistful, mystical, and sensuous. He loved me despite all his wisdom. What will happen? I haven't made him happy—I have made him restless. He was sometimes afraid of looking into me, so he teased me, made me suffer, made hard remarks about little things. I smiled—I always smile. He was moved.

If he can go on being merely witty, clever, brilliant after this, if he does not reach a profounder feeling of life and of woman, then he lacks the ultimate concept. I have faith in him. Today he does not understand me altogether, but he will later. I am so much older than he knows. Through an intensity of the imagination and of the body, millions of things have happened to me, and I know a great deal; I am old.

May 30. I have had few days as sad as yesterday, known few times when I could control myself as little. I cried in the street, walking home, and today it is worse. I miss him more than I ever imagined. I think of him every second. What surprised me most is that he inspired me to write about him, though it hurt me so much. A sorrowful desire for *preservation.* After I had done it I felt happier and had no more fears of *losing* it all.

In a way he knew best when he said the separation would have been unbearable if we had been more closely united. But I can't rejoice, because I know now it will never take place. And if I am glad of anything, it is that by the fact of his absence I may liberate myself from the need of him.

I don't do Hugh any harm. Ultimately what he wants is my love and me. He still has them. I have the power to multiply myself. I am not one woman. He has the greater part of me. I have never been so prodigal with anyone as I have with him. I have only one secret from him. Everything else he knows, he holds, is his. The strange paradox is that these last days he has loved me more—I don't know why. He finds me lovelier, he is astonished by new expressions, by my ideas, by the rayonnement physique et intellectuel [physical and intellectual radiance] which emanates from me. A discovery to madden me and make me doubt all truth.

John had said before the first kiss: "You look adventuresome, but your journal discloses another character. It is really a sad journal, because you are preoccupied with real values."

Notes

Text: *The Early Diary of Anaïs Nin, Volume 4, 1927-1931* (San Diego: Harcourt Brace Jovanovich, 1985), 184-93.

John is John Erskine. Hugh is Hugh Guiler. Lilith is a pseudonym for Adeline Lobdell Atwater (later Pynchon) (1887-1975), Erskine's mistress. "Une amitié passionée" means "an intense friendship." "Foire" means "fair." Enric is Enrique Madriguera (1904-1973), who briefly lived in the Nins' West 75th Street brownstone in New York; he went on to a significant musical career as violinist, composer ("Adios"), and band leader. Gustavo is Gustavo Morales, a Cuban composer with whom Nin flirted in Paris; he is best known for the ballet *The Royal Fandango* (1921). Mother is Rosa Culmell de Nin. Joaquin is Joaquín Nin-Culmell. Erskine's *Uncle Sam in the Eyes of His Family* was published in 1930. Lorraine Maynard (1897-1971) was the wife of Richard F. Maynard. Lapéruse is a Paris restaurant. Erskine's *Sonata and Other Poems* (1925) includes "The Sleeping Beauty"; Erskine's story of this title appeared in *Hearst's International-Cosmopolitan* (June 1930). Pauline Ives Erskine (ca. 1878-1960) was the wife of John Erskine; Graham Erskine (1911-1991) was their son. Rhoda Erskine (1893-1934), the youngest sibling of John Erskine, taught literature and history at what is now the Juilliard School of Music, which her brother served as president.

❧ HENRY AND JUNE ❧

(January 1932)
On June Miller

Context

Until Nin met Henry Miller and his wife, June, in December 1931, her life had been relatively tame, despite her father's desertion of the family, her moving from Europe to the United States, and her marriage to Hugh Guiler. Soon after meeting the Millers, sex became an important part of her life. She was first smitten by June

◆ ◆ ◆ ◆

January 1932. We met, June and I, at American Express. I knew she would be late, and I did not mind. I was there before the hour, almost ill with tenseness. I would see her, in full daylight, advance out of the crowd. Could it be possible? I was afraid that I would stand there exactly as I had stood in other places, watching a crowd and knowing no June would ever appear because June was a product of my imagination. I could hardly believe she would arrive by those streets, cross such a boulevard, emerge out of a handful of dark, faceless people, walk into that place. What a joy to watch that crowd scurrying and then to see her striding, resplendent, incredible, towards me. I hold her warm hand. She is going for mail. Doesn't the man at American Express see the wonder of her? Nobody like her ever called for mail. Did any woman ever wear shabby shoes, a shabby black dress, a shabby dark blue cape, and an old violet hat as she wears them?

I cannot eat in her presence. But I am calm outwardly, with that Oriental placidity of bearing that is so deceptive. She drinks and smokes. She is quite mad, in a sense, subject to fears and manias. Her talk, mostly unconscious, would be revealing to an analyst, but I cannot analyze it. It is mostly lies. The contents of her imagination are realities to her. But what is she building so carefully? An aggrandizement of her personality, a fortifying and glorifying of it. In the obvious and enveloping warmth of my admiration she expands. She seems at once destructive and helpless. I want to protect her. What a joke! I, protect her whose power is infinite. Her power is so strong that I actually believe it when she tells me her destructiveness is unintentional. Has she tried to destroy me? No, she walked into my house and I was willing to endure any pain from her hands. If there is any calculation in her, it comes

21

only afterwards, when she becomes aware of her power and wonders how she should use it. I do not think her evil potency is directed. Even she is baffled by it.

I have her in myself now as one to be pitied and protected. She is involved in perversities and tragedies she cannot live up to. I have at last caught her weakness. Her life is full of fantasies. I want to force her into reality. I want to do violence to her. I, who am sunk in dreams, in half-lived acts, see myself possessed by a furious intention: I want to grasp June's evasive hands, oh, with what strength, take her to a hotel room and realize her dream and mine, a dream she has evaded facing all her life.

I went to see Eduardo, tense and shattered by my three hours with June. He saw the weakness in her and urged me to act out my strength.

I could hardly think clearly because in the taxi she had pressed my hand. I was not ashamed of my adoration, my humility. Her gesture was not sincere. I do not believe she could love.

She says she wants to keep the rose dress I wore the first night she saw me. When I tell her I want to give her a going-away present, she says she wants some of that perfume she smelled in my house, to evoke memories. And she needs shoes, stockings, gloves, underwear. Sentimentality? Romanticism? If she *really* means it... Why do I doubt her? Perhaps she is just very sensitive, and hypersensitive people are false when others doubt them; they waver. And one thinks them insincere. Yet I want to believe her. At the same time it does not seem so very important that she should love me. It is not her role. I am so filled with my love of her. And at the same time I feel that I am dying. Our love would be death. The embrace of imaginings.

When I tell Hugo the stories June has told me, he says they are simply very cheap. I don't know.

Then Eduardo spends two days here, the demoniac analyst, making me realize the crisis I am passing through. I want to see June. I want to see June's body. I have not dared to look at her body. I know it is beautiful.

Eduardo's questions madden me. Relentlessly, he observes how I have humbled myself. I have not dwelt on the successes which could glorify me. He makes me remember that my father beat me, that my first remembrance of him is a humiliation. He had said I was ugly after having typhoid fever. I had lost weight and my curls.

What has made me ill now? June. June and her sinister appeal. She has taken drugs; she loved a woman; she talks the cops' language when she tells stories. And yet she has kept that incredible, out-of-date, uncallous sentimentalism: "Give me the perfume I smelled in your house. Walking up the hill to your house, in the dark, I was in ecstasy."

I ask Eduardo, "Do you really think I am a lesbian? Do you take this seriously? Or is it just a reaction against my experience with Drake?" He is not sure.

Hugo takes a definite stand and says he considers everything outside of our love extraneous—phases, passionate curiosities. He wants a security to live by. I rejoice in his finding it. I tell him he is right.

Finally Eduardo says I am not a lesbian, because I do not hate men—on the contrary. In my dream last night I desired Eduardo, not June. The night before, when I dreamed of June, I was at the top of a skyscraper and expected to walk down the façade of it on a very narrow fire ladder. I was terrified. I could not do it.

She came to Louveciennes Monday. I asked her cruelly, just as Henry had, "Are you a lesbian? Have you faced your impulses in your own mind?"

She answered me so quietly. "Jean was too masculine. I have faced my feelings, I am fully aware of them, but I have never found anyone I wanted to live them out with, so far." And she turned the conversation evasively. "What a lovely way you have of dressing. This dress—its rose color, its old-fashioned fullness at the bottom, the little black velvet jacket, the lace collar, the lacing over the breasts—how perfect, absolutely perfect. I like the way you cover yourself, too. There is very little nudity, just your neck, really. I love your turquoise ring, and the coral."

Her hands were shaking; she was trembling. I was ashamed of my brutality. I was intensely nervous. She told me how at the restaurant she had wanted to see my feet and how she could not bring herself to stare. I told her how I was afraid to look at her body. We talked brokenly. She looked at my feet, in sandals, and thought them lovely.

I said, "Do you like these sandals?" She answered that she had always loved sandals and worn them until she had become too poor to have them. I said, "Come up to my room and try the other pair I have."

She tried them on, sitting on my bed. They were too small for her. I saw she wore cotton stockings, and it hurt me to see June in cotton stockings. I showed her my black cape, which she thought beautiful. I made her try it on, and then I saw the beauty of her body, its fullness and heaviness, and it overwhelmed me.

I could not understand why she was so ill-at-ease, so timid, so frightened. I told her I would make her a cape like mine. Once I touched her arm. She moved it away. Had I frightened her? Could there be someone more sensitive and more afraid than I? I couldn't believe it. I was not afraid at that moment. I wanted desperately to touch her.

When she sat on the couch downstairs, the opening of her dress showed the beginning of her breasts, and I wanted to kiss her there. I was acutely upset and trembling. I was becoming aware of her sensitiveness and fear of her own feelings. She talked, but now I knew she talked to evade a deeper inner talk—the things we could not say.

We met the next day at American Express. She came in her tailored suit because I had said I liked it.

She had said she wanted nothing from me but the perfume I wore and my wine-colored handkerchief. But I insisted that she had promised to let me buy her sandals.

First I made her go to the ladies' room. I opened my bag and pulled out a pair of sheer stockings. "Put them on," I pleaded. She obeyed. Meanwhile I opened a bottle of perfume. "Put some on." The attendant was there, staring, waiting for her tip. I did not care about her. June had a hole in her sleeve.

I was terribly happy. June was exultant. We talked simultaneously. "I wanted to call you last night. I wanted to send you a telegram," June said. She had wanted to tell me she was very unhappy on the train, regretting her awkwardness, her nervousness, her pointless talk. There had been so much, so much she wanted to say.

Our fears of displeasing each other, of disappointing each other were the same. She had gone to the café in the evening as if drugged, full of thoughts of me. People's voices reached her from afar. She was elated. She could not sleep. What had I done to her? She had always been poised, she could always talk well, people never overwhelmed her.

When I realized what she was revealing to me, I almost went mad with joy. She loved me, then? June! She sat beside me in the restaurant, small, timid, unworldly, panic-stricken. She would say something and then beg forgiveness for its stupidity. I could not bear it. I told her, "We have both lost ourselves, but sometimes we reveal the most when we are least like ourselves. I am not trying to think any more. I can't think when I am with you. You are like me, wishing for a perfect moment, but nothing too long imagined can be perfect in a worldly way. Neither one of us can say just the right thing. We are overwhelmed. Let us be overwhelmed. It is so lovely, so lovely. I love you, June."

And not knowing what else to say I spread on the bench between us the wine-colored handkerchief she wanted, my coral earrings, my turquoise ring, which Hugo had given me and which it hurt me to give, but it was blood I wanted to lay before June's beauty and before June's incredible humility.

We went to the sandal shop. In the shop the ugly woman who waited on us hated us and our visible happiness. I held June's hand firmly. I commandeered the shop. I was the man. I was firm, hard, willful with the shopkeepers.

When they mentioned the broadness of June's feet, I scolded them. June could not understand their French, but she could see they were nasty. I said to her, "When people are nasty to you I feel like getting down on my knees before you."

We chose the sandals. She refused anything else, anything that was not symbolical or representative of me. Everything I wore she would wear, although she had never wanted to imitate anyone else before.

When we walked together through the streets, bodies close together, arm in arm, hands locked, I could not talk. We were walking over the world, over reality, into ecstasy. When she smelled my handkerchief, she inhaled me. When I clothed her beauty, I possessed her.

She said, "There are so many things I would love to do with you. With you I would take opium." June, who does not accept a gift which has no symbolical significance; June, who washes laundry to buy herself a bit of perfume; June, who is not afraid of poverty and drabness and who is untouched by it, untouched by the drunkenness of her friends; June, who judges, selects, discards people with severity, who knows, when she is telling her endless anecdotes, that they are ways of escape, keeping herself all the more secret behind that profuse talk. Secretly mine.

Hugo begins to understand. Reality exists only between him and me, in our love. All the rest, dreams. Our love is solved. I can be faithful. I was terrifyingly happy during the night.

But I must kiss her, I must kiss her.

If she had wanted to, yesterday I would have sat on the floor, with my head against her knees. But she would not have it. Yet at the station while we wait for the train she begs for my hand. I call out her name. We stand pressed together, faces almost touching. I smile at her while the train leaves. I turn away.

The stationmaster wants to sell me some charity tickets. I buy them and give them to him, wishing him luck at the lottery. He gets the benefit of my wanting to give to June, to whom one cannot give anything.

What a secret language we talk, undertones, overtones, nuances, abstractions, symbols. Then we return to Hugo and to Henry, filled with an incandescence which frightens them both. Henry is uneasy. Hugo is sad. What is this powerful magical thing we give ourselves to, June and I, when we are together? Wonder! Wonder! It comes with her.

Last night, after June, filled with June, I could not bear Hugo reading the newspapers and talking about trusts and a successful day. He understood—he does understand—but he couldn't share, he could not grasp the incandescent. He teased me. He was humorous. He was immensely lovable and warm. But I could not come back.

So I lay on the couch, smoking, and thinking of June. At the station, I had fainted.

The intensity is shattering us both. She is glad to be leaving. She is less yielding than I am. She really wants to escape from that which is giving her life. She does not like my power, whereas I take joy in submitting to her.

When we met for half an hour today to discuss Henry's future, she asked me to take care of him, and then she gave me her silver bracelet with a cat's-eye stone, when she has so few possessions. I refused at first, and then the joy of wearing her bracelet, a part of her, filled me. I carry it like a symbol. It is precious to me.

Hugo noticed it and hated it. He wanted to take it from me, to tease me. I clung to it with all my strength while he crushed my hands, letting him hurt me.

June was afraid that Henry would turn me against her. What does she fear? I said to her, "There is a fantastic secret between us. I only know about you through my own knowledge. Faith. What is Henry's knowledge to me?"

Then I met Henry accidentally at the bank. I saw that he hated me, and I was startled. June had said that he was uneasy and restless, because he is more jealous of women than of men. June, inevitably, sows madness. Henry, who thought me a "rare" person, now hates me. Hugo, who rarely hates, hates her.

Today she said that when she talked to Henry about me she tried to be very natural and direct so as not to imply anything unusual. She told him, "Anaïs was just bored with her life, so she took us up." That seemed crude to me. It was the only ugly thing I have heard her say.

Hugo and I yield entirely to each other. We cannot be without each other, we cannot endure discord, war, estrangement, we cannot take walks alone, we do not like to travel without each other. We have yielded in spite of our individualism, our hatred of intimacy. We have absorbed our egocentric selves into our love. Our love *is* our ego.

I do not think June and Henry have achieved that, because both their individualities are too strong. So they are at war; love is a conflict; they must lie to each other, mistrust each other.

June wants to go back to New York and do something well, be lovely for me, satisfy me. She is afraid of disappointing me.

We had lunch together in a softly lighted place which surrounded us with velvety closeness. We took off our hats. We drank champagne. June refused all sweet or tasteless food. She could live on grapefruit, oysters, and champagne.

We talked in half-spoken abstractions, clear to us alone. She made me realize how she eluded all of Henry's attempts to grasp her logically, to reach a knowledge of her.

She sat there filled with champagne. She talked about hashish and its effects. I said, "I have known such states without hashish. I do not need drugs. I carry all that in myself." At this she was a little angry. She did not realize that I achieved those states without destroying my mind. My mind must not die, because I am a writer. I am the poet who must see. I am not just the poet who can get drunk on June's beauty.

It was her fault that I began to notice discrepancies in her stories, childish lies. Her lack of coordination and logic left loopholes, and when I put the pieces together, I formed a judgment, a judgment which she fears always, which she wants to run away from. She lives without logic. As soon as one tries to coordinate June, June is lost. She must have seen it happen many times. She is like a man who is drunk and gives himself away.

We were talking about perfumes, their substance, their mixtures, their meaning. She said casually, "Saturday, when I left you, I bought some perfume for Ray." (Ray is a girl she has told me about.) At the moment I did not think. I retained the name of the perfume, which was very expensive.

We went on talking. She is as affected by my eyes as I am by her face. I told her how her bracelet clutched my wrist like her very fingers, holding me in barbaric slavery. She wants my cape around her body.

After lunch we walked. She had to buy her ticket for New York. First we went in a taxi to her hotel. She brought out a marionette, Count Bruga, made by Jean. He had violet hair and violet eyelids, a prostitute's eyes, a Pulcinella nose, a loose, depraved mouth, consumptive cheeks, a mean, aggressive chin, murderer's hands, wooden legs, a Spanish sombrero, a black velvet jacket. He had been on the stage.

June sat him on the floor of the taxi, in front of us. I laughed at him.

We walked into several steamship agencies. June did not have enough money for even a third-class passage and she was trying to get a reduction. I saw her lean over the counter, her face in her hands, appealing, so that the men behind the counter devoured her with their eyes, boldly. And she so soft, persuasive, alluring, smiling up in a secret way at them. I was watching her begging. Count Bruga leered at me. I was only conscious of my jealousy of those men, not of her humiliation.

We walked out. I told June I would give her the money she needed, which was more than I could afford to give, much more.

We went into another steamship agency, with June barely finishing some mad fairy tale before she stated her errand. I saw the man at the counter taken out of himself, transfixed by her face and her soft, yielding way of talking to him, of paying and signing. I stood by and watched him ask her, "Will you have a cocktail with me tomorrow?" June was shaking hands with him. "Three o'clock?" "No. At six." She smiled at him as she does at me. Then as we left she explained herself hurriedly. "He was very useful to me, very helpful. He is going to do a lot for me. I couldn't say no. I don't intend to go, but I couldn't say no."

"You must go, now that you said yes," I said angrily, and then the literalness and stupidity of this statement nauseated me. I took June's arm and said almost in a sob, "I can't bear it, I can't bear it." I was angry at some indefinable thing. I thought of the prostitute, honest because in exchange for money she gives her body. June would never give her body. But she would beg as I would never beg, promise as I would not promise unless I were to give.

June! There was such a tear in my dream. She knew it. So she took my hand against her warm breast and we walked, I feeling her breast. She was always naked under her dress. She did it perhaps unconsciously, as if to soothe an angry child. And she talked about things that were not to the point. "Would you rather I had said no, brutally, to the man? I am sometimes brutal, you know, but I couldn't be in front of you. I didn't want to hurt his feelings. He had been very helpful." And as I did not know what angered me, I said nothing. It was not a question of accepting or refusing a cocktail. One had to go back to the root of why she should need the help of that man. A statement of hers came back to me: "However bad things are for me I always find someone who will buy me champagne." Of course. She was a woman accumulating huge debts which she never intended to pay, for afterwards she boasted of her sexual inviolability. A gold digger. Pride in the possession of her own body but not too proud to humiliate herself with prostitute eyes over the counter of a steamship company.

She was telling me that she and Henry had quarreled over buying butter. They had no money and... "No money?" I said. "But Saturday I gave you 400 francs, for you and Henry to eat with. And today is Monday."

"We had things to pay up that we owed..."

I thought she meant the hotel room. Then suddenly I remembered the perfume, which cost 200 francs. Why didn't she say to me, "I bought perfume and gloves and stockings Saturday." She did not look at me when she intimated they had the rent to pay. Then I remembered another thing she had said. "People say to me that if I had a fortune, I could spend it in a day, and no one would ever know how. I can never account for the way I spend money."

This was the other face of June's fantasy. We walked the streets, and all the softness of her breast could not lull the pain.

I went home and was very heavy in Hugo's arms. I said to him, "I have come back." And he was very happy.

But yesterday at four, when I was waiting for her at American Express, the doorman said to me, "Your friend was here this morning and she said good-bye to me as if she were not coming back." "But we had agreed to meet here." If I were never again to see June walking towards me—impossible. It was like dying. What did it matter, all I thought the day before. She was unethical, irresponsible—it was her nature. I would not tamper with her nature. My pride about money matters was aristocratic. I was too scrupulous and proud. I would not change anything in June which was basic and at the root of her fantastic being. She alone was without fetters. I was a fettered, ethical being, in spite of my amoral intellect. I could not have let Henry go hungry. I accepted her entirely. I would not fight her. If only she would come and meet me for that last hour.

I had dressed ritually for her, in the very costume which created a void between me and other people, a costume which was a symbol of my individualism and which she alone would understand. Black turban, old rose dress with black lace bodice and collar, old rose coat with Medici collar. I had created a stir as I walked, and I was lonelier than ever because the reaction was partly hostile, mocking.

Then June came, all in black velvet, black cape and plumed hat, paler and more incandescent than ever, and carrying Count Bruga, as I had asked her to do. The wonder of her face and smile, her smileless eyes...

I took her to a Russian tearoom. The Russians sang as we felt. June wondered if they were really burning, as it seemed from their voices and intense playing. Probably they were not burning as June and I were.

Champagne and caviar with June. It is the only time one knows what champagne is and what caviar is. They are June, Russian voices and June.

Ugly, unimaginative, dead people surround us. We are blind to them. I look at June, in black velvet. June rushing towards death. Henry cannot rush on with her because he fights for life. But June and I together do not hold back. I follow her. And it is an acute joy to go along, giving in to the dissolution of the imagination, to her knowledge of strange experiences, to our games with Count Bruga, who bows to the world with the weeping willowness of his purple hair.

It is all over. In the street, June says regretfully, "I had wanted to hold you and caress you." I put her in a taxi. She sits there about to leave me and I stand by in torment. "I want to kiss you," I say. "I want to kiss you," says June, and she offers her mouth, which I kiss for a long time.

Notes

Text: *Henry and June: From the Unexpurgated Diary of Anaïs Nin* (San Diego: Harcourt Brace Jovanovich, 1986), 19-32.

June is June Miller; Eduardo, Eduardo Sánchez. June Miller probably left Paris for the United States in mid January 1932, soon after meeting Nin. Hugo is Hugh Guiler. Joaquín Nin frequently beat his children. Drake is Lawrence Drake (1900-ca. 1934), who tried to seduce Nin; the author of *Don't Call Me Clever* (1929), he was an assistant to Edward W. Titus (1870-1952), publisher of her first book, *D. H. Lawrence: An Unprofessional Study* (1932). Henry is Henry Miller. Jean is Jean Kronski, a sculptor, poet, and friend of June Miller. Pulcinella is a character from commedia dell'arte.

⊂ℬ *HENRY AND JUNE* ℬ

(March 1932)
On Henry Miller

Context

Impressed by Henry Miller's intelligence, Nin did her best to support this penurious writer by inviting him to her Louveciennes home and giving him necessities, including money. After his wife, June, left Paris for the United States, Nin became physically attracted to him and had, with him, her first consummated adulterous affair in March 1932. Here, she expresses delight in their uninhibited sex and philosophizes about the nature and necessity of love.

♦ ♦ ♦ ♦

March 1932. I see similarities between Henry and me in human relationships. I see our capacities for enduring pain when we love, our easily duped natures, our desire to believe in June, our quick rising to defend her from the hatred of others. He talks of beating June, but he would never dare. It is only a wish fulfillment, to dominate what he is dominated by. It is said in *Bubu de Montparnasse* that a woman submits to the man who beats her because he is like a strong government who can also protect her. But Henry's beating would be futile because he is not a protector of woman. He has let himself be protected. June has worked for him like a man, and so she can say, "I have loved him like a child." Yes, and it diminishes her passion. He has let her feel her own strength. And nothing of this can be changed, because it is engraved in both of them. All his life Henry will assert his manhood by destruction and hatred in his work; each time June appears he will bow his head. Now only hatred moves him. "Life is foul, foul," he cries. And with these words he kisses me and awakens me, I who have been sleeping one hundred years, with hallucinations hanging like curtains of spider webs over my bed. But the man who leans over my bed is soft. And he writes nothing about these moments. He doesn't even try to pull the spider webs down. How am I to be convinced the world is foul? "I am no angel. You have only seen me at my best, but wait..."

I was dreaming of reading all this to Henry, everything I have written about him. And then I laughed because I could hear Henry saying, "How strange; why is there so much gratefulness in you?" I didn't know why until

I read what Fred wrote about Henry: "Poor Henry, I feel sorry for you. You have no gratitude because you have no love. To be grateful one must first know how to love."

Fred's words added to my own about Henry's hatred hurt me. Do I or do I not believe in them? Do they explain the profound amazement I felt, while reading his novel, at the savagery of his attacks on Beatrice, his first wife? At the same time I thought it was I who was wrong, that people must fight and must hate each other, and that hatred is good. But I took love for granted; love can include hatred.

I have constant slips of the tongue and say "John" instead of "Henry" to Hugo. There is no resemblance whatsoever between them, and I cannot understand the association in my mind.

"Listen," I say to Henry, "don't leave me out of your book out of delicacy. Include me. Then we'll see what happens. I expect much."

"But meanwhile," says Henry, "it is Fred who has written three wonderful pages about you. He raves about you, he worships you. I am jealous of those three pages. I wish I had written them."

"You will," I say confidently.

"For example, your hands. I had never noticed them. Fred gives them so much importance. Let me look at them. Are they really as beautiful as that? Yes, indeed." I laugh. "You appreciate other things, perhaps."

"What?"

"Warmth, for instance." I'm smiling, but there are so many fine lacerations that Henry's words open. "When Fred hears me talk about June, he says I do not love you."

Yet he won't let me go. He calls out to me in his letters. His arms, his caresses, and his fucking are voracious. He says, with me, that no amount of thinking (Proust's words, or Fred's, or mine) will stop us from living. And what is living? The moment when he rings at Natasha's door (she is away and I have her place) and immediately desires me. The moment when he tells me he has had no thoughts of whores. I am so idiotically fair and loyal to June in every word I utter about her. How can I deceive myself about the extent of Henry's love when I understand and share his feelings about June?

He sleeps in my arms, we are welded, his penis still in me. It is a moment of real peace, a moment of security. I open my eyes, but I do not think. One of my hands is on his gray hair. The other hand is spread around his leg. "Oh, Anaïs," he had said, "you are so hot, so hot that I can't wait. I must shoot into you quickly, quickly."

Is how one is loved always so important? Is it so imperative that one should be loved absolutely or greatly? Would Fred say of me that I can love because I love others more than I love myself? Or is it Hugo who loves when he goes three times to the station to meet me because I have missed three trains? Or is it Fred, with his nebulous, poetic, delicate comprehension? Or do I love most when I say to Henry, "The destroyers do not always destroy. June has not destroyed you, ultimately. The core of you is a writer. And the writer is living.""

Henry, tell Fred we can go and get the curtains tomorrow."

"I'll come, too," said Henry, suddenly jealous.

"But you know Fred wants to see me, to talk with me." Henry's jealousy pleased me. "Tell him to meet me at the same place as last time."

"About four o'clock."

"No, at three." I was thinking we didn't have enough time together the last day we met. Henry's face is impenetrable. I never know by any sign on it what he feels. There are transitions, yes, when he is flushed and excited, or serious and chastened, or observant and introspective. The blue eyes are analytical, like a scientist's, or moist with feeling. When they are moist I am moved down to my toes because I remember a story about his childhood. His parents (his father was a tailor) used to take him with them on their Sunday outings, visiting, dragging the child along all day and late at night. They sat in the houses of their friends to play cards and smoke. The smoke would grow thick and hurt Henry's eyes. They would put him on the bed in the room next to the parlor, with wet towels over his inflamed eyes.

And now his eyes get tired with proofreading at the newspaper, and I would like to free him of it, and I can't.

Last night I couldn't sleep. I imagined being in Natasha's apartment again with Henry. I wanted to relive the moment when he came into me as we were standing. He taught me to encircle him with my legs. Such practices are so unfamiliar that they bewilder me. Afterwards, the joy bursts upon my senses, because it has unleashed a new kind of desire.

"Anaïs, I feel you, your hotness right down to my toes." In him, too, it is like lightning. He is always amazed by my moisture and my warmth.

Often, though, the passivity of the woman's role weighs on me, suffocates me. Rather than wait for his pleasure, I would like to take it, to run wild. Is it that which pushes me into lesbianism? It terrifies me. Do women act thus? Does June go to Henry when she wants him? Does she mount him? Does she wait for him? He guides my inexperienced hands. It is like a forest fire, to be with him. New places of my body are aroused and burnt. He is incendiary. I leave him in an unquenchable fever.

I have just been standing before the open window of my bedroom and I have breathed in deeply, all the sunshine, the snowdrops, the crocuses, the primroses, the crooning of the pigeons, the trills of the birds, the entire procession of soft winds and cool smells, of frail colors and petal-textured skies, the knotted gray-brown of old trees, the vertical shoots of young branches, the wet brown earth, the torn roots. It is all so savory that my mouth opens, and it is Henry's tongue which I taste, and I smell his breath as he sleeps, wrapped in my arms.

I expect to meet Fred, but it is Henry who comes to the rendezvous. Fred is working. My eyes open wide on Henry, the man who slept in my arms yesterday, and I have chill thoughts. I see his stained hat and the hole in his coat. Another day this would have moved me, but today I realize it is willed poverty, calculated, intentional, out of disdain for the bourgeois who holds a purse carefully. He talks marvelously about Samuel Putman and Eugene Jolas, and his work, and my work and Fred's. But then the Pernod affects him and he tells me of sitting in a café with Fred last night after work, and of whores talking to him, and of Fred's looking at him severely, because he had been with me that afternoon and shouldn't have been talking to those women; and they were ugly. "But Fred is wrong," I say, to Henry's surprise. "The whores complement me. I understand the relief a man must feel to go to a woman without demands on his emotions or feelings." And Henry adds, "You don't have to write them letters!" As I laugh he realizes that I understand completely. I even understand his preference for Renoiresque bodies. *Voilà.* Yet I keep this picture of an outraged Fred worshipping me. And Henry says, "That's the nearest I came to being unfaithful to you."

I don't know that I so much want Henry's faithfulness, because I am beginning to realize that the very word "love" tires me today. Love or no love. Fred's saying Henry doesn't love me. I understand the need for relief from complications, and I desire it for myself, only women cannot achieve such a state. Women are romantic.

Suppose I don't want Henry's love. Suppose I say to him, "Listen, we are two adults. I'm sick of fantasies and emotions. Don't mention the word 'love.' Let's talk as much as we want and fuck only when we want it. Leave love out of it." They are all so serious. Just this moment I feel old, cynical. I'm tired of demands, too. For an hour today I feel unsentimental. In a moment I could destroy the entire legend, from beginning to end, destroy everything, except the fundamentals: my passion for June and my worship of Hugo.

Perhaps my intellect is playing another prank. Is that what it is to feel a sense of reality? Where are yesterday's feelings and this morning's, and what about my intuition that Henry instead of Fred would meet me? And what has it all got to do with the fact that Henry was drunk, and that I, not realizing it, read to him about his power to "break" me. He didn't understand, of course, while swimming in the sulphur-colored Pernod.

The burlesque of that hurt me. I asked him, "What is Fred like when he is drunk?"

"Merry, yes, but always a bit contemptuous with the whores. They feel it."

"Whereas you get friendly?"

"Yes, I talk to them like a cart driver."

Well, I had no joy from all this. It makes me cold and blank inside. Once, I joked and said that someday I would send him a telegram saying: "Never meet again because you don't love me." Coming home, I thought, tomorrow we will not meet. Or if we meet, we will never lie together again. Tomorrow I'll tell Henry not to bother about love. But the rest?

Notes

Text: *Henry and June: From the Unexpurgated Diary of Anaïs Nin* (San Diego: Harcourt Brace Jovanovich, 1986), 97-103.

Henry is Henry Miller; June, June Miller. Charles-Louis Philippe (1874-1909) wrote *Bubu de Montparnasse* (1901), about the Parisian demimonde. Fred is Alfred Perlès. Beatrice is Beatrice Miller. John is John Erskine. Hugo is Hugh Guiler. Proust is Marcel Proust. Natasha is Princess Natasha Troubetskoia. Eugène Jolas (1894-1952) edited *transition* (1927-1938), an important literary magazine published initially in Paris but later in Colombay-les-deux-Églises.

ᘓ *HENRY AND JUNE* ᘔ

(April 1932)
Henry Miller and Nin on Guiler

Context

During her relationships with Henry Miller and June Miller, Nin was free to dally because Hugh Guiler worked all day as a banker. His income permitted him to pay for the upkeep of the Louveciennes house and the subsistence of his mother- and brother-in-law, as well as to give Nin an allowance, which she used to help support Henry Miller. Here, Nin examines her feelings for her husband.

◆ ◆ ◆ ◆

April 1932. One evening in Henry's kitchen—he and I alone—we talk ourselves empty. He takes up the subject of my red journal, tells me what faults I have to beware of, and then says, "Do you know what baffles me? When you write about Hugo, you write wonderful things, but at the same time they are unconvincing. You do not tell anything that would cause your admiration or love. It sounds strained."

I immediately become distressed, as if it were Allendy questioning me.

"It isn't for me to be asking questions, Anaïs," Henry continues, "but listen, I am not being personal now. I myself like Hugo. I think he is fine. But I am just trying to understand your life. I imagine that you married him when your character was not yet formed, or for the sake of your mother and brother."

"No, no, not for that. I loved him. For my mother and brother I should have married in Havana, in society, richly, and I couldn't do that."

"That day Hugo and I went out for a walk, I tried to grasp him. The truth is, if I had seen only him in Louveciennes, I would have come once, said here's a nice man, and forgotten all about it."

"Hugo is inarticulate," I said. "It takes time to know him." And all the while my old, secret, immense dissatisfaction wells up like a poison, and I keep saying foolish things about the bank subduing him, and how different he is on vacations.

Henry curses. "But it's so obvious that you are superior to him." Always that hateful phrase—from John, too. "Only in intelligence," I say.

"In everything," says Henry. "And listen, Anaïs, answer me. You are not just making a sacrifice. You're not really happy, are you? You want to run away from Hugo at times?"

I cannot answer. I bow my head and cry. Henry comes and stands over me.

"My life is a mess," I say. "You're trying to make me admit something I will not even admit to myself, as you could see by the journal. You sensed how much I *want* to love Hugo and in just what way I do. I'm all broken up with visions of what it might have been here, with you, for instance. How satisfied I have been, Henry."

"And now, only with me," says Henry, "you would blossom so quickly that you would soon exhaust all I can give and pass on to another. There are no limits to what your life could be. I have seen how you can swim in a passion, in a large life. Listen, if anybody else did the things you have done, I would call them foolish, but somehow or other you make them seem so terribly right. This journal, for instance, is so rich, so terribly rich. You say my life is rich but it is only full of events, incidents, experiences, people. What is really rich are these pages on so little material."

"But think what I would make of more material," I say. "Think of what you said about my novel, that the theme [faithfulness] was an anachronism. That stung me. It was like a criticism of my own life. Yet I cannot commit a crime, and to hurt Hugo would be a crime. Besides, he loves me as nobody has ever loved me."

"You haven't given anybody else a real chance."

I am remembering this while Hugo is gardening. And to be with him now seems as if I were living in the state of being I was in at twenty. Is it his fault, this youthfulness of our life together? My God, can I ask about Hugo what Henry asks about June? He has filled her. Have I filled Hugo? People have said there is nothing in him but me. His great capacity for losing himself, for love. That touches me. Even last night he talked about his inability to mix with other people, saying that I was the only one he was close to, happy with. This morning in the garden he was in bliss. He wanted me there, near him. He has given me love. And what else?

I love the past in him. But all the rest has seeped away.

After what I revealed to Henry about my life, I was in despair. It was as if I were a criminal, had been in jail, and were at last free and willing to work honestly and hard. But as soon as people discover your past they will not give you work and expect you to act like a criminal again.

I am finished with myself, with my sacrifices and my pity, with what chains me. I am going to make a new beginning. I want passion and pleasure and noise and drunkenness and all evil. But my past reveals itself inexorably, like a tattoo mark. I must build a new shell, wear new costumes.

While I wait for Hugo in the car I write on a cigarette box (on the back of the Sultanes there is a good bit of rosy space).

Hugo has found out that: I have not seen the gardener about the garden, the mason about the cracked pool, have not done my accounts, have missed my fitting for an evening dress, have broken all routine.

One evening Natasha calls up. I am supposed to have spent the nights in her studio. And she asks me, "What have you been doing these last ten days?" I cannot answer her or Hugo will hear me. "Why does Natasha call you up?" he asks.

Later, in bed. Hugo is reading. As I write, almost under his eyes, he cannot suppose that what I am writing is so treacherous. I am thinking the worst about him I have ever thought.

Today while we worked in the garden I felt as if I were in Richmond Hill again, wrapped up in books and in trances, with Hugo passing by, hoping for a glimpse of me. *Mon Dieu*, for a moment today, I was in love with him, with the soul and the virgin body of those earlier days. A part of me has grown immeasurably, while I have clung to my young love, to a memory. And now the woman lying naked in the vast bed watches her young love bending over her and does not want him.

Since that talk with Henry, when I admitted more than I had ever admitted to myself, my life has altered and become deformed. The restlessness which was vague and nameless has become intolerably clear. Here is where it stabs me, at the center of the most perfect, the most steadfast structure, marriage. When this shakes, then my whole life crumbles. My love for Hugo has become fraternal. I look almost with horror on this change, which is not sudden, but slow in appearing on the surface. I had closed my eyes to all the signs. Above all, I dreaded admitting that I didn't want Hugo's passion. I had counted on the ease with which I would distribute my body. But it is not true. It was never true. When I rushed towards Henry, it was all Henry. I am frightened because I have realized the full extent of my imprisonment. Hugo has sequestered me, fostered my love of solitude. I regret now all those years when he gave me nothing but his love and I turned into myself for the rest. Starved, dangerous years.

I should break up my whole life, and I cannot do it. My life is not as important as Hugo's, and Henry doesn't need me because he has June. But whatever in me has grown outside and beyond Hugo will go on.

Notes

Text: *Henry and June: From the Unexpurgated Diary of Anaïs Nin* (San Diego: Harcourt Brace Jovanovich, 1986), 139-43.

Henry is Henry Miller. During this period, in order to keep her husband from learning the truth about her relationship with Miller, Nin wrote two diaries, one with a red cover (which included her presumably truthful rendering of events) and one with a green cover (with entries written for her husband to read). Hugo is Hugh Guiler. Allendy is René Allendy. Miller and Nin refer to her mother, Rosa Culmell de Nin, and brother Joaquín Nin-Culmell. From both parents, Nin had Cuban roots. With Guiler in Europe and thinking he might never return, Rosa Culmell de Nin took her daughter to Havana in 1922, hoping she would marry a Cuban aristocrat. Upon learning of this, Guiler, to whom Nin considered herself engaged, sailed to Havana, where he and Nin were married on 3 March 1923. John is John Erskine. June is June Miller. Natasha is Princess Natasha Troubetskoia.

HENRY AND JUNE

(May-June 1932)
On René Allendy

Context

In April 1932, at the suggestion of Eduardo Sánchez, Nin became a patient of his psychoanalyst, René Allendy.

◆ ◆ ◆ ◆

May 1932. Allendy was a superman today. I will never be able to describe our talk. There was so much intuition, so much emotion throughout. To the very last phrase he was so human, so true.

I had come in a mood of confidence, of recklessness, thinking: I do not want Allendy to admire me unless he can do so when he knows me exactly as I am. My first effort at complete sincerity.

I tell him first of all that I was ashamed of what I had said last time about his wife. He laughed and said he had forgotten all about it and asks, "Is there anything else which worries you?"

"Nothing in particular, but I would like to ask you if my strong sensual obsession is a reaction against too much introspection? I have been reading Samuel Putnam, who writes that 'the quickest way out of introspection is a worship of the body, which leads to sexual intensity.'"

I cannot remember his exact answer, but I sense his connection of the word "obsession" with a frantic search for satisfaction. Why the effort? Why dissatisfaction?

Here, I feel an imperative need to tell him my biggest secret: In the sexual act I do not always experience an orgasm.

He had guessed this from the very first day. My talk on sex had been crude, bold, defiant. It did not harmonize with my personality. It was artificial. It betrayed an uncertainty.

"But do you know what an orgasm is?"

"Oh, very well, from the times I did experience it, and particularly from masturbation."

"When did you masturbate?"

"Once, in the summer, in St. Jean de Luz. I was dissatisfied and had a strong sexual urge." I am ashamed to admit that when I was alone for two days I masturbated four and five times a day, and also often in Switzerland, during our vacation, and in Nice.

"Why only once? Every woman does it and very often."

"I believe it is wrong, morally and physically. I was terribly depressed and ashamed afterwards."

"That's nonsense. Masturbation is not physically harmful. It is only the feeling of guilt we have about it that oppresses."

"I used to fear it would diminish my mental power, my health, and that I would disintegrate morally."

Here, I add other details, which he listens to silently, trying to coordinate them. I tell him things I have never entirely admitted to myself, and which I have not written in my journal, things I wanted to forget.

Allendy is piecing the fragments together and talks about my partial frigidity. He discovers that I also consider this an inferiority and believe it is due to my frail physique. He laughs. He attributes it to a psychic cause, a strong sense of guilt. Sixty out of a hundred women feel as I do and never admit it and, most important of all, Allendy says, if I only knew what little difference this makes to men and how unaware they are of it. He always transforms what I term an inferiority into a natural thing, or one whose curse can be easily removed. I immediately feel a great relief and lose my terror and secretiveness.

I tell him about June, of my desiring to be a *femme fatale*, of my cruelty towards Hugo and Eduardo, and my surprise that they should love me as much or more afterwards. We also discuss my frank, bold sex talk, how I reverse my true, innate modesty and exhibit a forced obscenity. (Henry says he doesn't like my telling obscene stories, because it doesn't suit me.)

"But I am full of dissonances," I say, feeling that strange anguish Allendy creates—half relief, because of his exactness, half sorrow for no specific reason, the feeling of having been discovered.

"Yes, and until you can act perfectly naturally, according to your own nature, you will never be happy. The *femme fatale* arouses men's passions, exasperates them, torments them, and they want to possess her, even to kill her, but they do not love her profoundly. You have already discovered that you are loved profoundly. Now you have also discovered that cruelty to both Eduardo and Hugo has aroused them, and they want you even more. This makes you want to play a game which is not really natural to you."

"I have always despised such games. I have never been able to conceal from a man that I loved him."

"But you tell me profound loves do not satisfy you. You crave to give and to receive stronger sensations. I understand, but that is only a phase. You can play the game now and then, to heighten passion, but profound loves are the loves which suit your true self, and they alone will satisfy you. The more you act like yourself the nearer you come to a fulfillment of your real needs. You are still terribly afraid to be hurt; your imaginary sadism shows that. So afraid to be hurt that you want to take the lead and hurt first. I do not despair of reconciling you to your own image."

These are his words, crudely restated and only half remembered. I was so overcome by the sensation of his loosening innumerable tensions, of liberating me. His voice was so gentle and compassionate. Before he had finished I was sobbing. My gratitude was immense. I wanted to tell him I admired him and finally did. He was silent while I sobbed, and then he asked me his gentle question: "I didn't say anything to hurt you?"

I would like to cover the last pages with yesterday's joys. Showers of kisses from Henry. The thrusts of his flesh into mine, as I arched my body to better weld it to his. If a choice were to be made today between June and me, he tells me, he would surrender June. He could imagine us married and enjoying life, together. "No," I say, half teasing, half serious. "June is the only one. I am making you bigger and stronger for June." A half truth; there is no choice. "You're too modest, Anaïs. You do not realize yet what you have given me. June is a woman who can be effaced by other women. What June gives I can forget with other women. But you stand apart. I could have a thousand women after you and they could not efface you."

I listen to him. He is elated, and so he exaggerates, but it is so lovely. Yes, I know, for a moment, June's rareness and mine. The balance leans towards me for the moment. I look at my own image in Henry's eyes, and what do I see? The young girl of the diaries, telling stories to her brothers, sobbing much without reason, writing poetry—the woman one can talk to.

June 1932. Last night Henry and I went to the movies. When the story became tragic, harrowing, he took my hand, and we locked fingers tightly. With every pressure I shared his response to the story. We kissed in the taxi, on the way to meet Hugo. And I could not tear myself away. I lost my head. I went with him to Clichy. He penetrated me so completely that when I returned to Louveciennes and fell asleep in Hugo's arms, I still felt it was Henry. All night it was Henry at my side. I curled my body around him in my dreams. In the morning I found myself tightly entangled with Hugo, and it took me a long time to realize it was not Henry. Hugo believes I was so loving last night, but it was Henry I loved, Henry I kissed.

Since Allendy has fully won my confidence I came ready to talk very frankly about frigidity. I confess this: that when I found pleasure in sexual intercourse with Henry I was afraid of having a baby and thought that I should not have an orgasm too frequently. But a few months ago a Russian doctor told me it could not happen easily; in fact, if I wanted a child I would have to subject myself to an operation. The fear of having a baby, then, was eliminated. Allendy said the very fact that I did not try to reassure myself on this score for seven years of my married life proved I did not really give it any importance, that I used it merely as an excuse for not letting go in coition. When this fear vanished, I was able to examine more closely the true nature of my feelings. I expressed a restlessness at what I termed the enforced passivity of women. Still, perhaps two times out of three, I kept myself passive, waiting for all the activity in the man, as if I did not want to be responsible for what I was enjoying. "That is to abate your sense of guilt," Allendy said. "You refuse to be active and feel less guilty if it is the other who is active."

After the previous talk with Allendy I had felt a slight change. I was more active with Henry. He noticed it and said, "I love the way you fuck me now." And I felt a keen pleasure.

What astonishes me most about June are Henry's stories of her aggressivity, her taking him, seeking him at her own will. When I occasionally try aggressivity, it gives me a feeling of distress, shame. I sense now an occasional psychic paralysis in me somewhat similar to Eduardo's, except that it is more serious for a man.

Allendy pressed me to admit that since the last analysis I had complete confidence in him and that I had become very fond of him. All is well, then, as this is necessary for the success of the analysis. At the end of the session he could use the word "frigidity" without offending me. I was even laughing.

One of the things he observed was that I was dressing more simply. I have felt much less the need of original costuming. I could almost wear ordinary tailored clothes now. Costume, for me, has been an external expression of my secret lack of confidence. Uncertain of my beauty, Allendy said, I designed striking clothes which would distinguish me from other women.

"But," I said, laughing, "if I become happy and banal, the art of costuming, which owes its existence purely to a sense of inferiority, will be mortally affected." The pathological basis of creation! What will become of the creator if I become normal? Or will I merely gain in strength, so as to live out my instincts more fully? I will probably develop different and more interesting illnesses. Allendy said that what was important was to become equal to life.

Notes

Text: *Henry and June: From the Unexpurgated Diary of Anaïs Nin* (San Diego: Harcourt Brace Jovanovich, 1986), 172-77.

Allendy is René Allendy. At a session with Allendy in May 1932, Nin described his wife, Yvonne Allendy (1890-1935), as "not beautiful." I cannot locate the source of Nin's quotation from Samuel Putnam. June is June Miller. Hugo is Hugh Guiler; Eduardo, Eduardo Sánchez. Henry is Henry Miller, who lived at 4, avenue Anatole France in Clichy.

✂ *INCEST* ✄

(23 June 1933)
In Valescure

Context

Before Nin reunited with her father in 1933, they had seldom seen each other since his desertion of the family in 1913. Together in Valescure, France, they spent, according to Nin's diary, nine days having sex. She rejoined him there in August, when they resumed their passion; they continued it in Louveciennes in October, and possibly at other times.

◆ ◆ ◆ ◆

June 23, 1933. First day of Father Story. King Father arrives after conquering a paralyzing lumbago. Pale. Suffering. Impatient to come. He appears cold and formal, but I will learn later that he is distressed that he and I should meet at the station—formally. He conceals his feelings. His face is a mask.

We set out immediately for a walk. He talks about the "system" we have constructed and live by. Our own. But we have found nobody to live it with. It works for ourselves. It is a world. We are alone in it. We have a peculiar way of looking at things. By current standards we are amoral. We have not been true to human beings but to ourselves. To an inner development. We are barbaric and subliminal. We have lived like civilized barbarians. The most barbaric and the most sublimated.

We are not talking. We are merely certifying each other's theories.

Our phrases interlock. There is not a tangential word. Focused...on the same attitude. He says, "Exactly. I have always wanted to be complete— that is, civilized, but barbaric also, strong but sensitive." This aim he has realized as no other man in this world has. His whole life is a masterpiece of equilibrium, where the greatest elements for unbalance gather. An equilibrium of extraordinary finesse, over the deepest abyss. I recognize in him the king—the leader of the mental world I created alone, and in which Henry triumphed by his force, livingness, Allendy by his abstractions. But the similitudes, the final complete synthesis, is in Father. I see in Father the whole—the finished, the created whole. I am dazzled.

We had soared for an hour. At lunch he was sober, and the "doctor." Again cold in appearance. I realized how this mask had terrorized me. The tense will, the criticalness, the severity. How as a child I had the obscure terror that this man could never be satisfied. I wonder what this sense of my Father's exactingness contributed to my haunting pursuit of perfection. I wonder what obscure awareness of his demands, expectations of life, moved me to the great efforts I made.

He did not let me help him unpack. He was humiliated by his stiffness. He treated me as his fiancée. (He had told Maria, "I must go and join my fiancée." He used to call me his betrothed after I sent him a photograph of myself at sixteen.) I saw his pride, his vanity, too, his hatred of showing himself weak, sick, at a disadvantage. And at the same moment that I saw these traits in Father, I saw them starkly in myself. The coquetry. The fear of intimacy. The inordinate respect of illusion. Yet in all the days of his illness there was not a moment of disillusion. He bore it with such grace and such dignity. Though it hurt him deeply to move, he took his bath, he shaved; his hair was perfumed, his nails immaculate.

I did not insist. I knew he would yield slowly to intimacy, to my care, to my tenderness.

He rested a while. He met me looking fresh, immaculate, dressed with an ultimate, subtle elegance. Walking stiffly, but head high, joking about his infirmity. The people of the hotel, all at his service, adoring him, catering to his whims.

He took me out in his beautiful car. And I saw the car was for him, as for me, a toy which gives a sense of power. He was proud of it. We attended first to those things he could not live without: certain biscuits, Quaker Oats for breakfast, syrup, etc. Here his world was inexorably ordained. Order. Order in details. The need to have things at all costs. All logical, part of a vast web. The biscuits a necessity of health. An arranged universe in which the struggle against bad health is constant. The sole tragic flaw in both of us. The health which fails to obey the tyranny of our aspirations.

I could see in him a more rigid pattern. At certain moments I can yield, do without everything. His life is more molded than mine. I love certain things like breakfast in bed, Sultane cigarettes, taxis, perfume, but at any moment I can surrender them.

In the car, then, Father organized the details of his life. And then he sped out along the sea, reveling in the lights, the colors. We sat on a rock, facing the sea.

This moment he had imagined, visualized, and he had set about realizing it. And there he talked about his love affairs as I do, mixing pleasure with creativity, interested in the creation of a human being through love. Playing with souls. And I watched him, I watched his face. And I knew he was telling me the truth, that he was talking to me as I talk to my journal. That he was giving me himself. This self was generous, imaginative, creative. And at certain moments, inevitably untrue. He abandoned the woman when she ceased to have a meaning for him, because he did not love her, as I did not love Allendy or Artaud.

Evening. In his room. He tells me about his life with Mother. It is a revelation, and I know it is all true because I recognize the traits in Mother which made such a life possible. I am profoundly shocked. First because it is strange to discover the sexual life of one's parents—one's mother. Secondly because Mother had seemed a Puritan to me...always. So reserved, so unsympathetic, so secretive about sex. Religion. Morality. Bourgeoisie.

And now I discovered a war, a sexual war, like the one between Lawrence and Frieda, June and Henry. Father trying to ascend as an artist; Mother the spider, voracious, bestial, not voluptuous, naturalistic, unromantic. Destroyer of illusion. Unkempt, dirty, without coquetry or taste. She could take off her wig before Father, lie about in kimonos.

Terrible list of crude details. Smell of perspiration, strong smell of unwashed sex. These things tortured my Father, the aristocrat, cursed besides with an excessive sense of smell—a passion for perfumes and refinements. The period bandages left in the night table, the underclothing not changed every day. Voracious then, sexually aroused to exasperation by Father's ardors (and that night I discovered his ardor, which I had sensed), for he was capable of taking Mother several times a day, and every day, and after the hardest work, and after a visit to a mistress—to calm her suspicion. Mother *understood nothing*, could not be reasoned with, was primitive in her jealousies, irritable, tyrannical. Terrible quarrels burst between them. Violent scenes in which Father wore out the energy he needed for other purposes. Finally, for the sake of peace, he would yield. He read at meals to evade quarrels (this was a detail which I had interpreted as indifference to us).

What prevented him from abandoning Mother was the children. Father has a strong Spanish clannishness, a sense of paternity, sacredness of family.

I cannot note down the entire story of Father's life as he told it to me. What I want is to seize him, the king, the solitary and obstinate visionary, visionary of balance, fairness, logic, transcendentalism.

The pity that this marriage aroused in me was replaced suddenly by a spark of ironic amusement. We were talking about our diabolicalness. I told Father about my liking to go with both Henry and Eduardo to the same hotel room (not at the same time!)—and why, I asked him? This simple statement revealed a world to him. He smiled: "I have done that, too." I could see the statement creating repercussions in him—revealing secrets. A secret, ironic pact of similarity between us.

When I left him I kissed him filially, without the feelings of a daughter. He suddenly bowed his head and kissed my neck.

As I walked down the hall to my room, he stood watching me, but I did not know it. Before entering, I turned back, expecting to see him. He was in too dark a recess, and I did not see him. But he had seen me turn around.

The next morning he could not move from his bed. He was in despair. I enveloped him in gaiety and tenderness. I finally unpacked his bags while he talked to me. And he continued the story of his life. Meals were brought to the room. I wore my satin negligee. The hours passed swiftly. I talked too—I told him the story of the flagellation.

When I described how I stood off and observed the commonness of the scene, Father was amazed. This fact seemed again to touch some secret spring of his own nature. He appeared for a moment not to listen, to be absorbed in the dream of his discovery—as I get with people. But then he said, "You are the synthesis of all the women I have loved."

He was watching me constantly. He said, "When you were a child you were beautifully made, formed. You had such a *dos cambré*. I loved taking photographs of you."

I sat all day at the foot of his bed. He caressed my foot.

Then he asked, "Do you believe in dreams?"

"Yes."

"I had a dream of you which frightened me. I dreamed that you masturbated me with jeweled fingers and that I kissed you like a lover. For the first time in my life I was terrified. It was after my visit to Louveciennes."

"I also had a dream of you."

"I don't feel toward you as if you were my daughter."

"I don't feel as if you were my Father."

"What a tragedy. What are we going to do about it? I have met *the* woman of my life, the ideal, and it is my daughter! I cannot even kiss you as I would like to. I'm in love with my own daughter!"

"Everything you feel, I feel."

After each one of these phrases there was a long silence. A heavy silence. A great simplicity of phrases. We did not even move. We looked at each other as in a dream, and I answered him with strange candor, directness.

"When I saw you in Louveciennes I was terribly upset by you. Did you feel it?" he said.

"I was disturbed by you."

"Bring Freud here, and all the psychologists. What could they say about this?"

Another suspense.

"I have been greatly afraid, too," I said.

"We must not let this fear make us unnatural toward each other. And I was all the more afraid, Anaïs, when I realized you are a liberated woman, an *affranchie*."

"I have already felt myself putting on the brakes."

"I have been desperately jealous of Hugo."

Father asked me to move nearer. He was lying on his back and could not move.

"Let me kiss your mouth." He put his arms around me. I hesitated. I was tortured by a complexity of feelings, wanting his mouth, yet afraid, feeling I was to kiss a brother, yet tempted—terrified and desirous. I was taut. He smiled and opened his mouth. We kissed, and that kiss unleashed a wave of desire. I was lying across his body and with my breast I felt his desire, hard, palpitating. Another kiss. More terror than joy. The joy of something unnameable, obscure. He so beautiful—godlike and womanly, seductive and chiseled, hard and soft. A hard passion.

"We must avoid possession," he said, "but, oh, let me kiss you." He caressed my breasts and the tips hardened. I was resisting, saying no, but my nipples hardened. And when his hand caressed me—oh, the knowingness of those caresses—I melted. But all the while some part of me was hard and terrified. My body yielded to the penetration of his hand, but I resisted, I resisted enjoyment. I resisted showing my body. I only uncovered my breasts. I was timid and unwilling, yet passionately moved. "I want you to enjoy, to enjoy," he said. "Enjoy." And his caresses were so acute, so subtle; but I couldn't, and to escape from him I pretended to. Again I lay over him and felt the hardness of his penis. He uncovered himself. I caressed him with my hand. I saw him quiver with desire.

With a strange violence, I lifted my negligee and I lay over him. "*Toi, Anaïs! Je n'ai plus de Dieu!*"

Ecstatic, his face, and I now frenzied with the desire to unite with him... undulating, caressing him, clinging to him. His spasm was tremendous, of his whole being. He emptied all of himself in me...and my yielding was immense, with my whole being, with only that core of fear which arrested the supreme spasm in me.

Then I wanted to leave him. Still, in some remote region of my being, a revulsion. And he feared the reaction in me. I wanted to run away. I wanted to leave him. But I saw him so vulnerable. And there was something terrible about his lying on his back, crucified, while yet so potent—something compelling. And I remembered how in all my loves there has been a reaction away—that I had always been so afraid.

And this flight, I would not hurt him with. No, not after the years of pain my last rejection had caused him. But at this moment, after the passion, I had at least to go to my room, to be alone. I was poisoned by this union. I was not free to enjoy the splendor of it, the magnificence of it. Some sense of guilt weighed down on my joy and continued to weigh down on me, but I could not reveal this to him. He was free—he was passionately free—he was older and more courageous. I would learn from him. I would at last be humble and learn something from my Father!

I went to my room, poisoned. The mistral was blowing, blowing, dry and hot. It had blown for days, from the moment I arrived. It racked my nerves. I thought of nothing. I was divided, and dying because of the division—the struggle to seize joy, and joy unattainable. The oppressive unreality. Life again receding, eluding me. I had the man I loved with my mind; I had him in my arms, in my body. I had the essence of his blood in my body. The man I sought throughout the world, who branded my childhood and haunted me. I had loved fragments of him in other men: the brilliance of John, the compassion of Allendy, the abstractions of Artaud, the creative force and dynamism of Henry—and the *whole* was there, body and face so beautiful, so ardent, with a greater force, all unified, synthesized, more brilliancy, more abstractions, and more force and more sensuality!

This man's love, because of the similitudes between us, because of the blood relation, atrophied my joy. And so life played on me its old trick of dissolving, of losing its palpableness, its normalcy. The mistral wind blew and the shape and savors were destroyed. The sperm was a poison, a love that was a poison...

When I told him in the morning that I wanted to run away, that I felt brakes on, hesitancies, he said simply, "You cannot do that. You must be stronger than that. You must have courage. We are living out something tremendous, fantastic, unique..."

"And if I resist you?"

"I will seduce you," he said, smiling.

"Do you regret nothing?"

"Nothing! Last night was the San Juan feast. A beautiful night for our union. We burned away all the prejudices. We flamed up with a new passion. I have never, never felt anything so absolute. How I gave myself to you! All the other moments of love, I realize now, were incomplete—a game. Last night I realized what love is. I poured my whole being into you."

It all seemed too wonderful to destroy.

We spent another day in his room. He moved with great difficulty and pain, yet he shaved and bathed. He sat in an armchair and read me his manuscript on musical opinions and sketches. In between, there were autobiographical sketches and poems—romantic poems. The whole book was romantic, idealistic, not as muscular or as dynamic as his own life. It is his own life which is a masterpiece.

At night—caresses. He begs me to undress and lie at his side. His caressing suppleness and mine, the feelings which run from head to toes—vibrations of all the senses, a thousand new vibrations...a new union, a unison of delicacies, subtleties, exaltations, keener awareness and perception and tentacles. A joy which spreads in vast circles, a joy for me without climax because of that deeper, inner holding back. Yet missing only the climax and revealing by this very absence what intensity he and I could bring to the envelopment, to the radius and rainbows of a climax.

We sat up until two or three, talking. "What a tragedy that I find you and cannot marry you." It was he who was preoccupied with enchanting me. It was he who talked, who was anxious, who displayed all his seductions. It was I who was being courted, magnificently. And he said, "How good it is that I should be courting you. Women have always sought me out, courted me: I have only been gallant with them."

Endless stories about women. Exploits. Teaching me at the same time the last expertness in love—the games, the subtleties, new caresses. I had at moments the feeling that here was Don Juan indeed, Don Juan who had possessed more than a thousand women, and I was lying there learning from him, and he was telling me how much talent I had, how amazing an amorous sensibility, how beautifully tuned and responsive I was. Amazed at the richness of my honey. "You walk like a courtesan from Greece. You seem to offer your sex when you walk."

When I walked down the dark hall to my room—with a handkerchief between my legs because his sperm is overabundant—the mistral was blowing, and I felt a veil between life and me, between joy and me. All this unfolded itself as it should, gloriously—but without the ultimate spark of joy, because at certain moments he was the unknown lover, the glamorous Spaniard expert in seductions, lover in love with his mind and his spirit and soul, and at other times too intimate, too like myself, with the same contractions of fear and lack of confidence, the same *survoltage*, the same exacerbated sensibilities. And what caused me anxiety were certain remarks: "I would like to replace your other lovers. I know I could have if I were forty instead of fifty-four. In a few years, perhaps, there will not be any more riquette, and then you will abandon me." Unbearable to me, his insecurity, he the lion, the jungle king, the most virile man I have known. For it amazes me to find a greater sensual force than Henry—to see him all day in a state of erection, and his *riquette*, his penis, so hard, so agile, so heavy.

The next night, when he was a little freer in his movements and he lay over me, it was an orgy, and he penetrated me three and four times without pausing and without withdrawing—his new strength, new desire, and new spurt coming like waves following each other. I sank into the dim, veiled, unclimaxed joy, into the mist of caresses, languors, into continuous excitation, experiencing at last, profoundly, a passion for this man, a passion founded on awe, admiration. It ceased to concern me, the attainment of my own joy. I plunged into the completion of his. I told him these had been the most beautiful nights of my life, and when I said this I saw he had wanted keenly to know if this were so. I poured out love, worship, awareness. And the fourth night was again different. He did not believe in excess, in exhaustion. He wanted the high exaltation preserved. I told him about the painting of Lot and his daughters. He said, "You are still a child." But I remembered he had said the first night, "*Je n'ai plus de Dieu*—I have lost God."

The mistral quieted down. We laughed together about the consumption of handkerchiefs. We laughed about obscene words I taught him in English. He went into a long fantastic tale, full of puns, about a speech he would make to Mother: "*Tu m'a pris souvent, mais tu ne savais pas comment me prendre. Anaïs sait. Je voudrais l'epouser.*" ["You have taken me often, but you did not know how to take me. Anaïs knows. I would like to marry her."] We laughed at the faces certain people would make if they knew.

With his will he was growing better. The first day he could go downstairs for lunch, he dressed to perfection, and with his alabaster skin, his clothes, his neat figure (he has small feet and hands), his soft hat, he looked so grandiose, so aristocratic, so unreal: a Spanish grandee, a king; walking slowly under a tropical sun, teaching me about the life of insects, the names of birds, and the distinctions between their cries, so that the world became peopled with new sounds, and everywhere I go now I cannot hear the cries of the swallows without remembering him and his walk and his face in the sun. *Le Roi Soleil.*

Once we sat in the blazing sun, alone in the garden. He had taken a chair in front of me. He observed that a stocking was wrinkled. I tightened my garter. The spectacle stirred him. He showed me his penis, tense. He asked me to lift my dress. I did so and began to undulate, moving as if in expectancy of a lancing. When we both could not bear the excitement any longer, we went to his room and he threw me on the bed and took me from behind.

"*Qué picara,*" he said. "*¡Tan picara como su padre!* Who do you take after, you little devil? Not me!"

One night we walked along the terrace in the moonlight. He looked twenty-five years old—like Joaquin. He said, "Even your height is what I dreamed. I always wanted a woman with eyes on a level with my own. And there you are. Tall, royal. A sun. You are a sun. You not only match and meet and equal my thoughts, you sometimes precede me! A match! I have found my match.

"Such a tenuous balance," he said. "We could easily be unbalanced. Our balance hangs on the most tenuous thread. All the more wonderful if we can maintain it. Look for the *light*, for clarity. Be more and more Latin!"

When the servant presented the mail and Father saw letters for me, he said, "Am I going to be jealous of your letters, too?"

Our last night. He did not want to go to the room. We stayed and talked to people. When we were in bed, naked, close, he began to sob. I was touched and so amazed. Nothing ever took me more by surprise. *He, he,* weeping because we were separating. He saying, "Now you see me weak like a woman."

Another man. The sensitive, the sentimental man. And I enshrouded in unreality, so that I realized acutely that in love there is always the one who gives and the one who receives. And how uneasy and strange I feel when I receive. Awkward. Yes, it was he who gave, who gave himself. I could not sleep. I felt ungenerous. It was he who had wept. I awoke early. I rushed to his room. I felt keen pangs of regret. I was amazed at my own self, that it was I who was leaving—yet he alone would have understood why. Fear of disillusion, fear that I should break physically, be less beautiful, less than all he expected. A flight from the most precious experience at a certain moment, always. *Trop pleine.* Like him, wanting all ecstasies to remain suspended— never satiation in love. Fear of satiation. Feeling our ecstasy had been timed perfectly, that since he was so much me, he too would want the pause.

To achieve this flight, which also meant keeping my word to Henry, I had to lie endlessly to everyone. A web of lies. Father had to believe I was returning to Paris. Hugo would understand that I should not return for reasons of health. But then if I returned to Paris I had to visit Father's wife. Thus I must pretend to go to London with Hugo's family. Hugo must think I was going to the mountains. But Henry expected me in Avignon. I had never hated my lies so. I was imprisoned in all my deceptions at once. I did not want Father to know I could go to Henry after nine days with him. I did not want Henry to know I did not want to join him.

After I saw Father vanishing at the station, a great misery and coldness overcame me. I sat inert, remembering obsessively. A suffocation. A leaden mood. Tumult, nervousness, chaos. I am leaving a man I feared to love—an unnatural love. From that moment, reality sank into the sea. I was living a dream. I was going to meet a man I had loved humanly, a natural love. I wanted clarity and wholeness and definiteness, and they eluded me. For five hours I thought of my *padre-amour*... unfocused...bewildered.

Notes

Text: *Incest: From "A Journal of Love," the Unexpurgated Diary of Anaïs Nin, 1932-1934* (New York: Harcourt Brace Jovanovich, 1992), 204-15.

Father is Joaquín Nin. Henry is Henry Miller. Allendy is René Allendy. Maria is María Luísa (Maruca) Rodríguez de Nin. Artaud is Antonin Artaud. Mother is Rosa Culmell de Nin. Frieda is Frieda Lawrence (1879-1956), wife of D. H. Lawrence. June is June Miller. Eduardo is Eduardo Sánchez. In mentioning flagellation, Nin refers to Allendy's whipping of her. "*Dos cambré*" means "arched back." Nin's father visited Louveciennes in May 1933. Freud is Sigmund Freud (1856-1939), the father of psychoanalysis. "*Affranchie*" means "freed one." Hugo is Hugh Guiler. "*Toi, Anaïs! Je n'ai plus de Dieu!*" means "You, Anaïs! I no longer have God." John is John Erskine. "*Survoltage*" means "boosting." "*Riquette*" implies "erection." Lot and his daughters have been rendered by several artists, including Bonifazio de' Pitati (1487-1553), Lucas Van Leyden (1494-1533), Hendrick Goltzius (1558-1617), Guido Reni (1575-1642), and Artemisia Gentileschi (1593-ca. 1653). "*Le Roi Soleil*" means "The Sun King." "*Qué picara. ¡Tan picara como su padre!*" means "How naughty. You're as mischievous as your father." Joaquin is Joaquín Nin-Culmell. "*Trop pleine*" means "too full." "*Padre-amour*" means "father-lover."

⊂ℜ *DIARY 1* ℬ

Remembering Paco Miralles

Context

In 1928, Nin took Spanish dancing lessons with Paco Miralles. Hugh Guiler did, too, in order to please her and possibly also to protect her against Miralles's advances. She based the opening pages of the novel *Children of the Albatross* (1947) on her experiences with Miralles.

◆ ◆ ◆ ◆

October, 1933. The death of Antonio Francisco Miralles in a hotel room, alone, of asthma. Miralles, my Spanish dancing teacher.

Whenever I stepped off the bus at Montmartre, I could hear the music of the merry-go-rounds at the fair, and I would feel my mood, my walk, my whole body transformed by its gaiety. I walked to a side street, knocked on a dark doorway opened by a disheveled concierge, and ran down the stairway to a vast room below street level, a vast cellar room with its walls covered with mirrors. It was the place where the little girls from the Opera Ballet rehearsed. When I came down the stairway I could hear the piano, feet stamping, and the ballet master's voice. When the piano stopped, there was always his voice scolding, and the whispering of smaller voices. As I entered, the class was dissolving and a flurry of little girls brushed by me in their moth ballet costumes, laughing and whispering, fluttering like moths on their dusty ballet slippers, flurries of snow in the darkness of the vast room, with drops of dew from exertion. I went down with them along the corridors to the dressing rooms. These looked like gardens, with so many ballet skirts, Spanish costumes hanging on pegs. It overflowed with the smell of cold cream, face powder, cheap cologne.

While they dressed for the street, I dressed for my Spanish dances. Miralles would already be rehearsing his own castanets. The piano, slightly out of tune, was beginning the dance of Granados. The floor was beginning to vibrate as other Spanish dancers tried out their heel work. Tap tap tap tap tap. Miralles was about forty, slender, erect, not handsome in face but graceful when dancing. His face was undefined, his features blurred.

I was the favorite.

He was like a gentle Svengali, and by his eyes, his voice, his hands, he had the power to make me dance as well as by his ordinary lessons. He ruled my body with a magnetic rule, master of my dancing.

One day he waited for me at the door, neat and trim. "Will you come and sit at the café with me?"

I followed him. Not far from there was the Place Clichy, always animated, but more so now, as the site of a permanent fair. The merry-go-rounds were turning swiftly. The gypsies were reading fortunes in little booths hung with Arabian rugs. Workmen were shooting clay pigeons and winning cut glass for their wives. The prostitutes were enjoying their loitering, and the men were watching them.

My dancing teacher was saying to me: "Anaïs, I am a simple man. My parents were shoemakers in a little village in the south of Spain. I was put to work in an iron factory where I handled heavy things and was on the way to becoming deformed by big muscles. But during my lunch hour, I danced. I wanted to be a dancer and I practiced every day, every night. At night I went to the gypsies' caverns, and learned from them. I began to dance in cabarets. And today, look!" He took out a cigarette case engraved with the names of all the famous Spanish dancers. "Today I have been the partner of all these women. If you would come with me, we could be happy. I am a simple man, but we could dance in all the cities of Europe. I am no longer young but I have a lot of dancing in me yet. We could be happy."

The merry-go-round turned and sang, and I imagined myself embarking on a dancing career with Miralles, dancing, which was so much like flying, from city to city, receiving bouquets, praise in newspapers, with joyous music at the center always, pleasure as colorful as the Spanish dresses, all red, orange, black and gold, gold and purple, and red and white.

Imagining...like amnesia. Forgetting who I was, and where I was, and why I could not do it. Not knowing how to answer so I would not hurt him, I said, "I am not strong enough."

"That's what I thought when I first saw you. I thought you couldn't take the discipline of a dancer's life. But it isn't so. You look fragile and all that, but you're healthy. I can tell healthy women by their skin. Yours is shining and clear. No, I don't think you have the strength of a horse, you're what we call a *petite nature*. But you have energy and guts. And we'll take it easy on the road."

Many afternoons, after hard work, we sat at this little café and imagined what a dancer's life might be.

Miralles and I danced in several places together, at a *haute couture* opening, at a millionaire Brazilian's open house, at a night club; but when I auditioned for the Opera, *Amor Brujo*, and was accepted and would have traveled all over the world, I gave up dancing [1928].

And Miralles died alone in his hotel room, of asthma. He had been saving his money to retire to his home town, Valencia. He was good, homely, and would say to me: "You know, I have no vices like the others. I would be good to you." Just because I listened to his gaudy stories of a gaudy past, he glowed, he went at his dancing with renewed vigor, he was rejuvenated, he bought himself a new suit.

For a while, it was as if I had lived in his shabby hotel room, with photographs of Spanish dancers pinned to the walls. I knew how it was in Russia, in music halls all over the world. The odor of the dancers, of dressing rooms, the pungent atmosphere of rehearsals. Lola, Alma Viva, L'Argentinita. I would wear bedroom slippers and flowered kimonos, big Spanish flowered cottons. I would open the door and my father would be standing there, saying: "Have you forgotten who you are? You are my daughter, you have forgotten your class, your name, your true stature in life."

One day I awakened from my amnesia. No longer a dancer. Miralles turned ashen and grey, was snuffed out. He became again an old, weary dancing teacher.

Notes

Text: *The Diary of Anaïs Nin, 1931-1934* (New York: Swallow Press/ Harcourt, Brace & World, 1966), 262-64.

Antonio Francisco (Paco) Miralles (d. 1933) was Nin's dancing teacher. Granados is Enrique Granados. Manuel de Falla's *El Amor Brujo* (1915) includes the famous "Ritual Fire Dance," which was popularized in dance by La Argentina, stage name of Antonia Mercé y Luque (1890-1936). Lola is probably Lola Montez (1821-1861). I cannot identify a dancer named Alma Viva, though Nin might refer to Countess Almaviva, a character in operas based on plays by Pierre Beaumarchais (1732-1799). La Argentinta, a different dancer from La Argentina, was Encarnación López Júlvez (1898-1945), known as "Queen of the Spanish Dance."

❧ *INCEST* ❧

Context

Probably in the spring of 1934, Nin became pregnant; months later, she had an abortion. Although she preferred thinking that Henry Miller impregnated her, Hugh Guiler could have. Nin used the abortion experience as the basis for fiction, most fully and artfully in the story "Birth."

◆ ◆ ◆ ◆

August 27, 1934. My life will always be a tragedy. Now I am in Louveciennes with Henry, packing books for our home, making plans, filing our manuscripts, and thinking all the while of Rank, yearning for his love, hoping Henry will not desire me. I don't really want to live with Henry, yet I have made this life myself. Today I want to live *alone*, because I love too many men.

It is Henry now who clings, who is jealous, but is he not being given what his egoism calls for? A half love.

Tuesday. Saw a doctor, who discovered the *sage-femme* has accomplished nothing. I have to be operated on, and the child is six months old, and alive and normal. It will be almost a childbirth. It will take over a week. I had begun to feel so heaving, and there were slight tremors inside of my womb. I look down and see the round white stomach. My breasts are full of milk, a milk that is not yet sweet. As I walk up the hill toward Rank I think of the child. I could give it away to Mother, and that might deliver Joaquin. But otherwise it would be nothing but a fetter. It does not belong in my life with Henry; it does not belong with Rank, who has a child and too many burdens already; it does not belong to Hugh because it is not his child and could only cause him sorrow. It belongs nowhere. I am a mistress. I have already too many children. There are too many men without hope and faith in the world. Too much work to do, too many to serve and care for. Already I have more than I can bear. I am trying to give to Hugh, to Henry, and to Rank.

When I got to Rank he was sad and brooding. He is being pushed to go to New York, offered plenty of money and a job. He had debts. But he wants to stay here. "How can I go there and just work, without living. My life is here with you. I don't want to go. I never wanted success. Now less than ever."

These conflicts, which he helps others to solve, he must solve alone. I cannot help him. It is not a question of six months or a year, but of an indefinite time. Why don't I come with him as assistant?

I would follow him anywhere.

I know I want to go with him. I love his sadness, his tenacity, his caring. We could face New York together, work together. "If I could be happy in my life," said Rank.

August 29. After seeing Rank so sad, only for an hour, I suddenly felt a great distress. Hugh was not arriving from London until midnight. I telephoned Henry, who was at the Lowenfelses', asking him to join me. He was slow and hesitant. It hurt me. I hung up brusquely. I went to Louveciennes. But this morning I went to him, meaning to call him a monster and remembering, for some unknown reason, the Henry who, while his wife was being operated on, was fucking a Negress on the table. His callousness. But the "monster" had left the Lowenfelses' last night all upset, had looked for me in several cafés, had come home at ten and waited for me, had a headache from worry, and looked quite ravaged. All my feelings about his imagined cruelty vanished. He would not let me have lunch with the Lowenfelses. He was terribly anxious about the abortion, terribly tender. But I would not let him take me. I was thinking of Rank, whom I was meeting at three.

Rank and I went to the boulevard Suchet apartment, which is empty. And we were overwhelmed with sadness. It stifled our desire. His going to London for four days seemed like a foretaste of his departure for America.

All night, neither one of us had slept.

I was awake, thinking I could not bear life without him, that again I had thrown myself into a purely physical passion and it was becoming love, a slavery, a whole. Not just the hour of possession. And pain and seriousness came with love.

I don't understand.

The violence of my feeling for Rank is almost terrifying.

When he left, I wandered through the place, restless and nervous. I occupied my hands. I thought how strange it was that Rank was living a block away when I lived on the boulevard Suchet, when my life was so empty and tragic. He was living and working where I often passed in my walks, in those walks I took desiring John and imagining John kissing me. Memories. The life in Suchet. The explosion of color and dancing, together with the starvation of soul and senses.

The place was lovely. I prepared the bed to receive the doctor tomorrow. I was glad of the soothing, glad of the decor in which the Princess was going to abort.

I sat in the studio, talking to my child. I told my child he should be glad not to be thrust into this black world in which even the greatest joys are tainted with pain, in which we are slaves to material forces. He kicked and stirred. So full of energy, oh, my child, my half-created child that I will thrust back into the *néant* again. Back into obscurity and unconsciousness, and the paradise of nonbeing. I have known you; I have lived with you. You are only the future. You are the abdication. I live in the present, with men who are closer to death. I want men, not a future extension of myself into a branch. My little one, not born yet, I feel your small feet kicking against my womb. My little one, not born yet, it is very dark in the room you and I are sitting in, just as dark as it must be for you inside of me, but it must be sweeter for you to be lying in the warmth than it is for me to be seeking in this dark room the joy of not knowing, not feeling, not seeing, the joy of lying still and quiet in utter warmth and darkness. All of us forever seeking again this warmth and this darkness, this being alive without pain, this being alive without anxiety or fear or aloneness. You are impatient to live; you kick with your small feet, my little one, not born yet; you ought to die. You ought to die before knowing light or pain or cold. You ought to die in warmth and darkness. You ought to die because you are fatherless.

You and I, my journal, alone, with the bottles of medicine, in the sumptuous bedroom. Hugh has gone to get medicine. The German doctor has been here. While he operates we talk about the persecution of the Jews in Berlin. I help him wash the instruments. I wear the "charm" which Rank gave me. I dream of him. In this same room, a few years ago, I suffered from the emptiness of my life. Now I am suffering from an overabundance! I got up so gaily, as if I were going on a voyage. I am so happy, no amount of physical pain can cower me. Life is full of wonder, even when I see the bloodstained rags. I thought this morning of how Henry greeted me once: "Here is the Princess Aubergine." And I telephoned him this morning: "Come and visit the palace of the Princess Aubergine, where the Prince Aubergin will be born." And an hour later I was opening my legs to instruments. The doctor said I could not have a child without a Caesarian operation. I am too small. I was not built for maternity. I am surrounded with so much love that it makes me weep.

You are a child without a father, just as I was a child without a father. You are born of man, but you have no father. This man who married me, it was he who fathered me. I could not bear it that he should take care of another and that I should be an orphan again. This care is the only care I have known. With everybody else it was I who did all the caring. I nursed the whole world. When there was a war I wept for all the wounds inflicted, and wherever there was injustice I struggled to return life, to re-create hope. The woman loved and cared too much. And inside of this woman there was still a child without a father, a child who did not die when it should have died. There was still the ghost of a little girl forever wailing inside, bewailing the loss of a father. This man who married me, he took care of her, and now, if you came, you would take him for a father and this little ghost would never let me alone. It would knock at the windows; it would cry at every caress he gave you. You are also the child of an artist, my child unborn. And this man is not a father; he is a child, he is the artist. He needs all the care, all the warmth, all the faith for himself. There is no end to his needs. He needs faith, indulgence, humor. He needs worship. He needs to be the only one in the world we created together. He is my child, and he would hate you. And if he did not hate you, he would hate your sickness, your wailing, and the woman who bore a child. I must nourish his creation and his hopes with all I have. He would cast you aside. He would run away from you, just as he ran away from his wife and his other little girl, because he is not a father. He feels awkward before a human child with needs. He does not understand the needs of others. He is too full of his own hunger. You would be abandoned, and you would suffer as I suffered when I was abandoned by my father, who was not a father but the artist, and the child. It would be better to die, my child, unborn; it would be better to die than to be abandoned, for you would spend your life haunting the world for this lost father, this fragment of your body and soul, this lost fragment of your very self. *There is no father on earth.* The father is this shadow of God the Father cast on the world, a shadow larger than man. This shadow you would worship and seek to touch, dreaming day and night of its warmth and of its greatness, dreaming of it covering you and lulling you, larger than a hammock, as large as the sky, big enough to hold your soul and all your fears, larger than man or woman, than church or house, the shadow of a magic father which is nowhere to be found—it is the shadow of God the Father. It would be better if you died inside of me, quietly, in the warmth and in the darkness.

Hugh drove us to the *clinique.* I was shaved and prepared for the major operation. I felt resigned, and yet, deep down, terrified of the anaesthetic. Remembrances of other anaesthetics. Feeling of oppression. Difficulty in breathing. Anxiety. Like a birth-trauma dream. Suffocation. Fear of death.

Fear of yielding to eternal sleep. Fear of dying. But I lay smiling and making jokes. I was wheeled to the operating room. Legs tied, raised, the pose of love, in an operating room, with the clatter of instruments and the smell of antiseptic, and the voice of the doctor, and I trembling with cold, blue with cold and anxiety.

The smell of ether. The cold numbness trickling through the veins. The heaviness, the paralysis, but the mind still clear and struggling against death, against sleep. The voices growing dimmer. The incapacity to answer. The desire to sigh, to sob, to murmur. "*Ça va, madame; ça va, madame? Ça va, madame, ça va madame ça va madame...*" The heart beats desperately, loudly, as if about to burst. Then you sleep, you fall, you roll, you dream, dream, dream; you are anxious. Dream of a drilling machine drilling between your legs, but into numbness. Drilling. You awake to voices. Vomiting. The voices growing louder: "*Ça va, madame? Elle vomit. Faut-il lui en donner encore? Non. C'est fini.*" I weep. The heart, the heart is pressed and weary. Breathing so difficult. My first thought is to reassure the doctor, so I say, "*C'est très bien, très bien, très bien.*"

I lie in my bed. When I see Hugh, I weep. I come back from death, from darkness, out of fear, an absence from life.

The doctor waits anxiously. At ten o'clock, he examines me again, probes me, hurts me. Exhausts me. The next morning, he has to operate again.

I have talked with Hugh about my fear of anaesthetic. He has urged me not to fight it, to let go, to think of it as a drug, as a forgetting. Had I not always wanted drugs, wanted to forget?

For the second time I yield to the ether. I yield to sleep. I resign myself to die. And the anxiety is lessened. I let myself go.

It is shorter this time. The awakening is less heavy with anxiety.

I had worn a towel, like a nun, so as not to wet my hair.

I felt that if Rank would only come everything would be well. But he was in London. Toward eight o'clock I had several spasms of pain. The doctor thought it would happen. He sent for a nurse. I made several fruitless efforts. He tormented me with his hands. I only ejected the balloon which he had placed inside of me during the operation. It was punctured and therefore ineffectual. He was in despair, tried to urge me to labor. I labored fruitlessly until midnight. I was exhausted. Then he began to prod me with his instruments. I was at the end of my endurance. I begged him only for a rest, just to let me sleep for a few hours. I could not bear any more. He let me.

I slept fitfully and called out to Rank, called him with all my being. In the morning, the doctor came and said he would let me rest all day. Early in the morning I had asked Hugh to telephone Rank to come. And as soon as he had done this, I was relieved. Rank said he would be in Paris that evening.

I combed my hair; I powdered, perfumed myself, painted my eyelashes. I sent for Henry. He came, looking haggard and desperate: "Oh, Anaïs, Anaïs, what torture. God, I don't know what to say, but I love you, I love you." We embraced. Hugh came. Eduardo.

At six o'clock Rank came. And this joy I felt was so terrible, so immense. All this love calling me back to life. He came. Overflowing with love. I was illumined. I revived. I felt his strength.

Sunday evening.

At eight o'clock I was taken to the operating room. I lay stretched on a table. I had no place to rest my legs. I had to keep them raised. Two nurses leaned over me. In front of me stood the German doctor with the face of a woman and eyes protruding with anger and fear.

For two hours I had been making violent efforts. The child inside of me was six months old, and yet it was too big for me. I was exhausted; the veins in me were swelling with the strain. I had pushed with my whole being, I had pushed as if I wanted this child out of my body and hurled into another world. "Push, push with all your strength!"

Was I pushing with *all* my strength? All my strength? No. A part of me did not want to push out the child. The doctor knew it. That is why he was angry, mysteriously angry. He knew.

A part of me lay passive, did not want to push anyone, not even this dead fragment of myself, out into the cold, outside of me. All of me which chose to keep, to lull, to embrace, to love, all of me which carried, preserved, and protected, all of me which imprisoned the whole world in its passionate tenderness, this part of me would not thrust the child out, nor this past which had died in me. Even though it threatened my life, I could not break, tear out, separate, surrender, open and dilate and yield up a fragment of a life like a fragment of the past; this part of me rebelled against pushing the child, or anyone, out into the cold, to be picked up by strange hands, to be buried in a strange place, to be lost.

He knew—the doctor. A few hours before, he loved me, adored me, served me. Now he was angry. And I was angry, with a black anger, at this part of me which refused to push, to kill, to separate, to lose. Push! Push! Push with all your strength! I pushed with anger, with despair, with frenzy, with the feeling that I would die pushing, as one exhales the last breath, that I would push out everything inside of me; and my soul with all the blood around it, and the sinews with my heart inside of them would choke, and my body itself would open and smoke would rise, and I would feel the ultimate incision of death.

The nurses leaned over me and they talked to each other while I rested. Then I pushed until I heard my bones cracking, until my veins swelled. I closed my eyes so hard I saw lightning and waves of red and purple.

There was a stir in my ears, a beating as if the tympana had burst. I closed my lips so tightly the blood was trickling. My legs felt enormously heavy, like marble columns, like immense marble columns crushing my body. I was pleading for someone to hold them. The nurse laid her knee on my stomach and shouted, "Push! Push! Push!" Her perspiration fell on me. The doctor paced up and down angrily and impatiently: "We will be here all night. Three hours now." The head was showing, but I had fainted. Everything was blue, then black. The instruments seemed to be gleaming before my closed eyes. Knives sharpened in my ears. Ice and silence.

Then I heard voices, at first talking too fast for me to understand. A curtain was parted; the voices still tripped over each other, falling fast like a waterfall, with sparks, and hurting my ears. The table was rolling gently, rolling. The women were lying in the air. Heads. Heads hung where the enormous white bulbs of the lamps hung. The doctor was still walking, the lamps moved, the heads came near, very near, and the words came more slowly.

They were laughing. One nurse was saying, "When I had my first child I was all ripped to pieces. I had to be sewed up again, and then I had another, and had to be sewed up, and then I had another."

The nurses talked. The words kept turning, like on a disk. They kept saying over and over again that the bag would not come out, that the child should have slipped out like a letter in a letter box, that they were so tired with so many hours of work. They laughed at what the doctor said. They said there was no more of that bandage, it was too late to get any. They washed instruments, and they talked, they talked, they talked.

"Please hold my legs! Please hold my legs! Please hold my legs! PLEASE HOLD MY LEGS!" I am ready again. By throwing my head back I can see the clock. I have been struggling four hours. It would be better to die. Why am I alive and struggling so desperately? I could not remember why I should want to live. Why *live*? I could not remember anything. I heard women talk. I saw eyes bulging out, and blood. Everything was blood and pain. What was it to *live*? How could one feel to *live*?

I have to push. I have to push. That is a black point, a fixed point in eternity. At the end of a long, dark tunnel. I have to push. A voice saying,

"Push! Push! Push!" A knee on my stomach, and the marble of the legs and the head too large, and I have to push. Am I pushing or am I dying? The light up there, the immense, round, blazing white light, is drinking me. It drinks me. It drinks me slowly, sucks me into space; if I do not close my eyes it will drink all of me. I seep upward, in long icy threads, too light, and yet inside there is a fire, too, the nerves are twisted; there is no repose from this long tunnel dragging me, or from me pushing myself out of the tunnel, or from the child being pushed out of me and the light drinking me. If I do not close my eyes, the light will drink my whole being, and I will no longer be able to push myself out of the tunnel.

Am I dying? The ice in the veins, the cracking of the bones, this pushing in blackness with a small shaft of light in the eyes like the edge of a knife, the feeling of a knife cutting the flesh, the flesh somewhere tearing as if it were burned through by a flame—somewhere my flesh is tearing and the blood is spilling out. I am pushing in the darkness, in utter darkness. I am pushing, pushing until I open my eyes and I see the doctor, who is holding a long instrument which he swiftly thrusts into me, and the pain makes me howl. A long animal howl.

"That will make her push," he says to the nurse. But it does not. It paralyzes me with pain. He wants to do it again. I sit up with fury and I shout at him, "If you do that again I won't push. Don't you dare do that again, don't you dare!" The heat of my anger warms me; all the ice and pain are melted in the fury. I have an instinct that what he has done is unnecessary, that he has done it because he is in a rage, because the needles on the clock keep turning, the dawn is coming, and the child does not come out and I am losing strength, and the injections do not produce the spasm. The body—neither the nerves nor the muscles do anything to eject this child. Only my will and my strength. My fury frightens him, and he stands away and waits.

These legs I opened to joy, this honey that flowed out in the joy—now the legs are twisted in pain and the honey flows with the blood. The same pose and the same wetness of passion, but this is dying and not loving.

I look at the doctor pacing up and down or bending to look at the head, which is barely showing. The legs like scissors, and the head barely showing. He looks baffled, as before a savage mystery, baffled by this struggle. He wants to interfere with his instruments, while I struggle with nature, with myself, with my child, and with the meaning I put in it all, with my desires to give and to hold, to keep and to lose, to live and to die. No instrument can help me. His eyes are furious. He would like to take a knife. He has to watch me and wait.

I want to remember all the time why I should want to live. I am all pain and no memory. The lamp has ceased drinking me. I am too weary to move even toward the light or to turn my head and look at the clock. Inside of my body there are fires, there are bruises, the flesh is in pain. The child is not a child; it is a demon lying half-choked between my legs, keeping me from living, strangling me, showing only its head, until I die in its grasp. The demon lies inert at the door of the womb, blocking life, and I cannot rid myself of it.

The nurses begin to talk again. I say, *"Let me alone."* I put my two hands on my stomach and very softly, with the tips of my fingers, I drum, drum, drum, on my stomach, in circles. Round and round, softly, with eyes open in great serenity. The doctor comes near and looks with amazement. The nurses are silent. Drum, drum, drum, drum, in soft circles, in soft, quiet circles. "Like a savage," they whisper. The mystery.

Eyes open, nerves quiet. I drum gently on my stomach for a long while. The nerves begin to quiver...a mysterious agitation. I hear the ticking of the clock...inexorably, separately. The little nerves awaken, stir. I say, "I can push now!" And I push violently. They are shouting, "A little more! Just a little more!"

Will the ice come, and the darkness, before I am through? At the end of the dark tunnel a knife gleams. I hear the clock and my heart. I say, "Stop!" The doctor holds the instrument, and he is leaning over. I sit up and shout at him with fury, "Don't you dare!" He is afraid again. "Let me alone, all of you!"

I lie back so quietly. I hear the ticking. Softly I drum, drum, drum. I feel my womb stirring, dilating. My hands are so weary, so weary, they will fall off. They will fall off, and I will lie there in darkness. The womb is stirring and dilating. Drum, drum, drum, drum. "I am ready!" The nurse puts her knee on my stomach. There is blood in my eyes, blood, blood. A tunnel. I push into this tunnel, I bite my lips and push. There is fire, flesh ripping, and no air. Out of the tunnel! All my blood is spilling out. "Push! Push! It is coming! It is coming!" I feel the slipperiness, the sudden deliverance; the weight is gone. Darkness.

I hear voices. I open my eyes. I hear them saying, "It was a little girl. Better not show it to her." All my strength is coming back. I sit up. The doctor shouts, "For God's sake, don't sit up, don't move!"

"Show me the child!"

"Don't show it," says the nurse. "It will be bad for her."

The nurses try to make me lie down. My heart is beating so loud I can hardly hear myself repeating, "Show it to me!" The doctor holds it up. It looks dark, and small, like a diminutive man. But it is a little girl. It has long eyelashes on its closed eyes; it is perfectly made, and all glistening with the water of the womb.

It was like a doll, or an old miniature Indian. About one foot long. Skin on bones. No flesh. But completely formed. The doctor told me afterward it had hands and feet exactly like mine, and long eyelashes. The head was bigger than the average. It was black. The child had died—strangled, perhaps, or from the operations. One more day and the tumor in its head would have infected me. I would have died. As I looked at the little Indian for a moment I hated it for all the pain it had caused me, and because it was a little girl and I had fancied it to be a boy.

It was only later that this flare of anger turned into great sadness, regrets, long dreams of what this little girl might have been. A dead creation, my first dead creation. The deep pain caused by any death and any destruction. The failure of my motherhood, of at least the embodiment of it, the abdication of one kind of motherhood for the sake of a higher one.

But all my hopes of real, human, simple, direct motherhood lying dead. The simple human flowering denied to me because of the dream, again, the sacrifice to other forms of creation. The necessity in me to produce more subtle flowerings. Nature conniving to keep me as Bilitis, as the Virgin. Nature arranging my destiny as man's woman, not child's woman. Nature shaping my body for passion alone, for the love of man. This child, which meant a simple, primitive connection with the earth, this child, a prolongation of myself, now cast off so that I would live out my destiny as the mistress, my life as a woman. This child, which meant self-sufficiency and separation from man. My child. My possession.

So wholly woman had I become that I became also the mother, the mother independent from the man she loves, with her flesh-and-blood image of the man she loves. But for man, for Henry, for love of Henry, or of my life as a woman, I killed the child. To protect Henry, to be free, I killed the child. Not to be abandoned, I killed the child. I did not give myself to the earth or to the lifelong task of nursing a child. I love man as lover and creator. Man as father I do not trust. I do not believe in man as father. I do not trust man as father. I stand by man the lover and creator. With him I feel an alliance. In man the father I feel an enemy, a danger.

This little girl, a prolongation of myself and of Henry, I reabsorbed into myself. It is to remain in me, a part of me. I gathered myself all together again. My womb did not remain dilated, open, bleeding for a selfless giving. I returned to life.

When I saw the child I thought that it looked like a diminutive Henry. The bald head, the thick, open mouth, the nose, the leanness of it, something almost nonhuman, not mental looking, a little bit monstrous. Or was the vision of Henry as my child definitely formed and associated with this creation of my flesh and blood? The womb love—a love that does not come from that flame between the legs at the petal external flowering of the womb's mouth, but from deeper beyond, inside the womb, like that little Indian who slipped out so easily, like a penis swimming in my overabundant honey.

I had sat up on the operating table to look at the child. The doctor and nurses were amazed by my aliveness and curiosity. They expected tears. I still had my eyelash makeup on. But afterward I lay back and almost fainted with weakness.

In my bed, when I saw Hugh again, I wept. He was terrified when he saw all the veins on my face cracked. We drank champagne. I fell asleep. Glory, glory of deliverance. The sleep of deliverance. Hugh had almost gone mad when he heard my screams.

Sleep. Morning toilette. Perfume. Powder. The face all well. I can see it in the long Egyptian hand mirror Hugh has given me with a poem. The rose silk jacket he bought me when I asked for an attractive hospital costume.

Rank came at eleven. We said very little. I saw Henry, Eduardo, Hugh as in a dream. Immense weakness. Henry and Hugh had suffered like primitive men, in their guts, with me. Henry said he had had terrible pains in his stomach all night.

The next day I suffered an intestinal poisoning. A bad night. Wednesday all was well. But a new anxiety appeared. The breasts began to hurt. Henry came and announced the coming out of *Tropic of Cancer*. I said, "Here is a birth which is of greater interest to me." Henry and Rank met. I felt nothing. Just languid. Everybody was amazed by my appearance. The morning after the birth: pure complexion, luminous skin, shining eyes. Henry was overwhelmed. He was awed. He said it made him weak to see me. He was vulnerable like a woman. Weeping and trembling like a woman. Eduardo brought me an orchid. The little nurse from the Midi left all her other patients waiting to comb my hair lovingly. All the nurses kissed and fondled me. I was bathing in love, feeling languid and calm and light, too.

And then my breasts got hard with the milk. Too much milk. An amazing amount of milk from such a small person. So hard and painful.

Thursday, Rank came and he was in despair to be going to New York.

The night was a nightmare. I felt again in the grip of some dark menace. I imagined my breasts spoiled forever. Ulcers. The nurses leaning over my bed seemed malevolent to me. The way they leaned over, examined me, predicted the worst things, it affected me, frightened me.

I could not sleep. I began to think about religion, about pain. I had not yet come to the end of pain. I thought of the God I had received with such fervor at Communion and whom I had confused with my Father. I thought of Catholicism. Wondering. Where was God, where was the fervor I had as a child? I got tired of thinking. I fell asleep with my hands folded on my breasts as for death. And I died again, as I had died again other times.

I died and was reborn again in the morning, when the sun came to the wall in front of my window. A blue sky, and the sun on the wall. The nurse had raised me to see the new day. I lay there feeling the sky, and myself—one with the sky, feeling the sun, and myself one with the sun, and abandoning myself to immensity and to God. God penetrated my whole body. I trembled and shivered with an immense, immense joy. Cold and fever and light, an illumination, a visitation, through the whole body, the shiver of a presence. The light and the sky in the body, God in the body, and I melting into God. I melted into God. No image. I felt space, gold, purity, ecstasy, immensity, a profound, ineluctable communion. I wept with joy. I knew everything then; I knew everything I had done was right. I knew that I needed no dogmas to communicate with Him; I needed but to live, to love, and to suffer. I needed no man or priest to communicate with Him. By living my life, my passions, my creation to the limit, I communed with the sky, the light, and with God. I believed in the transubstantiation of blood and flesh. I had come upon the infinite through the flesh and through the blood. Through flesh and blood and love, I was in the Whole, in God. I cannot say more. There is nothing more to say. The greatest communions come so simply. But from that moment on I have felt my connection with God, an isolated, wordless, individual, full connection which gives me an immense joy and a sense of the greatness of life, the elimination of human time and boundaries. Eternity. I was born. I was born woman. To love God and to love man supremely, and separately. I was born to a great quietude, a super-human joy above and beyond all my human sorrows, transcending pain and tragedy. This joy I found in love of man and in creation, completed in communion.

The doctor came, examined me, could not believe his eyes. I was intact, as if nothing had ever happened to me. I could leave the clinic. It was a soft summer day. I walked with joy at having escaped the great mouth of the monster.

Notes

Text: Incest: From *"A Journal of Love,"* the Unexpurgated Diary of Anaïs Nin, 1932-1934 (New York: Harcourt Brace Jovanovich, 1992), 371-85.

Henry is Henry Miller. Rank is Otto Rank. *"Sage-femme"* means "midwife," though Nin went to this woman for an abortion. Mother is Rosa Culmell de Nin; Joaquin is Joaquín Nin-Culmell. Hugh is Hugh Guiler. The Lowenfelses are Walter (1897-1976) and Lillian (1904-1975). With Michael Fraenkel, the poet Walter Lowenfels founded the Carrefour Press in Paris; Lillian helped her husband edit anthologies of poetry. Nin and Guiler lived (with her mother and brother Joaquín) at 47, boulevard Suchet, Paris, from July 1929 until November 1930, when they moved to 2 bis, rue Monbuisson, Louveciennes, though Guiler retained the lease on the previous residence. When it was not rented, Nin sometimes used it for trysting. John is John Erskine. By "Princess," Nin means herself. *"Néant"* means "nothingness," "nonbeing," "non-existence." "Princess Aubergine" is a story in *Tales of the Punjab* (1894), by Flora Annie Steel (1847-1929). "Aubergine" means "eggplant." In saying that Miller "ran away from his wife and his other little girl," Nin refers to his abandoning his first wife, Beatrice Miller, and their daughter, Barbara Miller. *"Ça va?"* means "Are you okay, madame?" *"Elle vomit. Faut-il lui en donner encore? Non. C'est fini"* means "She's vomiting. Should we give her some more? No, it's all over." Eduardo is Eduardo Sánchez. Bilitis is the name Pierre Louÿs (1870-1925) gives to a lesbian contemporary of Sappho in *Les Chansons de Bilitis* (1894). Nin paid for the publication of Miller's first novel, *Tropic of Cancer* (1934). Midi is an area in southern France. Father is Joaquín Nin.

⊂ℨ *FIRE* ℬ

(15 April 1935)
On Otto Rank

Context

In 1934, Otto Rank, Nin's analyst and lover, established his practice in New York. Nin joined him there in November. Hugh Guiler followed her, and Henry Miller arrived soon thereafter. Nin's account of the trip with Rank to Atlantic City, of which the selection here is a part, served as the basis for the conclusion of "The Voice" in *The Winter of Artifice* (1939).

◆ ◆ ◆ ◆

April 15, 1935. How I help Huck out of his differences and how he likes to be helped for a change. After a complete sexual bout in Atlantic City in the afternoon after our arrival, he again desired me at night when I didn't want it. He felt this but could not deny himself and so he took me as I lay passive. As I lay there letting him take his pleasure, I felt far away, as when I had to yield to Hugh; only, Hugh did not feel everything as Huck does—not as knowingly. So he was sad at the end, and I let him be sad—there was nothing I could say. My passivity was as natural as his desire. No way to reconcile them. And if I talked I felt that I might blame myself for indifference and thus betray the fact that I am fundamentally indifferent sexually to Huck. So I let him fall asleep, feeling a bit hard and reckless. Not until the afternoon of the next day, after a very warm, blind sexual fusion which had reassured him, did I feel in myself sufficient assurance to mention his sadness of the night before, saying, "Was it because I was passive last night that you were sad? Why should you mind that—I gave so much in the afternoon, it was so full. I just felt quiet and peaceful last night."

"Yes," said Huck. "When it is just sex, when it isn't an expression of our togetherness, then it makes me sad, for just sex is a separating thing, not a uniting one. I do know I should have left you alone last night. You were tired. I knew I was doing wrong because I can't enjoy it when you're passive. I just can't."

I talked about his clinging love, his clutching, saying, "You taught me to believe and not to clutch and now I want to give you that fearlessness you gave me." He said it was not fear but his age, his being closer to the end of his life, fear of coming to the end of his life. Whenever he talks about his age

71

ay marvelous things, and now: "Organically you're so young, because you haven't lived, you haven't burned yourself."

"But they say, on the contrary, that the organism gets atrophied by not living."

"I don't believe that at all. And I'm certainly the one to judge your organic youthfulness!"

The truth is that he is insatiable. He demands more than Henry.

Notes

Text: *Fire: From "A Journal of Love," the Unexpurgated Diary of Anaïs Nin, 1934-1937* (New York: Harcourt Brace, 1995), 63-64.

Huck is Otto Rank. Nin called him this because he admired Mark Twain, author of *Adventures of Huckleberry Finn* (1884). Hugh is Hugh Guiler. Henry is Henry Miller.

⊂ঙ *THE HOUSE OF INCEST* ৳০

(1936)

Context

Nin's first published fiction, *The House of Incest*, was published by Siana Editions ("Anais" spelled backwards), a press operated in Paris by Nin, Michael Fraenkel, Henry Miller, and Alfred Perlès. Subsequent editions omit the definite article. Usually considered a prose poem, this work deals with the narrator's inability to confront reality satisfactorily.

◆ ◆ ◆ ◆

ALL THAT I KNOW IS CONTAINED IN THIS BOOK WRITTEN WITHOUT WITNESS, AN EDIFICE WITHOUT DIMENSION, A CITY HANGING IN THE SKY.

The morning I got up to begin this book I coughed. Something was coming out of my throat: it was strangling me. I broke the thread which held it and yanked it out. I went back to bed and said: I have just spat out my heart.

There is an instrument called the quena made of human bones. It owes its origin to the worship of an Indian for his mistress. When she died he made a flute out of her bones. The quena has a more penetrating, more haunting sound than the ordinary flute.

Those who write know the process. I thought of it as I was spitting out my heart.

Only I do not wait for my love to die.

My first vision of earth was water veiled. I am of the race of men and women who see all things through this curtain of sea, and my eyes are the color of water.

I looked with chameleon eyes upon the changing face of the world, looked with anonymous vision upon my uncompleted self.

I remember my first birth in water. All round me a sulphurous transparency and my bones move as if made of rubber. I sway and float, stand on boneless toes listening for distant sounds, sounds beyond the reach of human ears, see things beyond the reach of human eyes. Born full of memories of the bells of the Atlantide.

Always listening for lost sounds and searching for lost colors, standing forever on the threshold like one troubled with memories, and walking with a swimming stride. I cut the air with wide-slicing fins, and swim through wall-less rooms.

Ejected from a paradise of soundlessness, cathedrals wavering at the passage of a body, like soundless music.

This Atlantide could be found again only at night, by the route of the dream. As soon as sleep covered the rigid new city, the rigidity of the new world, the heaviest portals slid open on smooth-oiled gongs and one entered the voicelessness of the dream. The terror and joy of murders accomplished in silence, in the silence of slidings and brushings. The blanket of water lying over all things stifling the voice. Only a monster brought me up on the surface by accident.

Lost in the colors of the Atlantide, the colors running into one another without frontiers. Fishes made of velvet, of organdie with lace fangs, made of spangled taffeta, of silks and feathers and whiskers, with lacquered flanks and rock crystal eyes, fishes of withered leather with gooseberry eyes, eyes like the white of egg. Flowers palpitating on stalks like sea-hearts. None of them feeling their own weight, the sea-horse moving like a feather...

It was like yawning. I loved the ease and the blindness and the suave voyages on the water bearing one through obstacles. The water was there to bear one like a giant bosom; there was always the water to rest on, and the water transmitted the lives and the loves, the words and the thoughts.

Far beneath the level of storms I slept. I moved within color and music as inside a sea-diamond. There were no currents of thoughts, only the caress of flow and desire mingling, touching, traveling, withdrawing, wandering—the endless bottoms of peace.

I do not remember being cold there, nor warm. No pain of cold and heat. The temperature of sleep, feverless and chilless. I do not remember being hungry. Food seeped through invisible pores. I do not remember weeping.

I felt only the caress of moving—moving into the body of another— absorbed and lost within the flesh of another lulled by the rhythm of water, the slow palpitation of the senses, the movement of silk.

Loving without knowingness, moving without effort, in the soft current of water and desire, breathing in an ecstasy of dissolution.

I awoke at dawn, thrown up on a rock, the skeleton of a ship choked in its own sails.

The night surrounded me, a photograph unglued from its frame. The lining of a coat ripped open like the two shells of an oyster. The day and night unglued, and I falling in between not knowing on which layer I was resting, whether it was the cold grey upper leaf of dawn, or the dark layer of night.

Sabina's face was suspended in the darkness of the garden. From the eyes a simoun wind shriveled the leaves and turned the earth over; all things which had run a vertical course now turned in circles, round the face, around HER face. She stared with such an ancient stare, heavy luxuriant centuries flickering in deep processions. From her nacreous skin perfumes spiraled like incense. Every gesture she made quickened the rhythm of the blood and aroused a beat chant like the beat of the heart of the desert, a chant which was the sound of her feet treading down into the blood the imprint of her face.

A voice that had traversed the centuries, so heavy it broke what it touched, so heavy I feared it would ring in me with eternal resonance; a voice rusty with the sound of curses and the hoarse cries that issue from the delta in the last paroxysm of orgasm.

Her black cape hung like black hair from her shoulders, half-draped, half-floating around her body. The web of her dress moving always a moment before she moved, as if aware of her impulses, and stirring long after she was still, like waves ebbing back to the sea. Her sleeves dropped like a sigh and the hem of her dress danced round her feet.

The steel necklace on her throat flashed like summer lightning and the sound of the steel was like the clashing of swords... Le pas d'acier... The steel of New York's skeleton buried in granite, buried standing up. Le pas d'acier... notes hammered on the steel-stringed guitars of the gypsies, on the steel arms of chairs dulled with her breath; steel mail curtains falling like the flail of hail, steel bars and steel barrage cracking. Her necklace thrown around the world's neck, unmeltable. She carried it like a trophy wrung of groaning machinery, to match the inhuman rhythm of her march.

The leaf fall of her words, the stained glass hues of her moods, the rust in her voice, the smoke in her mouth, her breath on my vision like human breath blinding a mirror.

Talk—half-talk, phrases that had no need to be finished, abstractions, Chinese bells played on with cotton-tipped sticks, mock orange blossoms painted on porcelain. The muffled, close, half-talk of soft-fleshed women. The men she had embraced, and the women, all washing against the resonance of my memory. Sound within sound, scene within scene, woman within woman—like acid revealing an invisible script. One woman within another eternally, in a far-reaching procession, shattering my mind into fragments, into quarter tones which no orchestral baton can ever make whole again.

The luminous mask of her face, waxy, immobile, with eyes like sentinels. Watching my sybaritic walk, and I the sibilance of her tongue. Deep into each other we turned our harlot eyes. She was an idol in Byzance, an idol dancing with legs parted; and I wrote with pollen and honey. The soft secret yielding of woman I carved into men's brains with copper words; her image I tattooed in their eyes. They were consumed by the fever of their entrails, the indissoluble poison of legends. If the torrent failed to engulf them, or did they extricate themselves, I haunted their memory with the tale they wished to forget. All that was swift and malevolent in woman might be ruthlessly destroyed, but who would destroy the illusion on which I laid her to sleep each night? We lived in Byzance. Sabina and I, until our hearts bled from the precious stones on our foreheads, our bodies tired of the weight of brocades, our nostrils burned with the smoke of perfumes; and when we had passed into other centuries they enclosed us in copper frames. Men recognized her always: the same effulgent face, the same rust voice. And she and I, we recognized each other; I her face and she my legend.

Around my pulse she put a flat steel bracelet and my pulse beat as she willed, losing its human cadence, thumping like a savage in orgiastic frenzy. The lamentations of flutes, the double chant of wind through our slender bones, the cracking of our bones distantly remembered when on beds of down the worship we inspired turned to lust.

As we walked along, rockets burst from the street lamps; we swallowed the asphalt road with a jungle roar and the houses with their closed eyes and geranium eyelashes; swallowed the telegraph poles trembling with messages; swallowed stray cats, trees, hills, hedges, Sabina's labyrinthian smile on the keyhole. The door moaning, opening. Her smile closed. A nightingale disleafing melliferous honeysuckle. Honey-suckled. Fluted fingers. The house opened its green gate mouth and swallowed us. The bed was floating.

The record was scratched, the crooning broken. The pieces cut our feet. It was dawn and she was lost. I put back the houses on the road, aligned the telegraph poles along the river and the stray cats jumping across the road. I put back the hills. The road came out of my mouth like a velvet ribbon—it lay there serpentine. The houses opened their eyes. The keyhole had an ironic curve, like a question mark. The woman's mouth.

I was carrying her fetiches, her marionettes, her fortune teller's cards worn at the corners like the edge of a wave. The windows of the city were stained and splintered with rainlight and the blood she drew from me with each lie, each deception. Beneath the skin of her cheeks I saw ashes: would she die before we had joined in perfidious union? The eyes, the hands, the senses that only women have.

There is no mockery between women. One lies down at peace as on one's own breast.

Sabina was no longer embracing men and women. Within the fever of her restlessness the world was losing its human shape. She was losing the human power to fit body to body in human completeness. She was delimiting the horizons, sinking into planets without axis, losing her polarity and the divine knowledge of integration, of fusion. She was spreading herself like the night over the universe and found no god to lie with. The other half belonged to the sun, and she was at war with the sun and light. She would tolerate no bars of light on open books, no orchestration of ideas knitted by a single theme; she would not be covered by the sun, and half the universe belonged to him; she was turning her serpent back to that alone which might overshadow her own stature giving her the joy of fecundation.

Come away with me, Sabina, come to my island. Come to my island of red peppers sizzling over slow braseros, Moorish earthen jars catching the gold water, palm trees, wild cats fighting, at dawn a donkey sobbing, feet on coral reefs and sea-anemones, the body covered with long seaweeds, Melisande's hair hanging over the balcony at the Opera Comique, inexorable diamond sunlight, heavy nerveless hours in the violaceous shadows, ash-colored rocks and olive trees, lemon trees with lemons hung like lanterns at a garden party, bamboo shoots forever trembling, soft-sounding espadrilles, pomegranate spurting blood, a flute-like Moorish chant, long and insistent, of the ploughmen, trilling, swearing, trilling and cursing, dropping perspiration on the earth with the seeds.

Your beauty drowns me, drowns the core of me. When your beauty burns me I dissolve as I never dissolved before man. From all men I was different, and myself, but I see in you that part of me which is you. I feel you in me; I feel my own voice becoming heavier, as if I were drinking you in, every delicate thread of resemblance being soldered by fire and one no longer detects the fissure.

Your lies are not lies, Sabina. They are arrows flung out of your orbit by the strength of your fantasy. To nourish illusion. To destroy reality. I will help you: it is I who will invent lies for you and with them we will traverse the world. But behind our lies I am dropping Ariadne's golden thread—for the greatest of all joys is to be able to retrace one's lies, to return to the source and sleep one night a year washed of all superstructures.

Sabina, you made your impression upon the world. I passed through it like a ghost. Does anyone notice the owl in the tree at night, the bat which strikes the window pane while others are talking, the eyes which reflect like water and drink like blotting paper, the pity which flickers quietly like candlelight, the understanding on which people lay themselves to sleep?

DOES ANYONE KNOW WHO I AM?

Even my voice came from other worlds. I was embalmed in my own secret vertigoes. I was suspended over the world, seeing what road I could tread without treading down even clay or grass. My step was a sentient step; the mere crepitation of gravel could arrest my walk.

When I saw you, Sabina, I chose my body.

I will let you carry me into the fecundity of destruction. I choose a body then, a face, a voice. I become you. And you become me. Silence the sensational course of your body and you will see in me, intact, your own fears, your own pities. You will see love which was excluded from the passions given you, and I will see the passions excluded from love. Step out of your role and rest yourself on the core of your true desires. Cease for a moment your violent deviations. Relinquish the furious indomitable strain.

I will take them up.

Cease trembling and shaking and gasping and cursing and find again your core which I am. Rest from twistedness, distortion, deformations. For an hour you will be me; that is, the other half of yourself. The half you lost. What you burnt, broke, and tore is still in my hands: I am the keeper of fragile things and I have kept of you what is indissoluble.

Even the world and the sun cannot show their two faces at once.

So now we are inextricably woven. I have gathered together all the fragments. I return them to you. You have run with the wind, scattering and dissolving. I have run behind you, like your own shadow, gathering what you have sown in deep coffers.

I AM THE OTHER FACE OF YOU

Our faces are soldered together by soft hair, soldered together, showing two profiles of the same soul. Even when I passed through a room like a breath, I made others uneasy and they knew I had passed.

I was the white flame of your breath, your simoun breath shriveling the world. I borrowed your visibility and it was through you I made my imprint on the world. I praised my own flame in you.

THIS IS THE BOOK YOU WROTE

AND YOU ARE THE WOMAN

I AM

Only our faces must shine twofold—like day and night—always separated by space and the evolutions of time.

The smoke sent my head to the ceiling: there it hung, looking down upon frog eyes, straw hair, mouth of soiled leather, mirrors of bald heads, furred monkey hands with ham colored palms. The music whipped the past out of its tomb and mummies flagellated my memory.

If Sabina were now a memory; if I should sit here and she should never come again! If I only imagined her one night because the drug made fine incisions and arranged the layers of my body on Persian silk hammocks, tipped with cotton each fine nerve and sent the radium arrows of fantasy through the flesh...

I am freezing and my head falls down through a thin film of smoke. I am searching for Sabina again with deep anguish through the faceless crowd.

I am ill with the obstinacy of images, reflections in cracked mirrors. I am a woman with Siamese cat eyes smiling always behind my gravest words, mocking my own intensity. I smile because I listen to the OTHER and I believe the OTHER. I am a marionette pulled by unskilled fingers, pulled apart, inharmoniously dislocated; one arm dead, the other rhapsodizing in mid-air. I laugh, not when it fits into my talk, but when it fits into the undercurrents of my talk. I want to know what is running underneath thus punctuated by bitter upheavals. The two currents do not meet. I see two women in me freakishly bound together, like circus twins. I see them tearing away from each other. I can hear the tearing, the anger and love, passion and pity. When the act of dislocation suddenly ceases—or when I cease to be aware of the sound—then the silence is more terrible because there is nothing but insanity around me, the insanity of things pulling, pulling within oneself, the roots tearing at each other to grow separately, the strain made to achieve unity.

It requires only a bar of music to still the dislocation for a moment; but there comes the smile again, and I know that the two of us have leaped beyond cohesion.

Greyness is no ordinary greyness, but a vast lead roof which covers the world like the lid of a soup pan. The breath of human beings is like the steam of a laundry house. The smoke of cigarettes is like a rain of ashes from Vesuvius. The lights taste of sulphur, and each face stares at you with the immensity of its defects. The smallness of a room is like that of an iron cage in which one can neither sit nor lie down. The largeness of other rooms is like a mortal danger always suspended above you, awaiting the moment of your joy to fall. Laughter and tears are not separate experiences, with intervals of rest: they rush out together and it is like walking with a sword between your legs. Rain does not wet your hair but drips in the cells of the brain with the obstinacy of a leak. Snow does not freeze the hands, but like ether distends the lungs until they burst. All the ships are sinking with fire in their bowels, and there are fires hissing in the cellars of every house. The loved one's whitest flesh is what the broken glass will cut and the wheel crush. The long howls in the night are howls of death. Night is the collaborator of torturers. Day is the light on harrowing discoveries. If a dog barks it is the man who loves wide gashes leaping in through the window. Laughter precedes hysteria. I am waiting for the heavy fall and the foam at the mouth.

A room with a ceiling threatening me like a pair of open scissors. Attic windows lie on a bed like gravel. All connections are breaking. Slowly I part from each being I love, slowly, carefully, completely. I tell them what I owe them and what they owe me. I cull their last glances and the last orgasm. My house is empty, sun-glazed, reflectively alive, its stillness gathering implications, secret images which some day will madden me when I stand before blank walls, hearing far too much and seeing more than is humanly bearable. I part from them all. I die in a small scissor-arched room, dispossessed of my loves and my belongings, not even registered in the hotel book. At the same time I know that if I stayed in this room a few days an entirely new life could begin— like the soldering of human flesh after an operation. It is the terror of this new life, more than the terror of dying, which arouses me. I jump out of bed and run out of this room growing around me like a poisoned web, seizing my imagination, gnawing into my memory so that in seven moments I will forget who I am and whom I have loved.

It was room number 35 in which I might have awakened next morning mad or a whore.

Desire which had stretched the nerve broke, and each nerve seemed to break separately, continuously, making incisions, and acid ran instead of blood. I writhed within my own life, seeking a free avenue to carry the molten cries, to melt the pain into a cauldron of words for everyone to dip into, everyone who sought words for their own pain. What an enormous cauldron I stir now; enormous mouthfuls of acid I feed the others now, words bitter enough to burn all bitterness.

Disrupt the brown crust of the earth and all the sea will rise; the sea-anemones will float over my bed, and the dead ships will end their voyages in my garden. Exorcise the demons who ring the hours over my head at night when all counting should be suspended; they ring because they know that in my dreams I am cheating them of centuries. It must be counted like an hour against me.

I heard the lutes which were brought from Arabia and felt in my breasts the currents of liquid fire which run through the rooms of the Alhambra and refresh me from the too clear waters.

The too clear pain of love divided, love divided...

I was in a ship of sapphire sailing on seas of coral. And standing at the prow singing. My singing swelled the sails and ripped them; where they had been ripped the edge was burnt and the clouds too were ripped to tatters by my voice.

I saw a city where each house stood on a rock between black seas full of purple serpents hissing alarms, licking the rocks and peering over the walls of their garden with bulbous eyes.

I saw the glass palm tree sway before my eyes; the palm trees on my island were still and dusty when I saw them deadened by pain. Green leaves withered for me, and all the trees seemed glassily unresponsive while the glass palm tree threw off a new leaf on the very tip and climax of its head.

The white path sprouted from the heart of the white house and was edged with bristly cactus long-fingered and furry, unmoved by the wind, ageless. Over the ageless cactus the bamboo shoots trembled, close together, perpetually wind-shirred.

The house had the shape of an egg, and it was carpeted with cotton and windowless; one slept in the down and heard through the shell the street organ and the apple vendor who could not find the bell.

Images—bringing a dissolution of the soul within the body like the rupture of sweet-acid of the orgasm. Images made the blood run back and forth, and the watchfulness of the mind watching against dangerous ecstasies was now useless. Reality was drowned and fantasies choked each hour of the day.

Nothing seems true today except the death of the goldfish who used to make love at ninety kilometers an hour in the pool. The maid has given him a Christian burial. To the worms! To the worms!

I am floating again. All the facts and all the words, all images, all presages are sweeping over me, mocking each other. The dream! The dream! The dream rings through me like a giant copper bell when I wish to betray it. If brushes by me with bat wings when I open human eyes and seek to live dreamlessly. When human pain has struck me fiercely, when anger has corroded me, I rise, I always rise after the crucifixion, and I am in terror of my ascensions. THE FISSURE IN REALITY. The divine departure. I fall. I fall into darkness after the collision with pain, and after pain the divine departure.

Oh, the weight, the tremendous weight of my head pulled up by the clouds and swinging in space, the body like a wisp of straw, the clouds dragging my hair like a scarf caught in a chariot wheel, the body dangling, colliding with the lantern stars, the clouds dragging me over the world.

I cannot stop, or descend.

I hear the unfurling of water, of skies and curtains. I hear the shiver of leaves, the breathing of the air, the wailing of the unborn, the pressure of the wind.

I hear the movements of the stars and planets, the slight rust creak when they shift their position. The silken passage of radiations, the breath of circles turning.

I hear the passing of mysteries and the breathing of monsters. Overtones only, or undertones. Collision with reality blurs my vision and submerges me into the dream. I feel the distance like a wound. It unrolls itself before me like the rug before the steps of a cathedral for a wedding or a burial. It is unrolled like a crimson bride between the others and me, but I cannot walk on it without a feeling of uneasiness, as one has at ceremonies. The ceremony of walking along the unrolled carpet into the cathedral where the functions unravel to which I am a stranger. I neither marry nor die. And the distance between the crowd, between the others and me, grows wider.

Distance. I never walked over the carpet into the ceremonies. Into the fullness of the crowd life, into the authentic music and the odor of men. I never attended the wedding or the burial. Everything for me took place either in the belfry where I was alone with the deafening sound of bells calling in iron voices, or in the cellar where I nibbled at the candles and the incense stored away with the mice.

I cannot be certain of any event or place, only of my solitude. Tell me what the stars are saying about me. Does Saturn have eyes made of onions which weep all the time? Has Mercury chicken feathers on his heels, and does Mars wear a gas mask? Gemini, the evolved twins, do they evolve all the time, turning on a spit, Gemini a la broche?

There is a fissure in my vision and madness will always rush through. Lean over me, at the bedside of my madness, and let me stand without crutches.

I am an insane woman for whom houses wink and open their bellies. Significance stares at me from everywhere, like a gigantic underlying ghostliness. Significance emerges out of dank alleys and sombre faces, leans out of the windows of strange houses. I am constantly reconstructing a pattern of something forever lost and which I cannot forget; I catch the odors of the past on street corners and I am aware of the men who will be born tomorrow. Behind windows there are either enemies or worshippers. Never neutrality or passivity. Always intention and premeditation. Even stones have for me druidical expressions.

I walk ahead of myself in perpetual expectancy of miracles.

I am enmeshed in my lies, and I want absolution. I cannot tell the truth because I have felt the heads of men in my womb. The truth would be death-dealing and I prefer fairy tales. I am wrapped in lies which do not penetrate my soul. As if the lies I tell were like costumes. The shell of mystery can break and grow again over night. But the moment I step into the cavern of my lies I drop into darkness. I see a face which stares at me like the glance of a cross-eyed man.

I remember the cold on Jupiter freezing ammonia and out of ammonia crystals came the angels. Bands of ammonia and methane encircling Uranus. I remember the tornadoes of inflammable methane on Saturn. I remember on Mars a vegetation like the tussock grasses of Peru and Patagonia, an ochrous red, a rusty ore vegetation, mosses and lichens. Iron bearing red clays and red sandstone. Light there had a sound and sunlight was an orchestra.

Dilated eyes, noble-raced profile, willful mouth. Jeanne, all in fur, with fur eyelashes, walking with head carried high, nose to the wind, eyes on the stars, walking imperiously, dragging her crippled leg. Her eyes higher than the human level, her leg limping behind the tall body, inert, like the chained ball of a prisoner.

Prisoner on earth, against her will to die.

Her leg dragging so that she might remain on earth, a heavy dead leg which she carried like the ball and chain of a prisoner.

Her pale, nerve-stained fingers tortured the guitar, tormenting and twisting the strings with her timidity as her low voice sang; and behind her song, her thirst, her hunger and her fears. As she turned the keys of her guitar, fiercely tuning it, the string snapped and her eyes were terror-stricken as by the snapping of her universe.

She sang and she laughed: I love my brother.

I love my brother. I want crusades and martyrdom. I find the world too small.

Salted tears of defeat crystallized in the corners of her restless eyes.

But I never weep.

She picked up a mirror and looked at herself with love.

Narcisse gazing at himself in Lanvin mirrors. The Four Horsemen of the Apocalypse riding through the Bois. Tragedy rolling on cord tires.

The world is too small. I get tired of playing the guitar, of knitting, and walking, and bearing children. Men are small, and passions are short-lived. I get furious at stairways, furious at doors, at walls, furious at everyday life which interferes with the continuity of ecstasy.

But there is a martyrdom of tenseness, of fever, of living continuously like the firmament in full movement and in full effulgence.

You never saw the stars grow weary or dim. They never sleep.

She sat looking at herself in a hand mirror and searching for an eyelash which had fallen into her eye.

I married a man, Jeanne said, who had never seen painted eyes weep, and on the day of my wedding I wept. He looked at me and he saw a woman shedding enormous black tears, very black tears. It frightened him to see me shedding black tears on my wedding night. When I heard the bells ringing I thought they rang far too loud. They deafened me. I felt I would begin to weep blood, my ears hurt me so much. I coughed because the din was immense and terrifying, like the time I stood next to the bells of Chartres. He said the bells were not loud at all, but I heard them so close to me that I could not hear his voice, and the noise seemed like hammering against my flesh, and I thought my ears would burst. Every cell in my body began to burst, one by one, inside of the immense din from which I could not escape. I tried to run away from the bells. I shouted: stop the bells from ringing! But I could not run away from them because the sound was all round me and inside me, like my heart pounding in huge iron beats, like my arteries clamping like cymbals, like my head knocked against granite and a hammer striking the vein on my temple. Explosions of sounds without respite which made my cells burst, and the echoes of the cracking and breaking in me rolled into echoes, struck me again and again until my nerves were twisting and curling inside me, and then snapped and tore at the gong, until my flesh contracted and shriveled with pain, and the blood spilled out of my ears and I could not bear any more... Could not bear to attend my own wedding, could not bear to be married to man, because, because, because...

I LOVE MY BROTHER!

She shook her heavy Indian bracelets; she caressed her Orient blue bottles, and then she lay down again.

I am the most tired woman in the world. I am tired when I get up. Life requires an effort which I cannot make. Please give me that heavy book. I need to put something heavy like that on top of my head. I have to place my feet under the pillows always, so as to be able to stay on earth. Otherwise I feel myself going away, going away at a tremendous speed, on account of my lightness. I know that I am dead. As soon as I utter a phrase my sincerity dies, becomes a lie whose coldness chills me. Don't say anything, because I see that you understand me, and I am afraid of your understanding. I have such a fear of finding another like myself, and such a desire to find one! I am so utterly lonely, but I also have such a fear that my isolation be broken through, and I no longer be the head and ruler of my universe. I am in great terror of your understanding by which you penetrate into my world; and then I stand revealed and I have to share my kingdom with you.

But Jeanne, fear of madness, only the fear of madness will drive us out of the precincts of our solitude, out of the sacredness of our solitude. The fear of madness will burn down the walls of our secret house and send us out into the world seeking warm contact. Worlds self-made and self-nourished are so full of ghosts and monsters.

Knowing only fear, it is true, such a fear that it chokes me, that I stand gaping and breathless, like a person deprived of air; or at other times, I cannot hear, I suddenly become deaf to the world. I stamp my feet and hear nothing. I shout and hear nothing of my shout. And then at times, when I lie in bed, fear clutches me again, a great terror of silence and of what will come out of this silence towards me and knock on the walls of my temples, a great mounting, choking fear. I knock on the wall, on the floor, to drive the silence away. I knock and I sing and I whistle persistently until I drive the fear away.

When I sit before my mirror I laugh at myself. I am brushing my hair. Here are a pair of eyes, two long braids, two feet. I look at them like dice in a box, wondering if I should shake them, would they still come out and be ME. I cannot tell how all these separate pieces can be ME. I do not exist. I am not a body. When I shake hands I feel that the person is so far away that he is in the other room, and that my hand is in the other room. When I blow my nose I have a fear that it might remain on the handkerchief.

Voice like a mistlethrush. The shadow of death running after each word so that they wither before she has finished uttering them.

When my brother sat in the sun and his face was shadowed on the back of the chair I kissed his shadow. I kissed his shadow and this kiss did not touch him, this kiss was lost in the air and melted with the shadow. Our love of each other is like one long shadow kissing, without hope of reality.

She led me into the house of incest. It was the only house which was not included in the twelve houses of the zodiac. It could neither be reached by the route of the milky way, nor by the glass ship through whose transparent bottom one could follow the outline of the lost continents, nor by following the arrows pointing the direction of the wind, nor by following the voice of the mountain echoes.

The rooms were chained together by steps—no room was on a level with another—and all the steps were deeply worn. There were windows between the rooms, little spying-eyed windows, so that one might talk in the dark from room to room, without seeing the other's face. The rooms were filled with the rhythmic heaving of the sea coming from many sea-shells. The windows gave out on a static sea, where immobile fishes had been glued to painted backgrounds. Everything had been made to stand still in the house of incest, because they all had such a fear of movement and warmth, such a fear that all love and all life should flow out of reach and be lost!

Everything had been made to stand still, and everything was rotting away. The sun had been nailed in the roof of the sky and the moon beaten deep into its Oriental niche.

In the house of incest there was a room which could not be found, a room without window, the fortress of their love, a room without window where the mind and blood coalesced in a union without orgasm and rootless like those of fishes. The promiscuity of glances, of phrases, like sparks marrying in space. The collision between their resemblances, shedding the odor of tamarisk and sand, of rotted shells and dying sea-weeds, their love like the ink of squids, a banquet of poisons.

Stumbling from room to room I came into the room of paintings, and there sat Lot with his hand upon his daughter's breast while the city burned behind them, cracking open and falling into the sea. There where he sat with his daughter the Oriental rug was red and stiff, but the turmoil which shook them showed through the rocks splitting around them, through the earth yawning beneath their feet through the trees flaming up like torches, through the sky smoking and smouldering red, all cracking with the joy and terror of their love. Joy of the father's hand upon the daughter's breast, the joy of the fear racking her. Her costume tightly pressed around her so that her breasts heave and swell under his fingers, while the city is rent by lightning, and spits under the teeth of fire, great blocks of a gaping ripped city sinking with the horror of obscenity and falling into the sea with the hiss of the eternally damned. No cry of horror from Lot and his daughter but from the city in flames, from an unquenchable desire of father and daughter, of brother and sister mother and son.

I looked upon a clock to find the truth. The hours were passing like ivory chess figures, striking piano notes and the minutes raced on wires mounted like tin soldiers. Hours like tall ebony women with gongs between their legs, tolling continuously so that I could not count them. I heard the tolling of my heart-beats; I heard the footsteps of my dreams and the beat of time was lost among them like the face of truth.

I came upon a forest of decapitated trees, women carved out of bamboo, flesh slatted like that of slaves in joyless slavery, faces cut in two by the sculptor's knife, showing two sides forever separate, eternally two-faced and it was I who had to shift about to behold the entire woman. Truncated undecagon figures, eleven sides, eleven angles, in veined and vulnerable woods, fragments of bodies, bodies armless and headless. The torso of a tube-rose, the knee of Achilles, tubercles and excrescences, the foot of a mummy in rotted wood, the veined docile wood carved into human contortions. The forest must weep and bend like the shoulders of men, dead figures inside of live trees. A forest animated now with intellectual faces, intellectual contortions. Trees become man and woman, two-faced, nostalgic for the shivering of leaves. Trees reclining, woods shining, and the forest trembling with rebellion so bitter I heard its wailing within its deep forest consciousness. Wailing the loss of its leaves and the failure of transmutation.

Further a forest of white plaster, white plaster eggs. Large white eggs on silver disks, an elegy to birth, each egg a promise, each half-shaped nascence of man or woman or animal not yet precise. Womb and seed and egg, the moist beginning being worshipped rather than its flowering. The eggs so white, so still gave birth to hope without breaking, but the cut-down tree lying there produced a green live branch that laughed at the sculptor.

Jeanne opened all the doors and searched through all the rooms. In each room the startled guest blinked with surprise. She asked them: "Please hang up something out of your windows. Hang up a shawl or a colored handkerchief, or a rug. I am going out into the garden. I want to see how many windows can be accounted for. I may thus find the room where my brother is hiding from me. I have lost my brother. I beg you, help me, every one of you." She pulled shawls off the tables, she took a red curtain down, a coral bedspread, a Chinese panel, and hung them out of the windows herself.

Then she rushed out into the garden of dead trees, over the lava paths, over the micha schist, and all the minerals on her path burned the muscovite like a bride, the pyrite, the hydrous silica, the cinnabar, the azurite like a fragment of benefic Jupiter, the malachite, all crushed together, pressed together, melted jewels, melted planets, alchemized by air and sun and time and space, mixed into mineral fixity, the fixity of the fear of death and the fear of life.

Semen dried into the silence of rock and mineral. The words we did not shout, the tears unshed, the curse we swallowed, the phrase we shortened, the love we killed, turned into magnetic iron ore, into tourmaline, into pyrite agate, blood congealed into cinnabar, blood calcinated, leadened into galena, oxidized, aluminized, sulphated, calcinated, the mineral glow of dead meteors and exhausted suns in the forest of dead trees and dead desires.

Standing on a hill of orthoclase, with topaz and argentite stains on her hands, she looked up at the facade of the house of incest, the rusty ore facade of the house of incest, and there was one window with the blind shut tight and rusty, one window without light like a dead eye, choked by the hairy long arm of old ivy.

She trembled with the desire not to shriek, an effort so immense that she stood still, her blood unseen for the golden pallor of her face.

She struggled with her death coming: I do not love anyone; I love no one, not even my brother. I love nothing but this absence of pain, this cold neutral absence of pain.

Standing still for many years, between the moment she had lost her brother and the moment she had looked at the facade of the house of incest, moving in endless circles round the corners of the dreams, never reaching the end of her voyage, she apprehended all wonder through the rock-agedness of her pain, by dying.

And she found her brother asleep among the paintings.

Jeanne, I fell asleep among the paintings, where I could sit for many days worshipping your portrait. I fell in love with your portrait, Jeanne, because it will never change. I have such a fear of seeing you grow old, Jeanne; I fell in love with an unchanging you that will never be taken away from me. I was wishing you would die, so that no one could take you away from me, and I would love the painting of you as you would look eternally.

They bowed to one part of themselves—only their likeness.

Good night, my brother!

Good night, Jeanne!

With her walked distended shadows, stigmatized by fear. They carried their compact like a jewel on their breast; they wore it proudly like their coat of arms.

I walked into my own book, seeking peace.

It was night, and I made a careless movement inside the dream; I turned too brusquely the corner and I bruised myself against my madness. It was this seeing too much, this seeing of a tragedy in the quiver of an eyelid, constructing a crime in the next room, the men and women who had loved before me on the same hotel bed.

I carry white sponges of knowledge on strings of nerves.

As I move within my book I am cut by pointed glass and broken bottles in which there is still the odor of sperm and perfume.

More pages added to the book but pages like a prisoner's walking back and forth over the space allotted him. What is it allotted me to say?

Only the truth disguised in a fairy tale, and this is the fairy tale behind which all the truths are staring as behind grilled mosque windows. With veils. The moment I step into the cavern of my lies I drop into darkness, and see a mask which stares at me like the glance of a cross-eyed man; yet I am wrapped in lies which do not penetrate my soul as if the lies I tell were like costumes.

LIES CREATE SOLITUDE

I walked out of my book into the paralytic's room.

He sat there among many objects under glass as in a museum. He had collected a box of paint which he never painted with, a thousand books with pages uncut, and they were covered with dust. His Spanish cape hung on the shoulders of a mannequin, his guitar lay with strings snapped like long disordered hair. He sat before a note book of blank pages, saying: I swallow my own words. I chew and chew everything until it deteriorates. Every thought or impulse I have is chewed into nothingness. I want to capture all my thoughts at once, but they run in all directions. If I could do this I would be capturing the nimblest of minds, like a shoal of minnows. I would reveal innocence and duplicity, generosity and calculation, fear and cowardice and courage. I want to tell the whole truth, but I cannot tell the whole truth because I would have to write four pages at once, like four long columns simultaneously, four pages to the present one, and so I do not write at all. I would have to write backwards, retrace my steps constantly to catch the echoes and the overtones.

His skin was transparent like that of a newborn child, and his eyes green like moss. He bowed to Sabina, to Jeanne, and to me: meet the modern Christ, who is crucified by his own nerves, for all our neurotic sins!

The modern Christ was wiping the perspiration which dripped over his face, as if he were sitting there in the agony of a secret torture. Pain-carved features. Eyes too open, as if dilated by scenes of horror. Heavy-lidded, with a world-heavy fatigue. Sitting on his chair as if there were ghosts standing beside him. A smile like an insult. Lips edged and withered by the black scum of drugs. A body taut like wire.

In our writings we are brothers, I said. The speed of our vertigoes is the same. We arrived at the same place at the same moment, which is not so with other people's thoughts. The language of nerves which we both use makes us brothers in writing.

The modern Christ said: I was born without a skin. I dreamed once that I stood naked in a garden and that it was carefully and neatly peeled, like a fruit. Not an inch of skin left on my body. It was all gently pulled off, all of it, and then I was told to walk, to live, to run. I walked slowly at first, and the garden was very soft, and I felt the softness of the garden so acutely, not on the surface of my body, but all through it, the soft warm air and the perfumes penetrated me like needles through every open bleeding pore. All the pores open and breathing the softness, the warmth, and the smells. The whole body invaded, penetrated, responding, every tiny cell and pore active and breathing and trembling and enjoying. I shrieked with pain. I ran. And as I ran the wind lashed me, and then the voices of people like whips on me. Being touched! Do you know what it is to be touched by a human being!

He wiped his face with his handkerchief.

The paralytic sat still in the corner of the room.

You are fortunate, he said, you are fortunate to feel so much; I wish I could feel all that. You are at least alive to pain, whereas I...

Then he turned his face away, and just before he turned away I saw the veins on his forehead swelling, swelling with the effort he made, the inner effort which neither his tongue nor his body, nor his thoughts would obey.

If only we could all escape from this house of incest, where we only love ourselves in the other, if only I could save you all from yourselves, said the modern Christ.

But none of us could bear to pass through the tunnel which led from the house into the world on the other side of the walls, where there were leaves on the trees, where water ran beside the paths, where there was daylight and joy. We could not believe that the tunnel would open on daylight: we feared to be trapped into darkness again; we feared to return whence we had come, from darkness and night. The tunnel would narrow and taper down as we walked; it would close around us, and close tighter and tighter around us and stifle us. It would grow heavy and narrow and suffocate us as we walked.

Yet we knew that beyond the house of incest there was daylight, and none of us could walk towards it.

We all looked now at the dancer who stood at the center of the room dancing the dance of the woman without arms. She danced as if she were deaf and could not follow the rhythm of the music. She danced as if she could not hear the sound of her castanets. Her dancing was isolated and separated from music and from us and from the room and from life. The castanets sounded like the steps of a ghost.

She danced, laughing and sighing and breathing all for herself. She danced her fears, stopping in the center of every dance to listen to reproaches that we could not hear, or bowing to applause that we did not make. She was listening to a music we could not hear, moved by hallucinations we could not see.

My arms were taken away from me, she sang. I was punished for clinging. I clung. I clutched all those I loved; I clutched at the lovely moments of life; my hands closed upon every full hour. My arms were always tight and craving to embrace: I wanted to embrace and hold the light, the wind, the sun, the night, the whole world. I wanted to caress, to heal, to rock, to lull, to surround, to encompass. And I strained and I held so much that they broke; they broke away from me. Everything eluded me then. I was condemned not to hold.

Trembling and shaking she stood looking at her arms now stretched before her again.

She looked at her hands tightly closed and opened them slowly, opened them completely like Christ; she opened them in a gesture of abandon and giving; she relinquished and forgave, opening her arms and her hands, permitting all things to flow away and beyond her.

I could not bear the passing of things. All flowing, all passing, all movement choked me with anguish.

And she danced; she danced with the music and with the rhythm of earth's circles; she turned with the earth turning, like a disk, turning all faces to light and to darkness evenly, dancing towards daylight.

Notes

Text: *House of Incest* ([New York]: Gemor Press, [1947]).

⚘ *FIRE* ❧

(3, 4, 10 January 1937)

On Gonzalo Moré and Henry Miller

Context

After writing in *The House of Incest* about living in a dream, Nin continued addressing this topic in her diary, as she does in the selections included here. She also discusses her feelings about two lovers, Henry Miller and Gonzalo Moré. Her relationship with Moré served as the basis for the novel *The Four-Chambered Heart* (1950).

◆ ◆ ◆ ◆

January 3, 1937. The secret of my seduction is the deviltry in me which none of my acts betray and which men sense—the mystery is my intelligence and acting and what I do with them. The enigma is the lie. The lie I told Gonzalo, intended to reassure him ("See, I give up Henry altogether"), turned into a drama because all he could think of was that Henry's attempt at suicide had made me ill, broken me down. All he could think of was how affected I was by what had happened. Then he heard, accidentally, that the day after the suicide Henry was eating heartily, and he deduced that Henry was playing on my feelings to win me back. He sensed all the time something false and twisted but could not tell what it was. From the time he was told about Henry's appetite to last night at eleven, when I met him, he was tortured by jealousy. He knocked his head against the wall, blind with fury and baffled by this dark corner in me, which he never could penetrate. Now, all afternoon I had been with Henry, who had received me with passion and tenderness. I had not responded to Henry, but I yielded to him. So Gonzalo's fears and doubts that Henry still has a hold on me are true—but not sexually, *creatively*. With Henry I enter a magic world of creation. We are still working together. We want to publish each other's works. When I meet Gonzalo and he talks to me about politics I feel cold. It is poetry I live with Henry.

What irony. Gonzalo pleads and entreats, "Oh, *chiquita*, I love you too much. I want you all to myself." The strange thing is that I feel such deep despair at the doubts of Gonzalo, despair that he should suffer, despair at seeing him withdrawn and tortured, that I really suffer with him deeply, and we get all entangled in useless words and chaotic emotions, all foggy and mad, and then suddenly, with tremendous vehemence, I say, "Oh, Gonzalo, how can such little things affect your faith in our love!"

"What little things?"

"A few vertigoes!" I say quickly, and we burst out laughing, irrepressibly, at what he calls my diabolical humor.

But deep down I am sad; I am as sad as if I were faithful to Gonzalo and he doubted me. Deep down I feel innocent. It seems to me that I can be faithful not to people but to cosmic life—to loves that are beyond men and individuals. I live in a mysterious world that faithfulness cannot encompass. I am alive, that is all I know—alive and feeling Gonzalo—alive in a different dream with Henry.

I couldn't sleep. I thought of our publication plans with Henry, our enjoyment of Durrell's writing, our banquet of ideas and inventions. And I thought of Gonzalo's politics and hated it.

"Don't you feel me all your own when I am with you..."

"Yes, *chiquita*, but as soon as you climb the little stairs out of the boat you enter another world."

Passing from world to world, giving to each my fullness, why is that treachery? You can only betray what *exists*. What there is in Gonzalo or between Gonzalo and me I do not betray. I do not give Henry the feelings I give Gonzalo—not even the same caresses. I do not take anything away from Henry, because I am still loyal to his creation, his life, and full of love and care.

It is I who could knock my head against the walls while composing this *absolute in space* not found in one man.

I am quite broken, quite broken now. No one would believe or understand.

Evening: I testify to the wonder of life, which surpasses all I have ever read. Rising haggard from the chaos of Gonzalo's jealousy, feeling in myself a conflict, or rather two. One: How can I prevent Gonzalo from suffering? Two: How can I poetize politics? For there lies the problem. *Life for me is a dream*. I mastered the mechanism of it, bending it to the will of the dream. I conquered details to make the dream more possible. With hammer and nails, paint, soap, money, typewriter, cookbooks, douchebags, I made a dream. That is why I renounce violence and tragedy. Reality. So, I made poetry out of science. I took psychoanalysis and made a myth of it. I mastered poverty and restrictions for the sake of the dream. I lived adroitly, intelligently, critically, for the sake of the dream. I lied for the sake of the dream. I sewed and mended for the sake of the dream, served the dream. I took all the elements of modern life and used them for the dream. I subjected New York to the service of the dream. And now it is all again a question of dream versus reality. In the dream nobody dies, in the dream no one suffers, no one is sick, nobody separates.

Now politics. Shall Gonzalo put my name down on the list? It gives him pride to do so. I am with him. He won me from my world. He tore me from tradition. He awakened me. Illusion. The dream. Let him put my name down, I say. Veils. Illusion. I shall make the poem. I can make the poem out of ragpickers. But neither Hugh nor my Father must know. Of course, Elena is a "Fascist." Elena, supremely intelligent, believes what I believe—beyond politics. The dream. Elena's friend is Delia del Carril. Delia is a friend of my Father and Maruca. Delia is "red." Delia is among the plotters.

Gonzalo asked me if I would come Wednesday evening. I said yes. I do not believe. I believe in love, illusion, and the dream. I entered the world of psychoanalysts, didn't I? With my seven veils.

The men who reduced all things—all but Rank—the great tearers of illusions, the great realists, the men who look at the phallus as you look at a lambchop. I entered their world, saw their files, read their books, found Rank the mystic among them, lived a poem, came out unscathed—free, a poet. Not all the stones tied around my analyzed neck can drown the poet. I laugh. Life is a dance to me, a profound, sacred, joyous, mysterious, symbolic, soulful dance. But it is a dance. Through the marketplaces, the whorehouses, the abattoirs, the butcher shops, the scientific laboratories, hospitals, Montparnasse, I walk with my dream unfurled and lose myself in my own labyrinths, and the dream unfurled carries me. Illusion. Politics. Here too I must dance my own rhythm. I will bring my white face, my faith (the immensity of my faith), my breath and passion. I am unbearably, profoundly, incredibly alone, alone, alone right in the furnace of love, right in the center of brilliant friends, glamorous excitement, continuous riches. Individual in my vision, I alone see and hear this way. It is my dream I hang on to. Is this the crime, to love, to love, to love and follow man in his mad ventures, touching mouths and bodies, mouths and hair, loving, adoring, laughing as I laughed last night, saying, "A few vertigoes"?

I have so much. And I must not hold on to everything. It is in my insistence on the dream that I am alone, when I take up my opium pipe and lie down and say, Politics, psychoanalysis—they never meant to me what they mean to others. Nor New York. Nor nightclubs. Nor anyone around me. Nor Montparnasse. Rank alone *knew*. He knows. It is like a secret.

It is my mystery. They always want me to become serious. I am passionate and fervent only for the dream, the poem. Whether I ally myself to the analysts to find I am not an analyst, or to Communists to find out I am not of the world, does not matter. I feel my solitude at the same instant as I make my greatest connection with human beings, the world, when I have a husband, two lovers, children, brothers, parents, friends, a stream of people passing around me; when I am in full motion, life and warmth; when I have reached the maximum of love!

Quand on danse on danse seule. When one practices witchcraft, one does so alone. One interviews the devil alone. One is Machiavellian alone. One is the lover alone. The loved one alone. And when you are attached profoundly, by blood, sex, soul, to human beings, you feel alone. *Ce qui m'amuse, ce sont les complications.* It's complications that amuse me. I laugh alone. Something is happening here of which I am not afraid. It is not insanity, but it is creating in space and loneliness. It is not schizophrenia, it is a vision, a city suspended in the sky, a rhythm which demands solitude. Creation issues only in separateness. The clay is sliced, the painting is begun with separate spots. Vision means separateness. Love means unity, wholeness.

Music swells my sails. *Nanankepichu* is afloat with a flag of fire, stained with the blood Gonzalo loves so much.

I feel hysterical, on the verge of ecstasy and madness. My body trembles with delight and despair.

January 4. Last night after I wrote this, I let Hugh fall asleep and I slipped out to *Nanankepichu.* Gonzalo, too, was worn out. We wanted softness and serenity after our orgy of emotions. Strange to watch a suffering you do not share. I see Gonzalo suffering all I suffered with Henry. Because I am all his happiness, his fear of losing me is tremendous. His joys, too, when after his sensual satisfaction he lies back and says, "You can't imagine what plenitude I feel! Everything is marvelous!"

I seem to be living over again all the joys and anguish I lived with Henry, their depth, the terror, and the ecstasy.

I am happy. After the fusion, which is always incomplete for me, I feel happiness. The joy Gonzalo feels goes through my body. I live inside of his body.

Rhythm requires this—just as in the sexual bout. *One* can be active and it forces the other into passivity. It is not a tragedy, but it makes one the lover and one the beloved. I was Henry's lover. June was his lover, too. And it is in my active role sexually that I found the orgasm.

In passivity I experience happiness, but no orgasm. But I am happy, happy, and I desire Gonzalo. I want him. When I see him with others and I cannot kiss him I get desperate.

I see Henry, who, when not sensually hungry, is cool and inexpressive. But today he is hungry. We get into bed. In spite of myself, I get aroused, so aroused—then I feel the sweetness and *éblouissement* Gonzalo felt last night. I smoke my cigarette voluptuously. I lie in a dream, and I dream of Gonzalo, Gonzalo. When I came in, I came in breezily, glowing, talking. I was telling Henry I was happy. I had received a letter from Rebecca West, who had shown my Father manuscript to a London publisher. The first reader got sick. It affected him like something lethal. The second one too! The publisher said it was a masterpiece, and the other partner too. But it remains uncertain—for puritanical reasons.

Henry, I know now definitely what I must do. In the diary I am natural, sincere. I must stay in the diary. In the novel I am artificial. I must take each volume separately and make it flower, fill it, complete it. That I must do.

Eduardo tells me over the telephone, "After seeing Gonzalo, Elena, you cannot rise any higher, you have the best. I am behind you in my friends."

I feel power. Power to seduce, to work, to love, and to be loved! Power. Power.

Sitting before Henry, thinking that I had only relinquished him imaginatively the night before, and seeing how we could talk and have sex, I was perplexed. Creation. Sex. No jealousy. Is it my *feelings* I have taken out of my life with Henry, my soul, my emotions which made our relationship intolerable? Is it my soul and feelings I have poured over Gonzalo, like a fire, which he takes for love? Is it love? I don't know. I will not question. All my feelings rush out toward Gonzalo, respond to his. A naked sexual exchange, a creative harmony, a bond with Henry—these persist.

Who has the best share? If I were Gonzalo I would prefer the feelings. It is, as he says, with time. I feel now that only the day I relinquish Henry will I experience the orgasm with Gonzalo which will make our rhythm complete. Mystery—how right his jealousy, his instinct. What a hold Henry has on me! How many men have tried to break it! How I have tried to break it myself! I have sometimes the feeling that my other loves are like anaesthetics to make my life with Henry bearable, because I could not bear the pain.

Accepting the mystery and trying *not to live too fast* with my terrible intelligence, losing myself in the moment, spending all I have each day, emptying myself, and sleeping profoundly at night: thus I live without anxiety or nerves, with less terror of this life which wounded me too deeply, with a greater faith. A day of assurance, of certainties, won by such great struggles. Marvelous to feel not one cell in one asleep, all of one's self burning. I feel my intelligence dancing. Gonzalo talks sometimes as if I were the one moving all the strings of our destinies. Because I *see*, sense, so far? Or because I like to play God, or because to create my own life, an *active* life, I stir so much blood around me?

I deny all calculation, all Machiavellian premeditation. But I have this strange pride and feeling that, yes, I have made all this. I have conquered the friends. I have won by love, devotion, and vision. I have truly constructed, with clairvoyance, mine and others' lives around me. Yes, a power to enslave, but not to make a slave; to make others fulfill themselves.

Why do I see so clearly, see so well the mischief, the trickery, and the play-acting with which I enact the most sincere and passionate of all destinies? When I leave the apartment, Hugh and Eduardo sitting there, to meet Gonzalo. When I see that Eduardo can see me go out from where he is sitting, and I not only wave at him but I show him the bottle of wine I am taking for Gonzalo, which makes Eduardo blush and call me perhaps a cynic! I feel not cynical but humorous.

January 10. My life is tragic only in relation to my unreal conception, my desire for a paradise—an artificial paradise. Henry taught me a great deal of acceptance of human life as it is—passivity. I learned to be happy, to enjoy. But I continued to create what I call an absolute in space, a paradise suspended in midair, made up of various elements, one composite heaven, disregarding faithfulness. I took Henry's elements, creation and sensuality, Gonzalo's soul and emotion, passion, love. For this reason I never talk about unfaithfulness. I gave Henry a whole love, but I suffered while I was having human life with its limitations, imperfections, tragedies. Then I grasped my dream with Gonzalo. Then human life demands choices—absolutes again. If Gonzalo suffers at my infidelity, I am baffled. I don't wish to cause suffering. Terrible, unanswerable aspirations, desires, push me out of human life. Terribly real anguish, real thirst and hunger. Then human life interferes. I may lose one of them, according to human laws, because I desire happiness, and all absolute is tragic.

Suffering horribly now at the possibility of separation from Henry, feeling probably I deserve it, seeing Elena's warm enthusiasm for him, hearing Elena saying, "He is so good, so winning. He resembles this man I loved so much."

Strange talk. Henry has just awakened from sleep. I am telling him that I have willed all the diary to him because we had been talking about who I would will it to, and Henry has been thinking I could not leave it to him because of my treacheries, but I said to Henry: "I am leaving it to you." I have nothing to be ashamed of. I have loved Henry even while I lay with other men. I have never been untrue to Henry. I would not mind if he read all my diary.

Then he told me again he thought I should stop writing in the diary and write a novel.

I am not natural outside of the diary. The diary is my form. I have no objectivity. I can only write while things are *warm* and happening. When I write later I become artificial. I stylize. I become unnatural. I have struggled enough against my neurosis. I am no longer neurotic. I know what I am. I am like the Chinese. I will write slender little books—outside of the diary. Live greatly and produce only a poem. I feel right with myself. I must perfect what is natural.

"When you look at it from such a superior aspect I have nothing to say. The diary is a drug, a narcotic," said Henry.

"Do you object to the Chinaman's opium? Is it not right in him?"

"Yes, there is nothing to say to that. But are you satisfied? Why do you seem to prefer what *I* do?"

"I prefer what you do—dynamic, objective, artistic, creative work—yes, of course. But the very fact of my devotion to it may prove I have not got that in myself. I accept what I have in myself. I am far beyond neurosis. I have lived reality, faced reality; I know reality—I am not cut off, I have no fears, no anxieties—but I prefer the dream. *La vida es sueño.* I repudiate violence, because I chose the dream. My nature, my temperament."

As I say this with quiet assurance, I move my hands with soft fatalism. Henry can no longer reproach me for not making sufficient *effort* in writing. I make all my efforts in life; all my dynamism is in life. In writing I am passive, flowing, drugged, yes, not because I cannot connect with reality, but because of my voluntary hatred of it.

My last night with Gonzalo, after I had imaginatively yielded up Henry, I responded to him sexually for the first time—but it is all in wanting not to love Henry. It is all with or against Henry. Just as I served Henry to escape from June! How ironic!

Let Henry read all this. As it is June's story, too.

I wanted to get inside of life. I got so deep inside that I cannot get out. Working on the old diaries is harrowing because I have made the past so warm and alive that it still hurts! No objectivity anywhere. No power to transform! Henry is at peace, transposing his life with June—*how* to tell it is his obsession. I am inside, with Gonzalo, who is inside. I cannot talk about creation with Gonzalo because he is personal, emotional. That is why we can have together a world of feelings which makes me happy.

Funny. When I met Henry I was objective. I became personal and emotional. Elena is now objective and detached. I know what is coming to her!

Gonzalo suffers because he reads a manuscript of mine and doesn't care how it is written—all he cares about is that *I*, his love, was kissed or taken, or that I kissed and loved. For that Gonzalo gives me the feeling of the you-and-I—alone and isolated right in the midst of life, crowds, wars, friends, popularity; and Henry rarely gave me that feeling—in fact only in Louveciennes, and in New York when he lost me for a while.

Working on the diary is too much like living. I touch real flesh, real tears; I hear real words. It is intolerable. Can people read it? It is warm, wet, it writhes, it exhales odors like flesh itself. Too near, too near. That is why I find Henry's world cold, Gonzalo's *warm!* No sensuality, no creation can create the same warmth as the feeling, a soul loving, a flesh loving in immediacy. Henry loves in space, in time, in imagination. Henry, contrary to all appearances, is not *in* life, not inside. *Il subit la vie.* He endures life. Passive. Never acts, but afterward spills out in writing.

Pas si vite! I am tearing through the skies of my inventions, disheveled! Nothing has happened. Under the calm surface of life I am always sensing demons! Underneath the fog and perfumes of the dream I sense the inexorable destruction and separation of life which I rebel against—against the evolution of time, when I evolved quicker than all the rest, when I projected myself out of Henry's life—and yet I can't accept definiteness—what a wrench! So it is the exactness I keep here, the breath and the odor, to keep everything alive! But we cannot bear to keep everything alive; that is why death was given us, because we cannot feel so much; we crack. Parts of us must die, must die to free us, to lighten us. How well parts of Henry die in him, because he possesses the gift of destruction. I can only gather life together until it becomes unbearable, the too-muchness of it, the intensity; and I explode in hysteria, into a million fragments, too much life! Too much feeling about life. Inside. It is torture to be *inside*, to hear and see so much, to know so much, to have no detachment or protection or refuge from being alive! Someone ought to make me unconscious! Kill me. Render me insensible, lethargic.

Parts of me ought to die, but how well I have prevented them from dying. The diary swarms with live things, cracks with reality, bursts with warmth!

Art. Where is the art that keeps us from insanity?

When Gonzalo thinks he will get money from his mother he says, "The first thing I will do is buy *Nanankepichu*." When we talk about his magazine, the printing press he wants, the publication of my work and the group's work, he is afraid of invasion and the loss of our intimacy. He wants to get a smaller boat, where he can be all alone with me and only water around us. He even resents René's presence on the *péniche*. I suggest we take refuge in the prow, a small painted room with two tiny square windows. We could cut it off from the room we now have, and enter it by a trapdoor on the top. Absolute secrecy. He preserves the two-ness.

Notes

Text: *Fire: From "A Journal of Love," the Unexpurgated Diary of Anaïs Nin, 1934-1937* (New York: Harcourt Brace, 1995), 367-77.

Gonzalo is Gonzalo Moré. Henry is Henry Miller; Durrell, Lawrence Durrell. Nin wrote the story "Ragtime" (1938) about ragpickers. Hugh is Hugh Guiler; Father is Joaquín Nin. Elena is Elena Hurtado, a South American painter who befriended Henry Miller in Paris and became a friend of Nin. Delia del Carril (1884-1989) was an Argentinean painter who studied with Fernand Léger (1881-1955) and married Pablo Neruda (1904-1973). Maruca is María Luísa Rodríguez de Nin. Rank is Otto Rank. "*Quand on danse on danse seule*" means "When one dances, one dances alone." *Nanankepichu* ("not at home") was a houseboat on the Seine that Nin rented and on which she and Moré conducted their affair. June is June Miller. "*Éblouissement*" means "dizziness." Rebecca West (1892-1983) was a major English literary figure; Nin used West's phrase "real and unmistakable genius" as a blurb in some of her books. Nin's "father" manuscript was published as "Lilith" in *The Winter of Artifice* (1939) and later as "Winter of Artifice." Eduardo is Eduardo Sánchez. "*La vida es sueño*" means "life is a dream." "*Pas si vite!*" means "Not so fast!" Nin bought Moré a printing press, on which he printed political documents. René was an orphan who worked on the *Nanankepichu*. "*Péniche*" means "barge."

⊂ℝ *DIARY 2* ℰ⅃

(August 1937)
On Lawrence Durrell and Henry Miller

Context

Upon arriving in Paris in 1937, Lawrence Durrell became friendly with Henry Miller and Nin. They critiqued each other's work and helped publish it.

◆ ◆ ◆ ◆

August, 1937. Beautiful flow between Durrell, Henry, Nancy and me. It is while we talk together that I discover how we mutually nourish each other, stimulate each other. I discover my own strength as an artist, for Henry and Durrell often ally themselves against me. Henry's respect is also reawakened by Durrell's admiration for me. My feeling for woman's inarticulateness is reawakened by Nancy's stutterings and stumblings, and her loyalty to me as the one who does not betray woman but seeks to speak for her. A marvelous talk, in which Henry unmasked Durrell and me, and when Durrell said: "And now we must unmask Henry," I answered: "We can't, because he has done it himself." Henry is the strongest because he is not afraid of being alone. Larry is afraid. I am afraid. And we confessed it.

They suddenly attacked my personal relation to all things, by personification of ideas. I defended myself by saying that relating was an act of life. To make history or psychology alive I personify it. Also everything depends on the nature of the personal relationship. My self is like the self of Proust. It is an instrument to connect life and the myth. I quoted Spengler, who said that all historical patterns are reproduced in individual man, entire historical evolutions are reproduced in one man in one lifetime. A man could experience, in a personal way, a Gothic, a Roman, or a Western period. Man is cheating when he sits for a whole evening talking about Lao-tze, Goethe, Rousseau, Spengler. It would be closer to the truth if he said, instead of Lao-tze, Henry—instead of Goethe, some poet we know now—instead of Rousseau, his contemporary equivalent. It would be more honest if Larry said that it is Larry who feels irritation because symbolical wine does not taste as good as plain wine.

When they discussed the problem of my diary, all the art theories were involved. They talked about the geological changes undergone with time, and that it was the product of this change we called art. I asserted that such a process could take place instantaneously.

Henry said: "But that would upset all the art theories."

I said: "I can give you an example. I can feel the potentialities of our talk tonight while it is happening as well as six months later. Look at the birth story. It varies very little in its polished form from the way I told it in the diary immediately after it happened. The new version was written three years later. Objectivity may bring a more rounded picture, but the absence of it, empathy, feeling with it, immersion in it, may bring some other kind of connection with it."

Henry asked: "But then, why did you feel the need of rewriting it?"

"For a greater technical perfection. Not to re-create it."

Larry, who before had praised me for writing as a woman, for not breaking the umbilical connection, said: "You must rewrite *Hamlet*."

"Why should I, if that is not the kind of writing I wish to do?"

Larry said: "You must make the leap outside of the womb, destroy your connections."

"I know," I said, "that this is an important talk, and that it will be at this moment that we each go different ways. Perhaps Henry and Larry will go the same way, but I will have to go another, the woman's way."

At the end of the conversation they both said: "We have a real woman artist before us, the first one, and we ought not to put her down."

I know Henry is the artist because he does exactly what I do not do. He waits. He gets outside of himself. Until it becomes fiction. It is all fiction.

I am not interested in fiction. I want faithfulness.

All I know is that I am right, right for me. If today I can talk both woman's and man's language, if I can translate woman to man and man to woman, it is because I do not believe in man's objectivity. In all his ideas, systems, philosophies, arts come from a personal source he does not wish to admit. Henry and Larry are pretending to be impersonal. Larry has the English complex. But it is a disguise.

Poor woman, how difficult it is to make her instinctive knowledge clear!

"Shut up," says Larry to Nancy. She looks at me strangely, as if expecting me to defend her, explain her. Nancy, I won't shut up. I have a great deal to say, for June, for you, for other women.

Notes

Text: *The Diary of Anaïs Nin, 1934-1939* (New York: Swallow Press/ Harcourt, Brace & World, 1967), 231-33.

Durrell is Lawrence Durrell; Nancy is Nancy Durrell (1912-1983), his wife. Nin dedicated *The Winter of Artifice* (1939) to the Durrells. Proust is Marcel Proust. Spengler is Oswald Spengler (1880-1936), a German author perhaps best known for *Der Untergang des Abendlandes* (*The Decline of the West*) (1918, 1923). Lao-Tze founded the Taoist religion. Johann Wolfgang von Goethe (1749-1832), a German, was one of the major authors and thinkers of his time; *Faust* (1808, 1832) is probably his most significant work. Jean-Jacques Rousseau (1712-1778), from Geneva, was a philosopher who emphasized the value of the emotions; his most influential book is *Du Contract Social* (*The Social Contract*) (1762). In referring to "the birth story," Nin means the story "Birth," which is based on her 1934 abortion. June is June Miller.

❧ *NEARER THE MOON* ❧

(6 March 1939)
On Thurema Sokol

Context

In New York, Nin knew Thurema Sokol, a married mother who once played with the Salzédo Harp Ensemble and the Lawrence Harp Quintet. Sokol visited Nin in Paris for a month in early 1939. In late 1941, Sokol lent Nin money to purchase type and paper for the Gemor Press in New York.

◆ ◆ ◆

March 6, 1939. Thurema. I never described her well. She was another liar who could not bear her real face in the mirror. All Thurema's acts were frenzied coverings of an erotic sexual appetite and lesbianism. Her white Negress face proclaimed her sensuality, her avid mouth, her provocative glance. But instead of yielding to it, she was ashamed of it, so she throttled it, and all this desire, lust, got twisted inside her and churned the poison of jealousy and envy. Whenever sensuality showed its flower head, Thurema hated it. She was jealous of everything, of everyone's loves. She bought a black lace nightgown like mine when she came to Paris. She remembered our nights in New York. She said she had bought it for a lover she had after I left New York, but the price tag was still fastened on it.

The night of her arrival, the valises piled into the taxi, the taxi lost in the darkness of the boulevard de Neuilly. I had to get out and walk to find the *péniche*. There was a little hill to descend in the dark. We slipped and fell with the valises. We laughed. In the room where so many times the passion of Gonzalo had blazed in many flames, I now found myself with a woman who had enchanted me in New York, attracted me by the same violence of feeling, the same savagery as Gonzalo. And now? I remember looking at Thurema then with something of the same ravishment. She had grown fatter. I could see the swelling of her breasts at the opening of her white blouse. I liked the vivid primitive eyes, the wild hair, the wide mouth, the round thick nose. A white Negress, with her husky voice, strong teeth, wide jaws, thick lips, vitality. A blue-eyed Negress, with hair in an aureole around her head. Every gesture one of disorder, forest gestures, as if you brought a lioness into the room, and the lioness tried to open a valise and smashed the locks, the lioness pulled out the perfume and jewelry to give me and almost threw them at me. She covered the bed with gifts. She wanted me to put all the jewelry on, smell all the perfumes at once. I was showered with gifts as in the fairy tales, only to each gift was tied a little cord of demand, exactingness, of debt, of domination. Thurema gave as the spider weaves its web. She did not give away objects but threads woven out of her own substance to hold and to fix. The gifts so lavishly displayed on my bed reminded me of Rank's gifts. They were not the fairy-tale gifts I expected all my life.

She brought me dresses, jewels, perfume, slippers. She wanted to dress me. But the dresses were not for me. They were little girls' dresses, Thurema's taste, and I did not like them. Her magnificence did not make me happy, it stifled me. She put too much violence and self into her gifts. I felt this. The night begun in gaiety began to thicken. It was a lovely summer night. The barge was steady. Water was trickling from the little hill, sewer water, but with the sound of a bubbling mountain stream. The island in front of us was dark and murmurous. The candlelight was steady. Thurema was flickering and leaping. We talked all night.

I explained all the discomforts of the barge because I did not want her to stay there without a bath and hot water. I took her to the Acropolis Hotel. We chose a room. I was full of plans to amuse Thurema. I thought she could choose between Gonzalo's world, friends, South Americans, Spaniards (Thurema speaks Spanish), artists, all of Montparnasse, or Henry's American friends, Henry's artists and painters. Or Hugo's more conventional world, American colony, American bank visitors. To meet Thurema the night before I had left a limping Henry getting into a taxi, Henry's first night out after his fall from the ladder. We had agreed that I would bring Thurema to lunch. Henry could not go out for errands yet. I had to get his food for him anyway. While Thurema was hanging up her clothes I told her Henry was expecting her. Her eyes flashed green danger signals, shone with anger. She hated Henry, she said. Hated him. Why? I asked. Her reasons were confused and inadequate. I could only make out that she hated him and did not want to see him. Bang! One door closed. No evenings with Henry and his friends at the Villa Seurat. I explained that he was helpless because of the fall from the ladder. I had to go out and buy him food at least, then I would return and take her out to lunch because she did not know French.

I thought I would have better luck with Gonzalo. She was willing to meet him. We sat at a café. They talked about the guitar, which they both play, they planned a "concours" to see which one could eat the most pimentos as Thurema was used to them from her childhood days in Mexico, the hottest pimentos of all. We had lunch together at a little Greek restaurant. I thought that they liked each other. I was even a little jealous because they both loved pimentos and because I remembered they were born under the same sign, and because, strangely, Thurema had a trick of sticking her right leg out of the bed to cool it off, like Gonzalo. But as soon as I was alone with Thurema I saw by her silence that she hated him too. I asked her if she didn't think he was handsome. She answered: "*Es mono!*" He's cute—which is the last word one could apply to Gonzalo. No, she didn't like him.

I was still in an innocent mood and I did not yet detect the true reason for these antagonisms.

When I saw Gonzalo alone he said: "Your friend is a maternal type, not attractive, and so common!"

After this failure Thurema and I were reduced to each other's company, which is what she wanted. We sat at cafés, we shopped, we strolled, we visited the barge in the daytime, we went to the *marché aux puces*. We went gift hunting. Then Hugo came. Thurema could not put him off. She had to endure him. The three of us went boating on the Seine. Thurema wore slacks and was very boyish, comical, delightful. I still found her fascinating. I liked to see her dress up for the evening with her barbaric jewelry. Her face wildly alive. She was not for Paris, for the cafés. She was for the African orgies, dances. But this white Negress was not a free Negress, rippling in natural undulations of pleasure and desire. If her mouth, body, legs, voice were made for sensuality, the true flow of sensuality was paralyzed in her. One felt it in her like a great fear. Between her legs she was impaled on a rigid pole of Puritanism. All the rest of her body was loose, provocative. She always looked as if she had just come from lying in bed with a lover, or as if she were about to lie down. She had circles under her eyes. And energy smoking from her whole body. Impatience. Avidity.

If I had not been so spellbound by Gonzalo, if Thurema had not been so tense and terrified, I might have had an adventure with her. I liked her body, the vigor and violence of it. But she very soon destroyed all my illusions. She had a gift for destruction. She told me stories which revolted me forever against her sexual self, minute descriptions of a disease she caught as a child sitting on a water closet in the *quartier reservé* of New Orleans, where her family stayed in a hotel not knowing it was a whorehouse, of other sicknesses, of hemorrhages, descriptions of her stormy periods. She indulged like Helba in all the exposures of intimate disorders and rottenness. This ended my sexual attraction. At the same time, with an ambivalence which was repelling, she did everything she thought would seduce me, exposing herself, raising her legs in bed when I sat at the foot of the bed so that I could see her sex, dropping her chemise or the bath towel, pretending she had not heard me come in and standing naked in the bathroom.

The nights when I wanted to be with Henry or Gonzalo became dramas. When I could I slept with her—but when I left her at midnight to join Gonzalo I would find her the next morning white and sick with jealousy. I displayed all my gifts for tenderness, consolation, humor, understanding, in vain. I set out to reveal her to herself, reveal her true nature. I spent nights awake to delicately guide her. I was playful, fantastic. Referring to her constant interpretation of everything that was said to her as an injury, I said I would write a Chinese dictionary for her where she could look up each time the real intention behind the phrases. I was patient with her scenes of jealousy, her childishness, her emotionalism. What she liked was that I kiss her on the lips more and more warmly until we both got excited. She thrived on this hysterical undertow without any culmination. I ceased this game soon after she came. I am too sensual for this and it would lead me into full sexual gestures. And my feelings for her were beginning to get mixed with antagonism. One night we went with Hugo to the Bal Tabarin. I admired the women, as I always do, with the appreciative aesthetics of a man. I enjoyed their beauty, their variety. I was enchanted. Thurema got drunk. And jealous. She got furious at my admiration. She leaned over and said: "If I were a man I would murder you." Mixed with everything was her sentimental pity, something more false and sentimental than my compassion. "Oh, poor Hugo, poor Hugo. Poor Hugo, he is so unhappy. Look at him. He is not enjoying himself." "You don't understand Hugo," I said. "He is happy in his own quiet way. I wish you would stop feeling sorry for everybody."

She began to weep. I had to put my arm around her and console her. Hugo was looking on baffled, as passersby look up suddenly at an unexpected, freakish storm. Here it was, chaotically upsetting the universe, coming from right and left, great fury and velocity, and why? She went home and wrote stuttering phrases on the back of a box of writing paper: "Anaïs, don't abandon me, if you abandon me I am lost."

This was the woman I had chosen for a friend. A woman, no, a child, the same egotistical devouring child of always, no better than Helba or Gonzalo. Will and selfishness, caprice and confusion.

I was exhausted. She was so possessive, so harassing, obsessive, oppressive, that when I was out with her for a whole evening I would go to the toilet in the café and sit there for a while just to be alone.

I was physically exhausted. Every word had consequences. If we talked about her children and Thurema reproached me for not having much interest in children and if I answered: "It's true, I am not the maternal type you are," then Thurema threw a fit in the middle of the street because she was "not the maternal type," she was "something else," and if later to soothe and please her I said: "You're a *femme fatale*," then she made a scene again, because she "never destroyed or hurt anyone." Thurema thought herself good, generous, and with a great capacity for love.

Finally I went to the beach alone with Hugo for a week.

And then Thurema invented a way to get me back. She got sick, serious strep throat. Sick, alone in a hotel, and not knowing French. I had to leave Hugo and return to Paris, call for the doctor, run out for medicines, buy fruit, magazines, then bring chicken soup. Stay in her room all day and all night, while outside the summer nights were passing like gay whores with a tinkle of cheap jewelry. Chained to Thurema's antics, Thurema clapping her hands and confessing: "Now at last I've got you to myself."

Finally Thurema got well. Hugo was angry and alone. I returned to the beach for the weekend.

All I could think of was that the day of Thurema's departure was approaching. By the time she left she had destroyed all my love. I could not bring myself to write her. From then on it has been a lie. I did not want to let her see what she had done. It's a dead love. I dread her coming again. We did not have one moment of pleasure together. Walking the streets her obsession was to see who was looking at us, or following us. In the shops it was anxiety about her plumpness. In the movies it was emotionalism. In the restaurant it was meals turned to poison by scenes and quarrels with the waiter if we were not waited upon instantly, scenes about the bill, a scene with all I said. In the café she sat denigrating all those who passed, dissected those sitting around us. The universe hinged on her injured and defeated self. Every act of hers pushed people away. She could not understand why everywhere we went I could get what I wanted with a soft voice and gentle ways, why I was always waited on first, why the saleswoman would show me what was hidden away, why I was not cheated, why the policeman stopped the traffic for me, why the taxi-driver was gallant and took the shortest route, why the hotel keeper was devoted.

Thurema's commands, attacks, terseness, cockiness, made everyone bristle. Antagonized everyone. As she appeared she brought dissonance. I wanted to make her a gift if possible which would arrest this wounding tension with the whole world. I softened her.

When she wrote me from New York she said: "I should have come to help you with your burdens, and instead I came and became one of your burdens myself—how selfish!" When she left I got sick.

Notes

Text: *Nearer the Moon: From "A Journal of Love," the Unexpurgated Diary of Anaïs Nin, 1937-1939* (New York: Harcourt Brace, 1996), 323-29.

Thurema is Thurema Sokol. In mentioning the nights Nin and Sokol spent together in New York, Nin refers to a period in 1936 when they had an intimate relationship to the degree that they caressed each other's breasts. "*Péniche*" means "barge"; Nin refers to her rented houseboat on the Seine. Gonzalo is Gonzalo Moré. Rank is Otto Rank. Henry is Henry Miller. Hugo is Hugh Guiler. Miller lived at 18, Villa Seurat, where he fell from a ladder. "Concours" means "competition." "*Marché aux puces*" means "flea market." From this description of Sokol, Nin used "impaled on a rigid pole of Puritanism" in "Lillian and Djuna" (1945), later titled "This Hunger," to describe the character Lillian, which is based on Sokol. "*Quartier reservé*" means "red-light district." Helba is Helba Huara. Bal Tabarin was a Paris cabaret.

“MANUEL”

(1940-1941)

Context

In spring 1940, Nin and some friends began writing erotica for a private collector. They were paid a dollar a page. Two volumes of Nin's erotica, *Delta of Venus* and *Little Birds*, were published posthumously.

◆ ◆ ◆

Manuel had developed a peculiar form of enjoyment that caused his family to repudiate him, and he lived like a bohemian in Montparnasse. When not obsessed with his erotic exigencies, he was an astrologer, an extraordinary cook, a great conversationalist and an excellent café companion. But not one of these occupations could divert his mind from his obsession. Sooner or later Manuel had to open his pants and exhibit his rather formidable member.

The more people there were, the better. The more refined the party, the better. If he got among the painters and models, he waited until everybody was a little drunk and gay, and then he undressed himself completely. His ascetic face, dreamy and poetic eyes and lean monklike body were so much in dissonance with his behavior that it startled everyone. If they turned away from him, he had no pleasure. If they looked at him for any time at all, then he would fall into a trance, his face would become ecstatic, and soon he would be rolling on the floor in a crisis of orgasm.

Women tended to run from him. He had to beg them to stay and resorted to all kinds of tricks. He would pose as a model and look for work in women's studios. But the condition he got into as he stood there under the eyes of the female students made the men throw him out into the street.

If he were invited to a party, he would first try to get one of the women alone somewhere in an empty room or on a balcony. Then he would take down his pants. If the woman was interested he would fall into ecstasy. If not, he would run after her, with his erection, and come back to the party and stand there, hoping to create curiosity. He was not a beautiful sight but a highly incongruous one. Since the penis did not seem to belong to the austere, religious face and body, it acquired a greater prominence—as it were, an apartness.

He finally found the wife of a poor literary agent who was dying of starvation and overwork, with whom he reached the following arrangement.

He would come in the morning and do all her housework for her, wash her dishes, sweep her studio, run errands, on condition that when all this was over he could exhibit himself. In this case he demanded all her attention. He wanted her to watch him unfasten his belt, unbutton his pants, pull them down. He wore no underwear. He would take out his penis and shake it like a person weighing a thing of value. She had to stand near him and watch every gesture. She had to look at his penis as she would look at a food she liked.

This woman developed the art of satisfying him completely. She would become absorbed in the penis, saying, "It's a beautiful penis you have there, the biggest I have seen in Montparnasse. It's so smooth and hard. It's beautiful."

As she said these words, Manuel continued to shake his penis like a pot of gold under her eyes, and saliva came to his mouth. He admired it himself. As they both bent over it to admire it his pleasure would become so keen that he would close his eyes and be taken with a bodily trembling from head to foot, still holding his penis and shaking it under her face. Then the trembling would turn into undulation and he would fall on the floor and roll himself into a ball as he came, sometimes all over his own face.

Often he stood at dark corners of the streets, naked under an overcoat, and if a woman passed he opened his coat and shook his penis at her. But this was dangerous and the police punished such behavior rather severely. Oftener still he liked to get into an empty compartment of a train, unbutton two of the buttons, and sit back as if he were drunk or asleep, his penis showing a little through the opening. People would come in at other stations. If he were in luck it might be a woman who would sit across from him and stare at him. As he looked drunk, usually no one tried to wake him. Sometimes one of the men would rouse him angrily and tell him to button himself. Women did not protest. If a woman came in with little schoolgirls, then he was in paradise. He would have an erection, and finally the situation would become so intolerable, the woman and her little girls would leave the compartment.

One day Manuel found his twin in this form of enjoyment. He had taken his seat in a compartment, alone, and was pretending to fall asleep when a woman came in and sat opposite him. She was a rather mature prostitute as he could see from the heavily painted eyes, the thickly powdered face, the rings under her eyes, the over-curled hair, the worn-down shoes, the coquettish dress and hat.

Through half-closed eyes he observed her. She took a glance at his partly opened pants and then looked again. She too sat back and appeared to fall asleep, with her legs wide apart. When the train started she raised her skirt completely. She was naked underneath. She stretched open her legs and exposed herself while, looking at Manuel's penis, which was hardening and showing through the pants and which finally protruded completely. They sat in front of each other, staring. Manuel was afraid the woman would move and try to get hold of his penis, which was not what he wanted at all. But no, she was addicted to the same passive pleasure. She knew he was looking at her sex, under the very black and bushy hair, and finally they opened their eyes and smiled at each other. He was entering his ecstatic state, but he had time to notice that she was in a state of pleasure herself. He could see the shining moisture appearing at the mouth of the sex. She moved almost imperceptibly to and fro, as if rocking herself to sleep. His body began to tremble with voluptuous pleasure. She then masturbated in front of him, smiling all the time.

Manuel married this woman, who never tried to possess him in the way of other women.

Notes

Text: *Delta of Venus* (New York: Harcourt Brace Jovanovich, 1977), 211-14.

❧ PREFACE TO *LITTLE BIRDS* ☙

(Undated)

Context

Nin wrote an introduction to the erotic story "Marianne" that was used as a preface to *Little Birds* (1979). In the preface, she comments about erotica in general and her experience writing it.

◆ ◆ ◆ ◆

It is an interesting fact that very few writers have of their own accord sat down to write erotic tales or confessions. Even in France, where it is believed that the erotic has such an important role in life, the writers who did so were driven by necessity—the need of money.

It is one thing to include eroticism in a novel or a story and quite another to focus one's whole attention on it. The first is like life itself. It is, I might say, natural, sincere, as in the sensual pages of Zola or of Lawrence. But focusing wholly on the sexual life is not natural. It becomes something like the life of the prostitute, an abnormal activity that ends by turning the prostitute away from the sexual. Writers perhaps know this. That is why they have written only one confession or a few stories, on the side, to satisfy their honesty about life, as Mark Twain did.

But what happens to a group of writers who need money so badly that they devote themselves entirely to the erotic? How does this affect their lives, their feelings towards the world, their writing? What effect has it on their sexual life?

Let me explain that I was the mother confessor for such a group. In New York everything becomes harder, more cruel. I had many people to take care of, many problems, and since I was in character very much like George Sand, who wrote all night to take care of her children, lovers, friends, I had to find work. I became what I shall call the Madame of an unusual house of literary prostitution. It was a very artistic *"maison,"* I must say, a one-room studio with skylights, which I painted to look like pagan cathedral windows.

Before I took up my new profession I was known as a poet, as a woman who was independent and wrote only for her own pleasure. Many young writers, poets, came to me. We often collaborated, discussed and shared the work in progress. Varied as they were in character, inclinations, habits and vices, all the writers had one trait in common; they were poor. Desperately poor. Very often my *"maison"* was turned into a cafeteria where they dropped in, hungry, saying nothing, and we ate Quaker Oats because that was the cheapest thing to make, and it was said to give strength.

Most of the erotica was written on empty stomachs. Now, hunger is very good for stimulating the imagination; it does not produce sexual power, and sexual power does not produce unusual adventures. The more hunger, the greater the desires, like those of men in prison, wild and haunting. So we had here a perfect world in which to grow the flower of eroticism.

Of course, if you get too hungry, too continuously, you become a bum, a tramp. Those men who sleep along the East River, in doorways, on the Bowery, they have no sexual life at all, it is said. My writers—some of them lived in the Bowery—had not reached that stage yet.

As for me, my real writing was put aside when I set out in search of the erotic. These are my adventures in that world of prostitution. To bring them into the light was at first difficult. The sexual life is usually enveloped in many layers, for all of us—poets, writers, artists. It is a veiled woman, half-dreamed.

Notes

Text: *Little Birds* (New York: Harcourt Brace Jovanovich, 1979), ix-xi.

Zola is Émile Zola; Lawrence, D. H. Lawrence. Nin probably refers to Mark Twain's *1601* (1880). George Sand had two children; the most famous of her lovers was Frédéric Chopin (1810-1849). *"Maison"* means "house."

☙ POSTSCRIPT TO THE PREFACE ❧ TO *DELTA OF VENUS*

(1976)

Context

Composed only four months before Nin died, the postscript to the preface to *Delta of Venus* distinguishes between erotica written by men and women.

◆ ◆ ◆ ◆

At the time we were all writing erotica at a dollar a page, I realized that for centuries we had had only one model for this literary genre—the writing of men. I was already conscious of a difference between the masculine and feminine treatment of sexual experience. I knew that there was a great disparity between Henry Miller's explicitness and my ambiguities—between his humorous, Rabelaisian view of sex and my poetic descriptions of sexual relationships in the unpublished portions of the diary. As I wrote in Volume Three of the *Diary*, I had a feeling that Pandora's box contained the mysteries of woman's sensuality, so different from man's and for which man's language was inadequate.

Women, I thought, were more apt to fuse sex with emotion, with love, and to single out one man rather than be promiscuous. This became apparent to me as I wrote the novels and the *Diary*, and I saw it even more clearly when I began to teach. But although women's attitude towards sex was quite distinct from that of men, we had not yet learned how to write about it.

Here in the erotica I was writing to entertain, under pressure from a client who wanted me to "leave out the poetry." I believed that my style was derived from a reading of men's works. For this reason I long felt that I had compromised my feminine self. I put the erotica aside. Rereading it these many years later, I see that my own voice was not completely suppressed. In numerous passages I was intuitively using a woman's language, seeing sexual experience from a woman's point of view. I finally decided to release the erotica for publication because it shows the beginning efforts of a woman in a world that had been the domain of men.

If the unexpurgated version of the *Diary* is ever published, this feminine point of view will be established more clearly. It will show that women (and I, in the *Diary*) have never separated sex from feeling, from love of the whole man.

Notes

Text: *Delta of Venus* (New York: Harcourt Brace Jovanovich, 1977), xvi-xvii. Nin's unexpurgated diary was published in five volumes: *Henry and June* (1986), *Incest* (1992), *Fire* (1995), *Nearer the Moon* (1996), and *Mirages* (2013).

☙ "HOUSEBOAT" ❧

(1941)

Context

In the early 1940s, Nin re-wrote a story that had appeared in two parts in little magazines in 1941 and titled it "Houseboat." It became the first selection in *Under a Glass Bell* (1944), a collection of stories.

♦ ♦ ♦ ♦

The current of the crowd wanted to sweep me along with it. The green lights on the street corners ordered me to cross the street, the policeman smiled to invite me to walk between the silver-headed nails. Even the autumn leaves obeyed the current. But I broke away from it like a fallen piece. I swerved out and stood at the top of the stairs leading down to the Quays. Below me flowed the river. Not like the current I had just broken from, made of dissonant pieces, colliding rustily, driven by hunger and desire.

Down the stairs I ran towards the water front, the noises of the city receding as I descended, the leaves retreating to the corner of the steps under the wind of my skirt. At the bottom of the stairs lay the wrecked mariners of the street current, the tramps who had fallen out of the crowd life, who refused to obey. Like me, at some point of the trajectory, they had all fallen out, and here they lay shipwrecked at the foot of the trees, sleeping, drinking. They had abandoned time, possessions, labor, slavery. They walked and slept in counter-rhythm to the world. They renounced houses and clothes. They sat alone, but not unique, for they all seemed to have been born brothers. Time and exposure made their clothes alike, wine and air gave them the same eroded skin. The crust of dirt, the swollen noses, the stale tears in the eyes, all gave them the same appearance. Having refused to follow the procession of the streets, they sought the river which lulled them. Wine and water. Every day, in front of the river, they reenacted the ritual of abandon. Against the knots of rebellion, wine and the river, against the cutting iron of loneliness, wine and water washing away everything in a rhythm of blurred silences.

They threw the newspapers into the river and this was their prayer: to be carried, lifted, borne down, without feeling the hard bone of pain in man, lodged in his skeleton, but only the pulse of flowing blood. No shocks, no violence, no awakening.

While the tramps slept, the fishermen in a trance pretended to be capturing fish, and stood there hypnotized for hours. The river communicated with them through the bamboo rods of their fishing tackle, transmitting its vibrations. Hunger and time were forgotten. The perpetual waltz of lights and shadows emptied one of all memories and terrors. Fishermen, tramps, filled by the brilliance of the river as by an anesthetic which permitted only the pulse to beat, emptied of memories as in dancing.

The houseboat was tied at the foot of the stairs. Broad and heavy on its keel, stained with patches of lights and shadows, bathing in reflections, it heaved now and then to the pressure of a deeper breathing of the river. The water washed its flanks lingeringly, the moss gathered around the base of it, just below the water line, and swayed like Naiad hair, then folded back again in silky adherence to the wood. The shutters opened and closed in obedience to the gusts of wind and the heavy poles which kept the barge from touching the shore cracked with the strain like bones. A shiver passed along the houseboat asleep on the river, like a shiver of fever in a dream. The lights and shadows stopped waltzing. The nose of the houseboat plunged deeper and shook its chains. A moment of anguish: everything was slipping into anger again, as on earth. But no, the water dream persisted. Nothing was displaced. The nightmare might appear here, but the river knew the mystery of continuity. A fit of anger and only the surface erupted, leaving the deep flowing body of the dream intact.

The noises of the city receded completely as I stepped on the gangplank. As I took out the key I felt nervous. If the key fell into the river, the key to the little door to my life in the infinite? Or if the houseboat broke its moorings and floated away? It had done this once already, breaking the chain at the prow, and the tramps had helped to swing it back in place.

As soon as I was inside of the houseboat, I no longer knew the name of the river or the city. Once inside the walls of old wood, under the heavy beams, I might be inside a Norwegian sailing ship traversing fjords, in a Dutch boyer sailing to Bali, a jute boat on the Brahmaputra. At night the lights on the shore were those of Constantinople or the Neva. The giant bells ringing the hours were those of the sunken Cathedral. Every time I inserted the key in the lock, I felt this snapping of cords, this lifting of anchor, this fever of departure. Once inside the houseboat, all the voyages began. Even at night with its shutters closed, no smoke coming out of its chimney, asleep and secret, it had an air of mysteriously sailing somewhere.

At night I closed the windows which overlooked the Quays. As I leaned over I could see dark shadows walking by, men with their collars turned up and their caps pushed over their eyes, women with wide long skirts, market women who made love with the tramps behind the trees. The street lamps high above threw no light on the trees and bushes along the big wall. It was only when the window rustled that the shadows which seemed to be one shadow split into two swiftly and then, in the silence, melted into one again.

At this moment a barge full of coal passed by, sent waves rolling behind it, upheaving all the other barges. The pictures on the walls swayed. The fishing net hung on the ceiling like a giant spider web swung, gently rocking a sea shell and a starfish caught in its meshes.

On the table lay a revolver. No harm could come to me on the water but someone had laid a revolver there believing I might need it. I looked at it as if it reminded me of a crime I had committed, with an irrepressible smile such as rises sometimes to people's lips in the face of great catastrophes which are beyond their grasp, the smile which comes at times on certain women's faces while they are saying they regret the harm they have done. It is the smile of nature quietly and proudly asserting its natural right to kill, the smile which the animal in the jungle never shows but by which man reveals when the animal re-enters his being and reasserts its presence. This smile came to me as I took up the revolver and pointed it out of the window, into the river. But I was so averse to killing that even shooting into the water I felt uneasy, as if I might kill the Unknown Woman of the Seine again—the woman who had drowned herself here years ago and who was so beautiful that at the Morgue they had taken a plaster cast of her face. The shot came faster than I had expected. The river swallowed it. No one noticed it, not from the bridge, not from the Quays. How easily a crime could be committed here.

Outside an old man was playing the violin feverishly, but no sound came out of it. He was deaf. No music poured from his instrument, no music, but tiny plaintive cries escaped from his trembling gestures.

At the top of the stairs two policemen were chatting with the prostitutes.

The windows overlooking the Quays now shut, the barge looked uninhabited. But the windows looking on the river were open. The dying summer breath entered into my bedroom, the room of shadows, the bower of the night. Heavy beams overhead, low ceilings, a heavy wooden sideboard along the walls. An Indian lamp threw charcoal patterns over walls and ceiling—a Persian design of cactus flowers, lace fans, palm leaves, a lamaist vajry-mandala flower, minarets, trellises.

(When I lie down to dream, it is not merely a dust flower born like a rose out of the desert sands and destroyed by a gust of wind. When I lie down to dream it is to plant the seed for the miracle and the fulfillment.)

The headboard opened like a fan over my head, a peacock feather opening in dark wood and copper threads, the wings of a great golden bird kept afloat on the river. The barge could sink, but not this wide heavy bed traveling throughout the nights spread over the deepest precipices of desire. Falling on it I felt the waves of emotion which sustained me, the constant waves of emotion under my feet. Burrowing myself into the bed only to spread fanwise and float into a moss-carpeted tunnel of caresses.

The incense was spiraling. The candles were burning with delicate oscillations of anguish. Watching them was like listening to a beloved heartbeat and fearing the golden hammer strokes might stop. The candles never conquered the darkness but maintained a disquieting duel with the night.

I heard a sound on the river, but when I leaned out of the window the river had become silent again. Now I heard the sound of oars. Softly, softly coming from the shore. A boat knocked against the barge. There was a sound of chains being tied.

I await the phantom lover—the one who haunts all women, the one I dream of, who stands behind every man, with a finger and head shaking— "Not him, he is not the one." Forbidding me each time to love.

The houseboat must have traveled during the night, the climate and the scenery were changed. Dawn was accelerated by a woman's shrieks. Shrieks interrupted by the sound of choking. I ran on deck. I arrived just as the woman who was drowning grasped the anchor's chain. Her shrieks grew worse as she felt nearer salvation, her appetite for life growing more violent. With the help of one of the drunken tramps, we pulled the chain up, with the woman clinging to it. She was hiccuping, spitting, choking. The drunken tramp was shouting orders to imaginary sailors, telling them what to do for the drowned. Leaning over the woman he almost toppled over her, which reawakened her aggressiveness and helped her to rise and walk into the barge where we changed her clothes.

The barge was traversing a dissonant climate. The mud had come to the surface of the river, and a shoal of corks surrounded the barge. We pushed them away with brooms and poles; the corks seemed to catch the current and float away, only to encircle the barge magnetically.

The tramps were washing themselves at the fountain. Bare to the waist, they soaked their faces and shoulders, and then they washed their shirts, and combed themselves, dipping their combs in the river. These men at the fountain, they knew what was going to happen. When they saw me on deck, they gave me the news of the day, of the approach of war, of the hope of revolution. I listened to their description of tomorrow's world. An aurora borealis and all men out of prison.

The oldest tramp of all, who did not know about tomorrow, he was in the prison of his drunkenness. No escape. When he was filled like a barrel, then his legs gave way and he could only fall down. When he was lifted by alcoholic wings and ready for flight, the wings collapsed into nausea. This gangplank of drunkenness led nowhere.

The same day at this post of anguish, three men quarreled on the Quays. One carried a ragpicker's bag over his shoulder. The second was brilliantly elegant. The third was a beggar with a wooden leg. They argued excitedly. The elegant one was counting out money. He dropped a ten-franc piece. The beggar placed his wooden leg on it and would not budge. No one could frighten him, and no one dared to push off the wooden leg. He kept it there all the time they argued. Only when the two others went off did he lean over to pick it up.

The street cleaner was sweeping the dead leaves into the river. The rain fell into the cracked letter box and when I opened my letters it looked as if my friends had been weeping when writing me.

A child sat on the edge of the river, his thin legs dangling. He sat there for two or three hours and then began to cry. The street cleaner asked him what was the matter. His mother had told him to wait there until she returned. She had left him a piece of dry bread. He was wearing his little black school apron. The street cleaner took his comb, dipped it in the river and combed the child's hair and washed his face. I offered to take him on the barge. The street cleaner said: "She'll never come back. That's how they do it. He's another for the Orphanage."

When the child heard the word orphanage he ran away so fast the street cleaner did not have time to drop his broom. He shrugged his shoulders: "They'll catch him sooner or later. I was one of them."

Voyage of despair.

The river was having a nightmare. Its vast whaleback was restless. It had been cheated of its daily suicide. More women fed the river than men—more wanted to die in winter than in summer.

Parasitic corks obeyed every undulation but did not separate from the barge, glued like waves of mercury. When it rained the water seeped through the top room and fell on my bed, on my books, on the black rug.

I awakened in the middle of the night with wet hair. I thought I must be at the bottom of the Seine; that the barge, the bed, had quietly sunk during the night.

It was not very different to look through water at all things. It was like weeping cool saltless tears without pain. I was not cut off altogether, but in so deep a region that every element was marrying in sparkling silence, so deep that I heard the music of the spinet inside the snail who carries his antennae like an organ and travels on the back of a harp fish.

In this silence and white communion took place the convolutions of plants turning into flesh, into planets. The towers were pierced by swordfishes, the moon of citron rotated on a sky of lava, the branches had thirsty eyes hanging like berries. Tiny birds sat on weeds asking for no food and singing no song but the soft chant of metamorphosis, and each time they opened their beaks the webbed stained-glass windows decomposed into snakes and ribbons of sulphur.

The light filtered through the slabs of mildewed tombs and no eyelashes could close against it, no tears could blur it, no eyelids could curtain it off, no sleep could dissolve it, no forgetfulness could deliver one from this place where there was neither night nor day. Fish, plant, woman, equally aware, with eyes forever open, confounded and confused in communion, in an ecstasy without repose.

I ceased breathing in the present, inhaling the air around me into the leather urns of the lungs. I breathed out into the infinite, exhaling the mist of a three-quarter-tone breath, a light pyramid of heart beats.

This breathing lighter than breathing, without pressure from the wind, like the windless delicacy of the air in Chinese paintings, supporting one winged black bird, one breathless cloud, bowing one branch, preceded the white hysteria of the poet and the red-foamed hysteria of woman.

When this inhaling of particles, of dust grains, of rust microbes, of all the ashes of past deaths ceased, I inhaled the air from the unborn and felt my body like a silk scarf resting outside the blue rim of the nerves.

The body recovered the calm of minerals, its plant juices, the eyes became gems again, made to glitter alone and not for the shedding of tears.

Sleep.

No need to watch the flame of my life in the palm of my hand, this flame as pale as the holy ghost speaking in many languages to which none have the secret.

The dream will watch over it. No need to remain with eyes wide open. Now the eyes are gems, the hair a fan of lace. Sleep is upon me.

The pulp of roots, the milk of cactus, the quicksilver drippings of the silver beeches is in my veins.

I sleep with my feet on moss carpets, my branches in the cotton of the clouds.

The sleep of a hundred years has transfixed all into the silver face of ecstasy.

During the night the houseboat traveled out of the landscape of despair. Sunlight struck the wooden beams, and the reflected light of the water danced on the wooden beams. Opening my eyes I saw the light playing around me and I felt as if I were looking through a pierced sky into some region far nearer to the sun. Where had the houseboat sailed to during the night?

The island of joy must be near. I leaned out of the window. The moss costume of the houseboat was greener, washed by cleaner waters. The corks were gone, and the smell of rancid wine. The little waves passed with great precipitation. The waves were so clear I could see the roots of the indolent algae plants that had grown near the edge of the river.

This day I landed at the island of joy.

I could now put around my neck the sea-shell necklace and walk through the city with the arrogance of my secret.

When I returned to the houseboat with my arms loaded with new candles, wine, ink, writing paper, nails for the broken shutters, the policeman stopped me at the top of the stairs: "Is there a holiday on the Quay?"

"A holiday? No."

As I ran down the stairs I understood. There was a holiday on the Quay! The policeman had seen it on my face. A celebration of lights and motion. Confetti of sun spots, serpentines of water currents, music from the deaf violinist. It was the island of joy I had touched in the morning. The river and I united in a long, winding, never-ending dream, with its deep undercurrents, its deeper undertows of dark activity, the river and I rejoicing at teeming obscure mysteries of river-bottom lives.

The big clock of the Sunken Cathedral rang twelve times for the feast. Barges passed slowly in the sun, like festive chariots throwing bouquets of lightning from their highly polished knobs. The laundry in blue, white and rose, hung out to dry and waving like flags, children playing with cats and dogs, women holding the rudder with serenity and gravity. Everything washed clean with water and light passing at a dream pace.

But when I reached the bottom of the stairs the festivity came to an abrupt end. Three men were cutting the algae plants with long scythes. I shouted but they worked on unconcerned, pushing them all away so that the current would sweep them off. The men laughed at my anger. One man said: "These are not your plants. Cleaning Department order. Go and complain to them." And with quicker gestures they cut all the algae and fed the limp green carpet to the current.

So passed the barge out of the island of joy.

One morning what I found in the letter box was an order from the river police to move on. The King of England was expected for a visit and he would not like the sight of the houseboats, the laundry exposed on the decks, the chimneys and water tanks in rusty colors, the gangplanks with teeth missing, and other human flowers born of poverty and laziness. We were all ordered to sail on, quite a way up the Seine, no one knew quite where because it was all in technical language.

One of my neighbors, a one-eyed cyclist, came to discuss the dispossessions and to invoke laws which had not been made to give houseboats the right to lie in the heart of Paris gathering moss. The fat painter who lived across the river, open-shirted and always perspiring, came to discuss the matter and to suggest we do not move at all as a form of protest. What could happen? At the worst, since there were no laws against our staying, the police would have to fetch a tugboat and move us all in a line, like a row of prisoners. That was the worst that could happen to us. But the one-eyed cyclist was overcome by this threat because he said his houseboat was not strong enough to bear the strain of being pulled between other heavier, larger barges. He had heard of a small houseboat being wrenched apart in such a voyage. He did not think mine would stand the strain either.

The next day the one-eyed man was towed along by a friend who ran one of the tourist steamers; he left at dawn like a thief, with his fear of collective moving. Then the fat painter moved, pulled heavily and slowly because his barge was the heaviest. He owned a piano and huge canvases, heavier than coal. His leaving left a vast hole in the alignment of barges, like a tooth missing. The fishermen crowded in this open space to fish and rejoiced. They had been wishing us away, and I believe it was their prayers which were heard rather than ours, for soon the letters from the police became more insistent.

I was the last one left, still believing I would be allowed to stay. Every morning I went to see the chief of police. I always believed an exception would be made for me, that laws and regulations broke down for me. I don't know why except that I had seen it happen very often. The chief of police was extremely hospitable; he permitted me to sit in his office for hours and gave me pamphlets to pass the time. I became versed in the history of the Seine. I knew the number of sunken barges, collided Sunday tourist steamboats, of people saved from suicide by the river police. But the law remained adamant, and the advice of the chief of police, on the sly, was for me to take my houseboat to a repair yard near Paris where I could have a few repairs made while waiting for permission to return. The yard being near Paris, I made arrangements for a tugboat to come for me in the middle of the day.

The tugboat's approach to the barge was very much like a courtship, made with great care and many cork protectors.

The tugboat knew the fragility of these discarded barges converted into houseboats. The wife of the tugboat captain was cooking lunch while the maneuvers were carried out. The sailors were untying the ropes, one was stoking the fire. When the tugboat and the barge were tied together like twins, the captain lifted the gangplank, opened his bottle of red wine, drank a very full gulp and gave orders for departure.

Now we were gliding along. I was running all over the houseboat, celebrating the strangest sensation I had ever known, this traveling along a river with all my possessions around me, my books, my diaries, my furniture, my pictures, my clothes in the closet. I leaned out of each little window to watch the landscape. I lay on the bed. It was a dream. It was a dream, this being a marine snail traveling with one's house all around one's neck.

A marine snail gliding through the familiar city. Only in a dream could I move so gently along with the small human heartbeat in rhythm with the tug tug heartbeat of the tugboat, and Paris unfolding, uncurling, in beautiful undulations.

The tugboat pulled its smokestacks down to pass under the first bridge. The captain's wife was serving lunch on deck. Then I discovered with anxiety that the barge was taking in water. It had already seeped through the floor. I began to work the pumps, but could not keep abreast of the leaks. Then I filled pails, pots and pans, and still I could not control the water, so I called out to the captain. He laughed. He said: "We'll have to slow down a bit." And he did.

The dream rolled on again. We passed under a second bridge with the tugboat bowing down like a salute, passed all the houses I had lived in. From so many of these windows I had looked with envy and sadness at the flowing river and passing barges. Today I was free, and traveling with my bed and my books. I was dreaming and flowing along with the river, pouring water out with pails, but this was a dream and I was free.

Now it was raining. I smelled the captain's lunch and I picked up a banana. The captain shouted: "Go on deck and say where it is you want to stop."

I sat on deck under an umbrella, eating the banana, and watching the course of the voyage. We were out of Paris, in that part of the Seine where the Parisians swim and canoe. We were traveling pass the Bois de Boulogne, through the exclusive region where only the small yachts were allowed to anchor. We passed another bridge, and reached a factory section. Discarded barges were lying on the edge of the water. The boat yard was an old barge surrounded with rotting skeletons of barges, piles of wood, rusty anchors, and pierced water tanks. One barge was turned upside down, and the windows hung half wrenched on the side.

We were towed alongside and told to tie up against the guardian barge, that the old man and woman would watch mine until the boss came to see what repairing had to be done.

My Noah's Ark had arrived safely, but I felt as if I were bringing an old horse to the slaughterhouse.

The old man and woman who were the keepers of this cemetery had turned their cabin into a complete concierge's lodge to remind themselves of their ancient bourgeois splendor: an oil lamp, a tile stove, elaborate sideboards, lace on the back of the chairs, fringes and tassels on the curtains, a Swiss clock, many photographs, bric-à-brac, all the tokens of their former life on earth.

Every now and then the police came to see if the roof was done. The truth was that the more pieces of tin and wood the boss nailed to the roof, the more the rain came in. It fell on my dresses and trickled into my shoes and books. The policeman was invited to witness this because he suspected the length of my stay.

Meanwhile the King of England had returned home, but no law was made to permit our return. The one-eyed man made a daring entry back and was expelled the very next day. The fat painter returned to his spot before the Gare d'Orsay—his brother was a deputy.

So passed the barge into exile.

Notes

Text: *Under a Glass Bell and Other Stories* (New York: Dutton, 1948), 11-25.

᜕ PROLOGUE TO *UNDER A GLASS BELL* ᜖

(1944)

Context

In the prologue to *Under a Glass Bell*, Nin explains why she wrote the stories as she did.

◆ ◆ ◆ ◆

Because these stories were written before the Spanish war I had thought first of all would destroy them, and then I understood truth which it might be good to state for others. The stories must be placed in the proper light for those who fail to see the relation between fantasy and reality, the past and the present. Everything is related and inter-active but at times we fail to see how, and consequently, fail to make a higher synthesis.

These stories represent the moment when many like myself had found only one answer to the suffering of the world: to dream, to tell fairytales, to elaborate and to follow the labyrinth of fantasy. All this I see now was the passive poet's only answer to the torments he witnessed. Being ignorant of the causes and therefore of a possibility of change, he sought merely a balm—art, the drug.

In the first story I took a houseboat and it became the Noah's Ark of a dream voyage. I sought the river as a lulling drug. In the story of the Mohican is resumed the mystical belief in astrology and the consequent fatalism. In the story of Pierre the poet's fantasy carries him into insanity, and this is the true story of what happened to many poets at that moment—the story of one of the most gifted of the surrealist poets: Antonin Artaud. In Under a Glass Bell I describe a brilliant and aristocratic family and its disintegration due to its isolation. It is in The Mouse that first appears the thread of humanity which was to lead me out of the dream: my feeling for the maid was human but I did not know what to do for her.

I did not stay in the world of the isolated dream or become permanently identified with it. The Spanish war awakened me. I passed out of romanticism, mysticism and neurosis into reality.

I see now there was no need to destroy the art that was produced under an evil social structure. But it is necessary to understand, to be aware of what caused the suffering which made such an opium essential and what this fantasy world concealed. And to this task I will devote the rest of my writing.

I am in the difficult position of presenting stories which are dreams and of having to say: but now although I give you these I am awake! Someone may say: then why don't you publish your new writing, and give us the new awareness? The answer to this I can best make through a story. I once saw a Russian film of dancers. One was a Mongolian woman most elaborately dressed in gold embroideries, with tasseled jewelry on her forehead, bells on her ankles and wrists. This was the traditional feast costume. However this Mongolian dancer was a Soviet and wanting to express the new spirit she felt she decided to do the Dance of the Girl Sewing in a Factory. In this elaborate accoutrement, the sediment of centuries of aesthetic refinements, she made the gestures of the girl sewing in a factory, occasionally forgetting her theme and shaking her shoulders and eyes in the old bizarre manner. Not wishing to be like this dancer I am merely presenting these dream dances while I change my costume.

Notes

Text: *Under a Glass Bell* (New York: Gemor Press, 1944), 2nd edition.

Nin refers to the Spanish Civil War (1936-1939). Some of Artaud's poems appear in *Tric trac du ciel* (1923).

ᘓ PROLOGUE TO *UNDER A GLASS BELL* ᘔ

(1968)

Context

Nin again addresses her stories in the preface to a later edition of them.

◆ ◆ ◆ ◆

There are two reasons why I agreed to let Peter Owen reprint these stories. One is that they were originally published in England during World War 2, at a most inauspicious time. There was then not enough paper, the limited edition looked prematurely aged, and there were insufficient reviewers and readers. A more important reason for me is that these stories broke a mould and used the distillation of poetry. I feel that a contemporary evaluation of them may come closer to their intention.

My *Journals*, covering the period during which the stories were written, and giving undistilled, human and authentic characters from which they were drawn, will also throw a new light upon them. The *Journals* supply the key to the mythical figures and assert the reality of what once may have seemed to be purely fantasy. Such a marriage of illusion and reality—or illusion as the key to reality—is a contemporary theme. Some of the stories are about people who became well known and influence our present life. They will now seem more familiar.

I am always reminded of the interplay between Debussy and Erik Satie: Debussy said to Satie that his compositions had no form. Satie responded by titling one: "Sonata in the Form of a Pear."

Notes

Text: *Under a Glass Bell and Other Stories* (London: Peter Owen, 1968).

Peter Owen (1927-) is one of Nin's English publishers. Nin errs in stating that the first English edition of *Under a Glass Bell* (London: Editions Poetry London, 1947) was published *"during World War 2,"* though this statement was corrected in the Penguin edition of the collection in 1978, the year after Nin died. In England, *The Diary of Anaïs Nin* is titled *The Journals of Anaïs Nin*. In response to the comment by Claude Debussy (1862-1918), Erik Satie (1866-1925) composed *Trois Morceaux en forme du poire* (*Three Pieces in the Shape of a Pear*) in 1903.

❦ *DIARY 3* ❧

(November 1941)
On Robert Duncan

Context

In 1940, Nin met Robert Duncan (1919-1988) through James Cooney (1909-1985) and Blanche Cooney (1917-1995) and became his friend. At the time of their meeting, Duncan was in his early twenties; Nin, her late thirties. As editor of *Ritual* and *Experimental Review*, he published some of Nin's short fiction. He appears as Donald in Nin's *Children of the Albatross, A Spy in the House of Love*, and "Elena."

◆ ◆ ◆

November, 1941. Reading Robert's diary was my only access to the inner Robert. Now that he can no longer work in my studio, and has taken his papers away, he wears a mask, he is detached. He felt I was throwing him out of the nest. The human contact, by way of the diaries, broke. One cannot reach him. Outside of the diary he is brittle, he is an actor.

While I read his diary we could communicate on a level where his cold rays could not reach, a level where playacting ceased.

In the diary he said he was devouring me like a food. It makes him write, to read my diary.

Man seems powerless to face the truth or the relative truth stripped of all adornment. Robert could not bear to look back, to examine, to interpret. His motives were oblique. He acted out illusions. He must have myths to love, but when they shatter, he stops loving. I argued this, that where the myth fails, human love begins. Then we love a human being, not our dream, but a human being with flaws. But Robert must peer forward into a new mirage. The moment we lost touch with the diaries, he lost his sincerity with me. Perhaps I lost mine, too. I would never have known Robert intimately if it had not been for his diary.

So now he exists outside, almost a stranger.

Robert thinks I am not writing a sketch book at all, that I am completing a work. "You are bringing in the characters fully, independently of you, and in person."

Scene with Robert. He came and asked for a loan for a trip. My eyes filled with tears.

"You weep only because you have no money?"

"I weep because I did not think you would ask me, knowing how indebted I am, how short I am. I thought you would spare me having to say no."

"Why do you weep? Just say *no* harshly, that's the end of it. I would have preferred that you get angry. Why don't you just get angry?" He made a grimace of disapproval. He said: "You are ineffectual in battle. You should *fight*."

The grin with which he invited me to battle was like a distortion, a Robert I did not know.

Because of my vision into the inner Robert I still refused to see how his behavior crystallized into coldness and selfishness. He always came in without a greeting. He went straight to the icebox. He was never concerned whether he finished the last carton of milk, or the last slice of bread, which meant I had to climb five flights of stairs to buy more of everything for dinner. He never helped to put away the dishes. He served himself, no one else. He monologued without regard for others' work or fatigue. I had to read all that he brought even if he found me writing. He invited his friends for lunch. At any time. When visitors came for me, he did not leave. Once, when he asked me for money, I showed him my empty pocketbook and he left without a word.

After breaking through the nonhuman Robert to reach the vulnerable Robert in his diary, again I had to learn I was casting my own reflections on him. I thought, With me he will be different. Knowing my struggles, he would not burden me. But he did. Furthermore, he demanded a harshness equal to his own. If I have to manufacture an equal hardness, then I do not want any friendship on such terms. I want to be able to trust, not live in perpetual self-defense.

When he rang the bell this morning I did not answer. I was in the kitchen when I heard him entering through the transom window.

I told him how I felt. He left angrily.

I made contact with the highest point of Robert's poetic intuitions, with the poet Robert, but all around this lay areas of confusion and coldness. This connection with the highest point of a human being can be dangerous to human life. You only love the potential and overlook the reality. Will I be able to love Robert as he is? Wasn't it I who told him, When you lose a myth about a person that is where human love begins?

Robert, *l'enfant terrible*, perverse and knowing. At times the softness of a boneless child makes him seem small, at others he stands up rigid and tall. His eyes are too widely opened, like a medium in a trance. His eyelids fall heavily, like a woman's, with a seductive sweep of the eyelashes, the feminine drawing of a veil; a man's eyelids never fall this way over the revealing landscape of the eyes. It is when a woman's eyes are about to reveal too much that the woman draws a veil, lowers the lid over the chamber of revelation. How often I have watched women cover the flame of mischief with a Venetian blind, especially the glint of jealousy, the flicker of envy, the gleam of anger.

Robert talked and wrote so much about his consuming hunger and his desire to be consumed in love, about his desire for renunciation and the protection of others. He talked about his quest for a father. With me he is not feminine.

My femininity annoys him. He loves me, but he would like me to be a boy. That must have been the meaning of the scene we had. He wanted a warrior, someone who would resist him. Not the softness of the woman.

Paul offered him a paradise somewhere, a beach where they could love each other freely, embrace day and night, a paradise of caresses. But this is not what Robert wanted. He was seeking the infernos of love, love mixed with suffering and obstacles. He wants to kill monsters (the parents), overcome obstacles (poverty), and know all the adventures of romantic, impossible loves.

At the same time, when he talked about Paul, there came to his face the same expression of obscene glee, of vain satisfaction, triumph, an inner uncontrollable celebration of his power to wound others, the female ruses and wiles and coquetries by which he had made Paul fall in love with him. The malicious feminine conspiracy to enchant, seduce and victimize.

He acted like a caricature of a woman. A bad imitation of woman.

The woman without a womb in which such great mysteries take place. Only this travesty of the invitation, like the prostitute's, which will never lead to a magnificent fusion. Why do men love this travesty of woman and not the real woman?

No great love could take place in this wombless femininity. Only a travesty of love. Robert's fury. His angry words: "He overlooked the masculinity in me completely. He treated me like a woman. I want to be saved from becoming a woman. He handled and possessed me like a woman."

Notes

Text: *The Diary of Anaïs Nin, 1939-1944* (New York: Harcourt, Brace & World, 1969), 168-71.

Robert is Robert Duncan. Paul is a pseudonym for Eduardo Sánchez, with whom Duncan had an affair.

♋ UNPUBLISHED DIARY ♋

(3-10 June 1943)
Affair with Albert Mangones

Context

At the time of the events depicted here, Nin was preparing *Under a Glass Bell* for publication with the Gemor Press. She was then associating with Haitians.

♦ ♦ ♦ ♦

June 3, 1943. They all came last night, [Jean] Brièrre, Albert, Josephine [Premice], Adele [Premice], Lionel Durant and Pierre Roumain. We sat on the porch. Albert. His hands were on the drum. I could not resist placing mine on the drum. He only touched the tip of my finger. I felt his feeling following me if I sat by Lionel—his feelings welcoming me when I moved towards him, drawing me to the seat beside him. He said: "I wish I had a gift to make you." I said: "There is something I want—the photo of you drumming in the fields..." He immediately gave it to me, though he had only one. I said I would have one made for him. I took it to the light. He followed me. We were alone in the studio. We leaned over Hugo's pictures. Then the emotion caught us together. I had taken his arm. He pressed mine. Our bodies touched. As we could be seen from the window we walked away—his arm about my waist. Forever and forever I shall feel how he pressed his temple against mine and said: *"Je sais, Anaïs, je sais."* Delicate brushings, charged with feelings, tensions. A moment later others came. We put on the radio. Albert opened his arms and we danced...he held me tightly. Simple acts.

But after they left, I turned out the light, and I fell back into the summer night drunk. Over and over again I repeated the scene, the movements, from the very first—the hands on the drum—to the dance—feelings each time anew the strong current, the ecstasy—the most marvelous moment of all life—more marvelous even than possession!

Albert, tu sais. Je sais, Anaïs... Je sais, Anaïs...

Evening: Albert and I went to the Blue Angel to present Josephine at an audition. When it was over, while Josephine was dressing, Albert and I sat at the bar. He first of all kissed my hand. His face when he becomes passionate is beautiful, ardent and joyous. We touched cheeks, temples, and then could

133

not resist the impulse and kissed. His full, so full, so rich mouth taking mine, the grating of our teeth...

He was not free to stay with me: Pussy had arranged an evening. But he came back home with me, carrying the drum upstairs. And for the first time we were alone, facing each other, body to body. A marvelous rhythm took place, some secret harmony—which made each gesture exactly alike, a new firmness, like a premeditated graceful dance—I cannot tell of it—but it was a dream embrace. We stood up, the bodies fitted so closely I felt his desire—a strength came out of our similar softness and graceful violence. Such intensity, but no brusqueness. How beautiful it must have been to see. First we stood up, until, beside himself, he broke away and went to wash his face. But when he was fresh and clean to leave and sat on the drum, I moved towards him and then with passion, he laid his head on my breast and I kissed his bowed head, his hair... Then again we separated. "I must leave." But I stood by the window, leaning against the table and Albert held me again, so powerfully, with his beautiful face resplendent—crushing me so I lost my breath.

And then he left. And I was full of him, his face, his mouth, his strength— so perfect the caress that I felt possession almost too much—so *possessive* were the caresses!

June 4. Black hairs again, lost among mine. Black curled hair. Albert's high brow—his slanting upward eyes, his high cheek bones (his father was a white Spaniard from Columbia), his round nose, and his full finely chiseled mouth always slightly open. Beautiful teeth. His mouth the magnet. His carriage. With all the gentle fullness of his body, the indolent form of it, the soft outlines, he has an erect carriage of pride. Pride, joy, perfection. No perversions or deformities. He reflects dance and music and the sun. His skin is the color of the sun.

J'ai peur de l'aimer trop...

For a night and day after this I was in ecstasy, an ecstasy so powerful that I thought it would break me. Everything was illuminated, lightened, the air, the light, the sky... The intensity of the desire carried me out of the world and out of reality! I thought too it would carry Albert out of his entanglements with the continuous presence of Pussy and the "group"—for they live a kind of tribal life, always in groups together. But he sweetly, gently, and realistically yielded to the difficulties.

By nighttime—not having heard from him—the ecstasy turned to pain— anguish. I thought everything was lost, that my passionate responsiveness had frightened him. Again the next day, such anxiety that I telephoned him—

when I didn't want to—only to find him sweet and soft and pliant.

I made him come at six—for five minutes, I said. Found a pretext. Felt I could not go to the Haitian dance that evening without seeing him. He came. I was trembling with anxiety. He came quietly, passively accepting the difficulties, but just as passionate. While I talked, he was the one who began to kiss me. We embraced and kissed and he said: "*Tout cela ne nous avance à rien...nous ne pouvons pas être ensemble.*" His brother had arrived. He was surrounded, encircled.

I was reassured by his embrace, but disappointed. It was what I had feared... Softness and the lack of audacity. Lack of intensity too—he is tranquil and passionate without tension.

At least my suffering ceased, my fear. I felt gay again. We went to the dance. The evening was lovelier than the last, more intimate, no whites but ourselves. I was taken out to dance constantly—and then...

Brièrre, whom I call the Port de Prince, Brièrre the Hindu Prince, so black, so intense, nervous, fiery, Brièrre took me dancing. As soon as he clasped me for the dance, there was a conflagration! Such a burning fire came from him, and from me. He held me closer and closer. He danced almost without moving across the room—we swung our hips. His knee, nervous, wiry, hard, rhythmically moved between my legs with such a sensual simulation of a caress. My knee moved closer between his legs and I felt his desire firm and strong.

A darker, more violent feeling than with Albert.

Brièrre danced with me several times. Each time he aroused me. Once I looked up into his eyes and his black fiery glance was more like a stab. Those dances were like a sexual act, and I yielded to the drug.

At times I would move my face away...for Jean Brièrre's temple touched mine...and look for Albert—look at Albert. Albert, in contrast to Jean, looked more and more tender, gentle, idealized, purer. My feelings went out to his gentleness, but the nervous, fiery intensity of Jean compelled me.

What a beautiful evening! How far I was from the parties of surrealists and artists, men without beauty or sex. How often I have commented lately on the complete absence of magnetism, of coquetry between the men and women. Last night I felt beautiful not in an abstract way as I felt before, but beautiful and desirable—a woman. The women were beautiful and desirable. We lived in the dancing and singing. My body was joyous and flowering. But what a division again between my nature and my feelings. My feelings go to Albert, and my nature goes to Jean whom I do not love, because he is cynical and vain of his great beauty, because he is affected and literary. I love the great simplicity of Albert.

Dream of Haiti
Varied and beautiful faces. Aristocratic sensuality, emotion, subtlety.

My unhappy Venus wills that both Albert and Jean are returning home to not be drafted!

June 6. Great fall tonight—from the ecstasies.

Seeing Albert at the Premices' singing, wanting to caress him, seeing him with Pussy at his heels, not being able to be with him. Caressing him endlessly within myself and realizing I am going to lose him. In a few weeks he returns home.

Jean Brièrre too—leaving in a week. Filled with promises, drum beating, singing, knowing here is life, revolted by Catherine and Michel and all the whites...but I will lose it all like a dream, in a few weeks.

All but Premice's affection.

My only pleasure, to arouse a sensation always when I come in—the Haitians see me as beautiful. I feel desired. But I cannot reach any happiness.

An hour with Gonzalo, dragged into the past. Finally in a strong talk, I make it clear to him that it is destructive to dwell in the past—that my role is to make him react and live in the present. A greater understanding was reached even to the deep differences of character and attitude which differentiate and separate me from Helba as the deep cause of discord, and I proved to him how it was just that I should react against the stifling, crushing past to save him—and Helba.

But as I gave him strength I realized how far I am moving away from him.

Le sang se nourrit de danse et de musique. How deeply right the Haitians are—and I with them—in wanting talk only between two or three, but the group always gives itself to music—I always wanted deep, important, creative talk with certain persons, where an active relationship takes place. But the music and dance—instead of the disjointed lifeless talk that takes place in white talk. Oh those evenings without music and dancing—the lifeless evenings. Irina so intent on talking while the Fête was going on—and I wanted to dance. The deep life of the body so nourishing and vital.

At the Premices'—the generous hospitality, the childish atmosphere, naïve and simple, the joyousness and playfulness.

June 7. Jean came to the Press at eleven. He was shy. And I was frightened—I was frightened of my impulsiveness, frightened of my élans which carry me into abysms, frightened to give him the sign... I let him read me poems and look into my face. And then he sat down and wrote me a poem.

Eduardo came at twelve—we went to lunch together, with Pierre Roumain too.

I have a feeling Albert was jealous to see me dance with Jean. (I looked so white that night of the dance, ivory white. Our bodies fit together so... And Jean so utterly black...) Was he jealous to see us together today when we called for Pierre? Albert was going to work.

No word from Albert—and I have not sufficient faith. My ecstasy is shattered. I have lost my audacity, my courage. I cannot give Jean a sign (though in the dance I yielded to the passion which possessed us). The dark sensual Jean of the dance and the mannered timid Jean of daylight.

Suddenly, because of Jean's darker life (he was fifteen months in prison in Haiti for revolutionary activity) and Albert's joyous one, I saw them as the two facets of Gonzalo—and I realized I was not free of Gonzalo yet.

This afternoon Gonzalo took me. I was without feeling for him, saying to myself: Well, here is a very handsome man! But he seems to have killed my tenderness. Last night I spoke to him strongly, not tenderly, regardless of consequence (consequence was that he took me!).

June 8. What a torment this mirage of love, soon to vanish altogether. What a cruel torment, this passion for both Jean and Albert. To Jean I could have given a great passion.

I am burning—continuously, as I have never burned. From head to toe like a torch. I am sensitive and open to all. Even in Eduardo I aroused and released a deep emotion, delivered him of his fear of expressing it, and our parting today was in itself like a romance. A true wave of feeling. It is sad too that I have my greatest power of fascination, just at this moment, when I cannot pour the passion into anyone, when I am imprisoned in a mirage. Albert is my soft dream and Jean my violent one.

The beauty of Jean is royal. He is slender, nervous, a little taller than I am (Albert is the same height but rounder, softer, fuller). His carriage is tense, nervous. Albert is relaxed, tranquil. Jean is as black as he can be—with a finely chiseled head—the close short Negro hair, but the fine straight nose, the full, rich, but not exaggerated, mouth. He looks somber—smiles rarely. Albert's mouth is open and smiling. Jean is torturous, labyrinthian and perverse.

June 9. At the most anguished moment of my watch for Albert's telephone, I lay back and said to myself: I *deserve* happiness. I deserve it!

Days passed. Last Thursday we embraced. No word from him after his visit Saturday. I began to tremble, to doubt, to suffer. Then came Jean. And Jean's poem. And the darkness again. Then this morning I called Jaeger, needing her. My heart hurt me. My being wanted Albert—not Jean. A moment after I spoke with Jean, Albert called. His voice rich, deep and intimate—"Pussy is not well. I shall go and see her but could be free at ten. *Mais je crains que toi, maintenant, tu ne soit pas libre. Viens chez moi.*"

Je viendrai.

My happiness inundated me. But I was still shaking and trembling. I took my anguish to my mythological mother. She quieted my heart, unknotted my nerves, magically. Something wonderful is being born. In birth there is struggle. Passion is being born, purified of its masculinity.

Passion free of guilt.

Again I found Albert's mouth, sweeter than Jean. Again I felt the strength concealed in his softness which is aroused by my strength concealed in softness. I seek his quietness and integrity. I move towards Albert and the light. Out of my prison...

June 10. Again the bathing, the sandalwood soap, the perfume in the hair, copper on the nails, the black lace panties, the turquoise green dress Albert liked, hair loose. I walked fast, lightly to him, like an arrow. But I did not enter his room directly. I stood in the street looking up at his two lighted windows. Then I felt: a beautiful lover is awaiting me. And I walked around the block, to find the lighted windows again, the anticipation...

"*Tu as les cheveux fous,*" he said, kissing me. I said, "*J'ai marché vite.*"

No violence but quietness and sureness and strength. Aware it is Albert, it is Anaïs, we called the names... Supple caresses like his dancing. He did not linger enough. His desire impelled him, and soon he had taken his pleasure. But all my pleasure spread in the caresses. For each nook and form of the body there was an answer, a nook, a form. Cat-like, languorous, voluptuous. The taste of sweetness, of fruit perfection. We lay in the dark. He said: "*Tu es contente?*" I said yes. Later he asked me why I was amoureuse de lui much as if he did not believe it. I said: "*Pour beaucoup, beaucoup des choses—j'aime tout en toi, comme tu penses, je sens ton caractère en ton bon visage, tu es lumineux.*"

The rolling softness, warmth we bathed in—then after a while I slid down and took his sex in my mouth. All that I knew of caresses I gave him in this—I felt it stirred him—he lay back sighing. He placed his hand on my hair and then he moved with my mouth with a soft continuous undulation, until his pleasure increased and rose to a climax. How I enjoyed giving him this, seeing his body yielding, abandoned, hearing his cry, a greater pleasure than the first. I lay over him, now. The silkiness of his skin, the softness and down, the tranquility, the perfection of the rhythm. My lasciviousness matching his.

Oh, Albert, how I wanted to know if you felt this as a miracle. Was it new to you? Were you warmed to the depths of your being, caressed so intimately that the remembrance lingered? I felt near to him—not as in other adventures, strange or separated, but near, near.

I said: "I am heavy."

He answered: *"Non—reste là. Est-ce bon?"*

"Oui, c'est bon."

"Alors reste."

Simple words. Simple, simple. The body and soul can learn happiness, joy. This was joy, fragrant and miraculous. My own youth, my quietness, before love became a torment. Oh the sweetness, the sweetness! The lightness I felt, I felt washed of pain and darkness, washed, luminous and clear. I could have slept at his side as quietly as he slept after his pleasure. I felt as if he had transmitted his youth to me, his fresh skin and glossy live curls, his laughter and his singing.

What will he remember of this? My body remembers him. My body did not remember Canada [Lee], or Chinchilito [Edward Graeffe]. Balm and fragrance on my soul, a sexual act like a dance. What did I leave on his skin, in his nerves, what flavor, what magnetic waves? He left his fragrance, like his songs. *Douceur, mollesse, chaleur, force souple, force enroulante*, the mysterious currents passing through two bodies, out in the night—light of foot. "Don't you see me through a prism?" he asked.

I didn't notice then.

What does he mean?

Does he think I dream him?

He does not dream.

He is content, he is sleepy, he is hungry, he smokes, he tells me to wear his slippers to the bathroom, he moves quietly, free, beautiful... Very beautiful. More beautiful than Gonzalo, because Gonzalo's beauty is marred by the weakness of the mouth—in Albert the mouth is rich and full—his face is balanced—Gonzalo's hands and feet are strong and coarse. Albert's are delicate. His body has the savor of his songs...the Creole gentleness.

Albert—I took you into my arms, and I take you into my diary, into my devastated life now blossoming anew because of you. Singing and drumming but with pale hands and without savagery you come, soft like your songs, tender like your climate, tranquil like your island, vibrant like your plants, rich like your earth, Albert, I take you into my arms again, into my diary, your innocence and your purity, your luminousness. I take you, take you, take you bending over me, and pray and wish you felt as much as I did... remember, retain, absorbed. What I gave you was only the perfume of all my suffering, for there is a suffering that can bear a perfume, a magnificent fragrance of soul. There is a suffering that is without bitterness, like mine, which can give birth to a deeper knowledge of joy, to a deeper reception of joy, to a deeper love for Albert than those who eluded the pain. In each caress of joy there was the magnetic miracle of love that knows the beauty of what it is caressing—knows it more deeply, for all its deprivations, for all its sacrifices, for all its openness to pain... What my hands and mouth know of your fragrance only pain could have made possible. Exquisite joy created by past suffering. To better know Albert, the childlikeness of his laughter, his fragrance, his fragrance.

Notes

Text: "Dances of Love and Desire: From the Unpublished Diary," in *A Café in Space: The Anaïs Nin Literary Journal* 2 (2004): 88-95. Republished in *Mirages* (2013).

Jean-Fernand Brièrre (1909-1992) was a Haitian poet. Albert is Albert Mangones (1917-2002), a Haitian architect and sculptor. Josephine Premice (1926-2001) was an actress and singer who, in the late 1940s, drummed and chanted on a recording of Nin reading some of Nin's fiction; Adèle Premice was her sister. I cannot identify Lionel Durant and Pierre Roumain. Hugo is Hugh Guiler. *"Je sais, Anaïs, je sais"* means "I know, Anaïs, I know." *"Albert, tu sais"* means "Albert, you know." The Blue Angel was a New York nightclub. Pussy is Mangones's girlfriend. *"J'ai peur de l'aimer trop"* means "I am afraid of loving him too much." *"Tout cela ne nous avance à rien...nous ne pouvons pas être ensemble"* means "That's not getting us anywhere...we can't be together." Nin refers to the family of Lucas Premice (1892-1977). Catherine was an English potter living in Greenwich Village. I cannot identify Michel. Gonzalo is Gonzalo Moré; Helba, Helba Huara. The Press is Nin's Gemor Press, where Moré worked. *"Le sang se nourrit de danse et de musique"* means "The blood is nourished by dance and music." Irina was a friend of Nin. Eduardo is Eduardo Sánchez. Jaeger is Martha Jaeger (1894-1963), Nin's analyst. *"Mais je crains que toi, maintenant, tu ne soit pas libre. Viens chez moi"* means "But I fear that now you may not be free. Come to my place." *"Je viendrai"* means "I will come." *"Tu as les cheveux fous"* means "Your hair is a mess." *"J'ai marché vite"* means "I walked fast." *"Tu es contente?"* means "Are you happy?" *"Amoureuse de lui"* means "In love with him." *"Pour beaucoup, beaucoup des choses— j'aime tout en toi, comme tu pense[s], je sens ton caractère en ton bon visage, tu es lumineux*" means "For many, many things—I love everything about you; as you know, I feel your warmth shining through your handsome face." "*Non—reste là. Est-ce bon?*" means "No—stay here. Are you comfortable?" "*Oui, c'est bon*" means "Yes, I'm fine." "*Alors reste*" means "Then stay." Nin had affairs with actor Canada Lee (1907-1952) and singer Edward Graeffe (ca. 1909-1969). "*Douceur, mollesse, chaleur, force souple, force enroulante*" means "Sweetness, softness, warmth, supple strength, imprisoning strength."

⌘ *DIARY 4* ☙

(April 1945)
On Joaquín Nin-Culmell

Context

Here, Nin reflects on the music and goodness of her younger brother, Joaquín Nin-Culmell.

◆ ◆ ◆ ◆

April, 1945. Joaquin's "Quintet for Piano and Strings" was played at the Museum of Modern Art.

In my brother's music there is always a sense of space, air, as if the lyrical experience had been distilled into a light essence and become transparent. The color gold is always a part of it. Emotion is contained, but always clear and strong.

Joaquin's piano recitals and his compositions are a permanent motif in my life, confirming my convictions that music is the highest of the arts.

When he was five years old, a spirited and restless child no one could tame, he would spend hours absolutely still on the staircase of our home in Brussels, listening to the musicians rehearsing. That was the sign of his vocation. We both listened. I can still hear the lines of Bach which were most often repeated. Joaquin became a musician, and in me music was channeled into writing.

In New York, in the brownstone on Seventy-fifth Street, he studied piano with an eccentric old maid, Emilia Quintero, whom I often described in my childhood diary. She kept a white silk scarf of Sarasate's as others keep a memento of a saint. She had loved him secretly and hopelessly. Some of this love was transferred to the handsome Joaquin.

His music was always there. In Richmond Hill he practiced every hour he did not spend in school. In Paris he practiced all day, in spite of delicate health. In Louveciennes he had his studio in a large, beautiful attic room. There was not only the practicing, but even in childhood there were moments of improvisation, the forerunners of his later compositions.

In Paris we had adjoining apartments. He was studying piano with Paul Braud at the Schola Cantorum, and privately with Alfred Cortot and Ricardo Viñes. He studied harmony, counterpoint, and fugue with Jean and Noel Gallon of the Paris Conservatory. He studied musical composition with

Paul Dukas at the Paris Conservatory, and privately with Manuel de Falla in Granada, Spain.

I heard him study and compose by the hour. In Louveciennes, when he grew weary of the discipline, he would visit my mother in her apartment, and then me at my typewriter, and ask *"Tu m'aime?"*

Satisfied and recharged, he would go back to work. He drew his strength from his love, never from hatred, and later it was his capacity for love, understanding, and forgiveness which kept the family from estrangements. He was always trying to reunite and reconstruct the family unit. He never took sides, judged, or turned a hostile back on anyone.

He gave concerts in Spain, France, Switzerland, Italy, Belgium, Denmark, England, the United States, Canada, and Cuba.

He is proud and modest, unassuming and yet uncompromising, unable to cripple a rival, push anyone aside, or assert himself.

When he whistles, it means he is standing by his piano writing down his compositions, correcting his scores.

Once, in Paris, he destroyed one movement of a quintet whose motif I loved. He commented it was too romantic. Perhaps I heard in it the wistful adolescent parting from adolescent sorrows. Perhaps he had, musically, very good reasons for casting it off, to reach a more austere modernism. But I felt the loss as emotional, and its disappearance as a part of Joaquin himself that he was shedding for more rigorous standards. It coincided with the burning of his diaries. Ten years later, during a period of psychoanalysis, I came out singing the entire melodic theme, I who am not a musician and who cannot read music. This proved to me how deeply his music penetrated an unconscious universe. Even when apparently forgotten, lost, this fragment had remained imbedded in me.

In my father there was a distinct faithfulness to Spanish folklore. Spain was recognizable in the themes he embroidered on and harmonized for concert use. With Joaquin something else happened, which brought his music into the realm of modern universal compositions. The Spanish themes became transformed into something more abstract, more unconscious, not the cliché Spain. He modernized the colors, the fervors, the richness of Spain into daring abstractions. It was a far more complex and subtle Spain. There was a tension between simplicity, the single line, and the highly evolved complexities of colors and tones. The intricacies, like the Moorish lacework of Granada, were always unified into the single wistful chant of *"Cante Jondo."*

I spoke of the color gold. There is always a crystalline quality, the transparencies of truth, a strange faculty for musical sincerity which never reaches a common, explicit statement. The composition always spirals away deftly from a familiar statement. It appeals to a third ear, an unborn ear, the ears of today, more intricate but always true: he has a perfect pitch of the soul.

He explores constantly for daring juxtapositions, daring multiplicities, and superimpositions. He achieves radiations, luminosities, and sparkle. The human being and the composer are one. The sources are good humor, generosity, hidden sorrows he does not burden others with, gray days and joyous days, back-breaking labor and early morning whistling.

Joaquin never slides into anger, caricature, or emptiness, or into any of the artifices and pretensions of some of his contemporaries.

I am sure that listening to his music directed my choice of words, my search for rhythm, my ear for tonalities, my use of the unconscious as a many-voiced symphony. I am sure he is the orchestra conductor who quietly and modestly indicates the major theme of the diary; words similar to music which can penetrate the feelings and bypass the mind. His music, far from being in the background of my life, was in the foreground. It was he as a musician who accomplished what I dreamed of, and I followed as well as I could with the inferior power of words. The ear is purer than the eye, which reads only relative meaning into words. Whereas the distillation of experience into pure sound, a state of music, is timeless and absolute.

As a human being, he is the strongest influence in my life, for it is not the failed relationships which influence our life—they influence our death. With Joaquin I had the model of the best relationship I had throughout childhood and adolescence. True, I had to take care of him; he was five years younger. True, it was he who lived out the wildness, the freedom, the independence, while I had to become responsible for his safety, his well-being. But in return he gave the greatest responsiveness and tenderness. He was loving and loyal. We never quarreled. Once, when I lost some money given to me for marketing (when we had little enough), he offered to take the blame. He was ten years old. He set the pattern for the many little brothers I was to have, whose life I must watch over but who return an immense care and tenderness. He never passed judgment, he was never critical. Our lives were different, but we kept an immense respect for each other.

Notes

Text: *The Diary of Anaïs Nin, 1944-1947* (New York: Harcourt Brace Jovanovich, 1971), 49-52.

Joaquin is Joaquín Nin-Culmell. The Nin family lived in Uccle, outside Brussels, from 1909 until 1913. Following Joaquín Nin's 1913 abandonment of the family, Rosa Culmell de Nin took the children ultimately to New York, where they lived on West 75th Street before settling in Richmond Hill. In 1924, they—now including Anaïs's husband, Hugh Guiler—moved to Paris and then, without Anaïs's brother Thorvald, to Louveciennes. Emilia Quintero (1864-1934) lived in the Nins' 75th Street brownstone; she accompanied singers at the Metropolitan Opera and was young Joaquín's first piano teacher. Pablo de Sarasate (1844-1908) was a Spanish composer and violinist. Among Nin-Culmell's music teachers were Paul Braud (b. 1860), Alfred Cortot (1877-1962), Ricardo Viñes (1875-1943), the brothers Jean Gallon (1878-1959) and Noel Gallon (1891-1966), Paul Dukas (1865-1935), and Manuel de Falla. "*Tu m'aime[s]?*" means "Do you love me?" "*Cante Jondo*" literally means "deep song," but is used to mean a flamenco song.

⋆ "THIS HUNGER" ⋆

(September 1945)

Context

Nin published "Lillian and Djuna" in *This Hunger* (1945) and *Ladders to Fire* (1946) before changing its title to "This Hunger" and making it the first section of *Ladders to Fire* when published in *Cities of the Interior* (1959) "This Hunger" introduces characters and themes that resonate throughout the remainder of the novel and the other volumes of Nin's continuous novel.

◆ ◆ ◆ ◆

Lillian was always in a state of fermentation. Her eyes rent the air and left phosphorescent streaks. Her large teeth were lustful. One thought of a negress who had found a secret potion to turn her skin white and her hair red.

As soon as she came into a room she kicked off her shoes. Necklaces and buttons choked her and she loosened them, scarves strangled her and she slackened them. Her hand bag was always bursting full and often spilled over.

She was always in full movement, in the center of a whirlpool of people, letters, and telephones. She was always poised on the pinnacle of a drama, a problem, a conflict. She seemed to trapeze from one climax to another, from one paroxysm of anxiety to another, skipping always the peaceful region in between, the deserts and the pauses. One marveled that she slept, for this was a suspension of activity. One felt sure that in her sleep she twitched and rolled, and even fell off the bed, or that she slept half sitting up as if caught while still talking. And one felt certain that a great combat had taken place during the night, displacing the covers and pillows.

When she cooked, the entire kitchen was galvanized by the strength she put into it; the dishes, pans, knives, everything bore the brunt of her strength, everything was violently marshaled, challenged, forced to bloom, to cook, to boil. The vegetables were peeled as if the skins were torn from their resisting flesh, as if they were the fur of animals being peeled by the hunters. The fruit was stabbed, assassinated, the lettuce was murdered with a machete. The flavoring was poured like hot lava and one expected the salad to wither, shrivel instantly. The bread was sliced with a vigor which recalled heads falling from the guillotine. The bottles and glasses were knocked hard against each other as in bowling games, so that the wine, beer, and water were conquered before they reached the table.

What was concocted in this cuisine reminded one of the sword swallowers at the fair, the fire-eaters and the glass-eaters of the Hindu magic sects. The same chemicals were used in the cooking as were used in the composition of her own being: only those which caused the most violent reaction, contradiction, and teasing, the refusal to answer questions but the love of putting them, and all the strong spices of human relationship which bore a relation to black pepper, paprika, soybean sauce, ketchup and red peppers. In a laboratory she would have caused explosions. In life she caused them and was afterwards aghast at the damage. Then she would hurriedly set about to atone for the havoc, for the miscarried phrase, the fatal honesty, the reckless act, the disrupting scene, the explosive and catastrophic attack. Everywhere, after the storms of her appearance, there was emotional devastation. Contacts were broken, faiths withered, fatal revelations made. Harmony, illusion, equilibrium were annihilated. The next day she herself was amazed to see friendships all askew, like pictures after an earthquake.

The storms of doubt, the quick cloudings of hypersensitivity, the bursts of laughter, the wet furred voice charged with electrical vibrations, the resonant quality of her movements, left many echoes and vibrations in the air. The curtains continued to move after she left. The furniture was warm, the air was whirling, the mirrors were scarred from the exigent way she extracted from them an ever unsatisfactory image of herself.

Her red hair was as unruly as her whole self; no comb could dress it. No dress would cling and mould her, but every inch of it would stand out like ruffled feathers. Tumult in orange, red and yellow and green quarreling with each other. The rose devoured the orange, the green and blue overwhelmed the purple. The sport jacket was irritated to be in company with the silk dress, the tailored coat at war with the embroidery, the everyday shoes at variance with the turquoise bracelet. And if at times she chose a majestic hat, it sailed precariously like a sailboat on a choppy sea.

Did she dream of being the appropriate mate for the Centaur, for the Viking, for the Pioneer, for Attila or Genghis Khan, of being magnificently mated with Conquerors, the Inquisitioners or Emperors?

On the contrary. In the center of this turmoil, she gave birth to the dream of a ghostly lover, a pale, passive, romantic, anaemic figure garbed in grey and timidity. Out of the very volcano of her strength she gave birth to the most evanescent, delicate and unreachable image.

She saw him first of all in a dream, and the second time while under the effects of ether. His pale face appeared, smiled, vanished. He haunted her sleep and her unconscious self.

The third time he appeared in person in the street. Friends introduced them. She felt the shock of familiarity known to lovers.

He stood exactly as in the dream, smiling, passive, static. He had a way of greeting that seemed more like a farewell, an air of being on his way.

She fell in love with an extinct volcano.

Her strength and fire were aroused. Her strength flowed around his stillness, encircled his silence, encompassed his quietness.

She invited him. He consented. Her whirlpool nature eddied around him, agitating the fixed, saturnian orbit.

"Do you want to come...do you?"

"I never know what I want," he smiled because of her emphasis on the "want," "I do not go out very much." From the first, into this void created by his not wanting, she was to throw her own desires, but not meet an answer, merely a pliability which was to leave her in doubt forever as to whether she had substituted her desire for his. From the first she was to play the lover alone, giving the questions and the answers too.

When man imposes his will on woman she knows how to give him the pleasure of assuming his power is greater and his will becomes her pleasure; but when the woman accomplishes this, the man never gives her a feeling of any pleasure, only of guilt for having spoken first and reversed the roles. Very often she was to ask: "Do you want to do this?" And he did not know. She would fill the void, for the sake of filling it, for the sake of advancing, moving, feeling, and then he implied: "You are pushing me."

When he came to see her he was enigmatic. But he was there.

As she felt the obstacle, she also felt the force of her love, its impetus striking the obstacle, the impact of the resistance. This collision seemed to her the reality of passion.

He had been there a few moments and was already preparing for flight, looking at the geography of the room, marking the exits "in case of fire," when the telephone rang.

"It's Serge asking me to go to a concert," said Lillian with the proper feminine inflection of: "I shall do your will, not mine." And this time Gerard, although he was not openly and violently in favor of Lillian, was openly against Serge, whoever he was. He showed hostility. And Lillian interpreted this favorably. She refused the invitation and felt as if Gerard had declared his passion. She laid down the telephone as if marking a drama and sat nearer to the Gerard who had manifested his jealousy.

The moment she sat near him he recaptured his quality of a mirage: paleness, otherworldliness, obliqueness. He appropriated woman's armor and defenses, and she took the man's. Lillian was the lover seduced by obstacle and the dream. Gerard watched her fire with a feminine delectation of all fires caused by seduction.

When they kissed she was struck with ecstasy and he with fear.

Gerard was fascinated and afraid. He was in danger of being possessed. Why in danger? Because he was already possessed by his mother and two possessions meant annihilation.

Lillian could not understand. They were two different loves, and could not interfere with each other.

She saw, however, that Gerard was paralyzed, that the very thought of the two loves confronting each other meant death.

He retreated. The next day he was ill, ill with terror. He sought to explain. "I have to take care of my mother."

"Well," said Lillian, "I will help you."

This did not reassure him. At night he had nightmares. There was a resemblance between the two natures, and to possess Lillian was like possessing the mother, which was taboo. Besides, in the nightmare, there was a battle between the two possessions in which he won nothing but a change of masters. Because both his mother and Lillian (in the nightmare they were confused and indistinguishable), instead of living out their own thoughts, occupying their own hands, playing their own instruments, put all their strength, wishes, desires, their wills on him. He felt that in the nightmare they carved him out like a statue, they talked for him, they acted for him, they fought for him, they never let him alone. He was merely the possessed. He was not free.

Lillian, like his mother, was too strong for him. The battle between the two women would be too strong for him. He could not separate them, free himself and make his choice. He was at a disadvantage. So he feared: he feared his mother and the outcries, the scenes, dramas, and he feared Lillian for the same reason since they were of the same elements: fire and water and aggression. So he feared the new invasion which endangered the pale little flame of his life. In the center of his being there was no strength to answer the double challenge. The only alternative was retreat.

When he was six years old he had asked his mother for the secret of how children were born. His mother answered: "I made you."

"You made me?" Gerard repeated in utter wonder. Then he had stood before a mirror and marveled: "You made this hair? You made this skin?"

"Yes," said his mother. "I made them."

"How difficult it must have been, and my nose! And my teeth! And you made me walk, too." He was lost in admiration of his mother. He believed her. But after a moment of gazing at the mirror he said: "There is one thing I can't believe. I can't believe that you made my eyes!"

His eyes. Even today when his mother was still making him, directing him, when she cut his hair, fashioned him, carved him, washed his clothes, what was left free in this encirclement of his being were his eyes. He could not act, but he could see.

But his retreat was inarticulate, negative, baffling to Lillian. When she was hurt, baffled, lost, she in turn retreated, then he renewed his pursuit of her. For he loved her strength and would have liked it for himself. When this strength did not threaten him, when the danger was removed, then he gave way to his attraction for this strength. Then he pursued it. He invited and lured it back, he would not surrender it (to Serge or anyone else). And Lillian who suffered from his retreat suffered even more from his mysterious returns, and his pursuits which ceased as soon as she responded to them.

He was playing with his fascination and his fear.

When she turned her back on him, he renewed his charms, enchanted her and won her back. Feminine wiles used against woman's strength like women's ambivalent evasions and returns. Wiles of which Lillian, with her straightforward manly soul, knew nothing.

The obstacle only aroused Lillian's strength (as it aroused the knights of old) but the obstacle discouraged Gerard and killed his desire. The obstacle became his alibi for weakness. The obstacle for Gerard was insurmountable. As soon as Lillian overcame one, Gerard erected another. By all these diversions and perversions of the truth he preserved from her and from himself the secret of his weakness. The secret was kept. The web of delusion grew around their love. To preserve this fatal secret: you, Lillian, are too strong; you, Gerard, are not strong enough (which would destroy them), Gerard (like a woman) wove false pretexts. The false pretexts did not deceive Lillian. She knew there was a deeper truth but she did not know what it was.

Weary of fighting the false pretexts she turned upon herself, and her own weakness, her self-doubts, suddenly betrayed her. Gerard had awakened the dormant demon doubt. To defend his weakness he had unknowingly struck at her. So Lillian began to think: "I did not arouse his love. I was not beautiful enough." And she began to make a long list of self-accusations. Then the harm was done. She had been the aggressor so she was the more seriously wounded. Self-doubt asserted itself. The seed of doubt was implanted in Lillian to work its havoc with time. The real Gerard receded, faded, vanished, and was reinstated as a dream image. Other Gerards will appear, until...

After the disappearance of Gerard, Lillian resumed her defensive attitude towards man, and became again the warrior. It became absolutely essential to her to triumph in the smallest issue of an argument. Because she felt so insecure about her own value it became of vital importance to convince and win over everyone to her assertions. So she could not bear to yield, to be convinced, defeated, persuaded, swerved in the little things.

She was now afraid to yield to passion, and because she could not yield to the larger impulses it became essential also to not yield to the small ones, even if her adversary were in the right. She was living on a plane of war. The bigger resistance to the flow of life became one with the smaller resistance to the will of others, and the smallest issue became equal to the ultimate one. The pleasure of yielding on a level of passion being unknown to her, the pleasure of yielding on other levels became equally impossible. She denied herself all the sources of feminine pleasure: of being invaded, of being conquered. In war, conquest was imperative. No approach from the enemy could be interpreted as anything but a threat. She could not see that the real issue of the war was a defense of her being against the invasion of passion. Her enemy was the lover who might possess her. All her intensity was poured into the small battles; to win in the choice of a restaurant, of a movie, of visitors, in opinions, in analysis of people, to win in all the small rivalries through an evening.

At the same time as this urge to triumph continuously, she felt no appeasement or pleasure from her victories. What she won was not what she really wanted. Deep down, what her nature wanted was to be made to yield.

The more she won (and she won often for no man withstood this guerrilla warfare with any honors—he could not see the great importance that a picture hung to the left rather than to the right might have) the more unhappy and empty she felt.

No great catastrophe threatened her. She was not tragically struck down as others were by the death of a loved one at war. There was no visible enemy, no real tragedy, no hospital, no cemetery, no mortuary, no morgue, no criminal court, no crime, no horror. There was nothing.

She was traversing a street. The automobile did not strike her down. It was not she who was inside of the ambulance being delivered to St. Vincent's Hospital. It was not she whose mother died. It was not she whose brother was killed in the war.

In all the registers of catastrophe her name did not appear. She was not attacked, raped, or mutilated. She was not kidnapped for white slavery.

But as she crossed the street and the wind lifted the dust, just before it touched her face, she felt as if all these horror had happened to her, she felt the nameless anguish, the shrinking of the heart, the asphyxiation of pain, the horror of torture whose cries no one hears.

Every other sorrow, illness, or pain is understood, pitied, shared with all human beings. Not this one which was mysterious and solitary.

It was ineffectual, inarticulate, unmoving to others as the attempted crying out of the mute.

Everybody understands hunger, illness, poverty, slavery and torture. No one understood that at this moment at which she crossed the street with every privilege granted her, of not being hungry, of not being imprisoned or tortured, all these privileges were a subtler form of torture. They were given to her, the house, the complete family, the food, the loves, like a mirage. Given and denied. They were present to the eyes of others who said: "You are fortunate," and invisible to her. Because the anguish, the mysterious poison, corroded all of them, distorted the relationships, blighted the food, haunted the house, installed war where there was no apparent war, torture where there was no sign of instruments, and enemies where there were no enemies to capture and defeat.

Anguish was a voiceless woman screaming in a nightmare.

She stood waiting for Lillian at the door. And what struck Lillian instantly was the aliveness of Djuna: if only Gerard had been like her! Their meeting was like a joyous encounter of equal forces.

Djuna responded instantly to the quick rhythm, to the intensity. It was a meeting of equal speed, equal fervor, equal strength. It was as if they had been two champion skiers making simultaneous jumps and landing together at the same spot. It was like a meeting of two chemicals exactly balanced, fusing and foaming with the pleasure of achieved proportions.

Lillian knew that Djuna would not sit peacefully or passively in her room awaiting the knock on her door, perhaps not hearing it the first time, or hearing it and walking casually towards it. She knew Djuna would have her door open and would be there when the elevator deposited her. And Djuna knew by the swift approach of Lillian that Lillian would have the answer to her alert curiosity, to her impatience; that she would hasten the elevator trip, quicken the journey, slide over the heavy carpet in time to meet this wave of impatience and enthusiasm.

Just as there are elements which are sensitive to change and climate and rise fast to higher temperatures, there were in Lillian and Djuna rhythms which left them both suspended in utter solitude. It was not in body alone that they arrived on time for their meetings, but they arrived primed for high living, primed for flight, for explosion, for ecstasy, for feeling, for all experience. The slowness of others in starting, their slowness in answering, caused them often to soar alone.

To Djuna Lillian answered almost before she spoke, answered with her bristling hair and fluttering hands, and the tinkle of her jewelry.

"Gerard lost everything when he lost you," said Djuna before Lillian had taken off her coat. "He lost life."

Lillian was trying to recapture an impression she had before seeing Djuna. "Why, Djuna, when I heard your voice over the telephone I thought you were delicate and fragile. And you look fragile but somehow not weak. I came to...well, to protect you. I don't know what from."

Djuna laughed. She had enormous fairy tale eyes, like two aquamarine lights illumining darkness, eyes of such depth that lit first one felt one might fall into them as into a sea, a sea of feeling. And then they ceased to be the pulling, drawing, absorbing sea and they became beacons, with extraordinary intensity of vision, of awareness, of perception. Then one felt one's chaos illumined, transfigured. Where the blue, liquid balls alighted every object acquired significance.

At the same time their vulnerability and sentience made them tremble like delicate candlelight or like the eye of the finest camera lens which at too intense daylight will suddenly shut black. One caught the inner chamber like the photographer's dark room, in which sensitivity to daylight, to crudity and grossness would cause instantaneous annihilation of the image.

They gave the impression of a larger vision of the world. If sensitivity made them retract, contract swiftly, it was not in any self-protective blindness but to turn again to that inner chamber where the metamorphosis took place and in which the pain became not personal, but the pain of the whole world, in which ugliness became not a personal experience of ugliness but the world's experience with all ugliness. By enlarging and situating it in the totality of the dream, the unbearable event became a large, airy understanding of life which gave to her eyes an ultimately triumphant power which people mistook for strength, but which was in reality courage. For the eyes, wounded on the exterior, turned inward, but did not stay there, and returned with the renewed vision. After each encounter with naked unbearable truths, naked unbearable pain, the eyes returned to the mirrors in the inner chambers, to the transformation by understanding and reflection, so that they could emerge and face the naked truth again.

In the inner chambers there was a treasure room. In it dwelt her racial wealth of Byzantine imagery, a treasure room of hierarchic figures, religious symbols. Old men of religion, who had assisted at her birth and blessed her with their wisdom. They appeared in the colors of death, because they had at first endangered her advance into life. Their robes, their caps, were made of the heavily embroidered materials of rituals illumined with the light of eternity. They had willed her their wisdom of life and death, of past and future, and therefore excluded the present. Wisdom was a swifter way of reaching death. Death was postponed by living, by suffering, by risking, by losing, by error. These men of religion had at first endangered her life, for their wisdom had incited her in the past to forego the human test of experience, to forego the error and the confusion which was living. By knowing she would reach all, not by touching, not by way of the body. There had lurked in these secret chambers of her ancestry a subtle threat such as lurked in all the temples, synagogues, churches—the incense of denial, the perfume of the body burnt to sacrificial ashes by religious alchemy, transmuted into guilt and atonement.

In the inner chamber there were also other figures. The mother madonna holding the child and nourishing it. The haunting mother image forever holding a small child.

Then there was the child itself, the child inhabiting a world of peaceful, laughing animals, rich trees, in valleys of festive color. The child in her eyes appeared with its eyes closed. It was dreaming the fertile valleys, the small warm house, the Byzantine flowers, the tender animals and the abundance. It was dreaming and afraid to awaken. It was dreaming the lightness of the sky, the warmth of the earth, the fecundity of the colors.

It was afraid to awaken.

Lillian's vivid presence filled the hotel room. She was so entirely palpable, visible, present. She was not parceled into a woman who was partly in the past and partly in the future, or one whose spirit was partly at home with her children, and partly elsewhere. She was here, all of her, eyes and ears, and hands and warmth and interest and alertness, with a sympathy which surrounded Djuna—questioned, investigated, absorbed, saw, heard...

"You give me something wonderful, Lillian. A feeling that I have a friend. Let's have dinner here. Let's celebrate."

Voices charged with emotion. Fullness. To be able to talk as one feels. To be able to say all.

"I lost Gerard because I leaped. I expressed my feelings. He was afraid. Why do I love men who are afraid? He was afraid and I had to court him. Djuna, did you ever think how men who court a woman and do not win her are not hurt? And woman gets hurt. If woman plays the Don Juan and does the courting and the man retreats she is mutilated in some way."

"Yes, I have noticed that. I suppose it's a kind of guilt. For a man it is natural to be the aggressor and he takes defeat well. For woman it is a transgression, and she assumes the defeat is caused by the aggression. How long will woman be ashamed of her strength?"

"Djuna, take this."

She handed her a silver medallion she was wearing. "Well, you didn't win Gerard but you shook him out of his death."

"Why," said Lillian, "aren't men as you are?"

"I was thinking the same thing," said Djuna.

"Perhaps when they are we don't like them or fear them. Perhaps we like the ones who are not strong..."

Lillian found this relation to Djuna palpable and joyous. There was in them a way of asserting its reality, by constant signs, gifts, expressiveness, words, letters, telephones, an exchange of visible affection, palpable responses. They exchanged jewels, clothes, books, they protected each other, they expressed concern, jealousy, possessiveness. They talked. The relation-ship was the central, essential personage of this dream without pain. This relationship had the aspect of a primitive figure to which both enjoyed presenting proofs of worship and devotion. It was an active, continuous ceremony in which there entered no moments of indifference, fatigue, or misunderstandings or separations, no eclipses, no doubts.

"I wish you were a man," Lillian often said.

"I wish you were."

Outwardly it was Lillian who seemed more capable of this metamorphosis. She had the physical strength, the physical dynamism, the physical appearance of strength. She carried tailored clothes well; her gestures were direct and violent. Masculinity seemed more possible to her, outwardly. Yet inwardly she was in a state of chaos and confusion. Inwardly she was like nature, chaotic and irrational. She had no vision into this chaos: it ruled her and swamped her. It sucked her into miasmas, into hurricanes, into caverns of blind suffering.

Outwardly Djuna was the essence of femininity...a curled frilled flower which might have been a starched undulating petticoat or a ruffled ballet skirt moulded into a sea shell. But inwardly the nature was clarified, ordered, understood, dominated. As a child Djuna had looked upon the storms of her own nature—jealousy, anger, resentment—always with the knowledge that they could be dominated, that she refused to be devastated by them, or to destroy others with them. As a child, alone, of her own free will, she had taken on an oriental attitude of dominating her nature by wisdom

155

and understanding. Finally, with the use of every known instrument—art, aesthetic forms, philosophy, psychology—it had been tamed.

But each time she saw it in Lillian, flaring, uncontrolled, wild, blind, destroying itself and others, her compassion and love were aroused. "That will be my gift to her," she thought with warmth, with pity. "I will guide her."

Meanwhile Lillian was exploring this aesthetic, this form, this mystery that was Djuna. She was taking up Djuna's clothes one by one, amazed at their complication, their sheer femininity. "Do you wear this?" she asked, looking at the black lace nightgown. "I thought only prostitutes wore this!"

She investigated the perfumes, the cosmetics, the refined coquetries, the veils, the muffs, the scarves. She was almost like a sincere and simple person before a world of artifice. She was afraid of being deceived by all this artfulness. She could not see it as aesthetic, but as the puritans see it: as deception, as immorality, as belonging with seduction and eroticism.

She insisted on seeing Djuna without make-up, and was then satisfied that make-up was purely an enhancement of the features, not treachery.

Lillian's house was beautiful, lacquered, grown among the trees, and bore the mark of her handiwork all through, yet it did not seem to belong to her. She had painted, decorated, carved, arranged, selected, and most of it was made by her own hands, or refashioned, always touched or handled or improved by her, out of her very own activity and craftsmanship. Yet it did not become her house, and it did not have her face, her atmosphere. She always looked like a stranger in it. With all her handiwork and taste, she had not been able to give it her own character.

It was a home; it suited her husband, Larry, and her children. It was built for peace. The rooms were spacious, clear, brightly windowed. It was warm, glowing, clean, harmonious. It was like other houses.

As soon as Djuna entered it, she felt this. The strength, the fervor, the care Lillian spent in the house, on her husband and children came from some part of her being that was not the deepest Lillian. It was as if every element but her own nature had contributed to create this life. Who had made the marriage? Who had desired the children? She could not remember the first impetus, the first choice, the first desire for these, nor how they came to be. It was as if it had happened in her sleep. Lillian, guided by her background, her mother, her sisters, her habits, her home as a child, her blindness in regard to her own desires, had made all this and then lived in it, but it had not been made out of the deeper elements of her nature, and she was a stranger in it.

Once made—this life, these occupations, the care, the devotion, the family—it never occurred to her that she could rebel against them. There was no provocation for rebellion. Her husband was kind, her children were lovable, her house was harmonious; and Nanny, the old nurse who took care of them all with inexhaustible maternal warmth, was their guardian angel, the guardian angel of the home.

Nanny's devotion to the home was so strong, so predominant, and so constantly manifested that the home and family seemed to belong to her more than to Lillian. The home had a reality for Nanny. Her whole existence was centered on it. She defended its interests, she hovered, reigned, watched, guarded tirelessly. She passed judgments on the visitors. Those who were dangerous to the peace of the home, she served with unappetizing meals, and from one end of the meal to the other, showed her disapproval. The welcome ones were those her instinct told her were good for the family, the home, for their unity. Then she surpassed herself in cooking and service. The unity of the family was her passionate concern: that the children should understand each other and love each other; that the children should love the father, the mother; that the mother and father should be close. For this she was willing to be the receiver of confidences, to be the peacemaker, to reestablish order.

She was willing to show an interest in any of Lillian's activities as long as these ultimately flowed back to the house. She could be interested in concerts if she brought the overflow of the music home to enhance it. She could be interested in painting while the results showed visibly in the house.

When the conversation lagged at the table she supplied diversion. If the children quarreled she upheld the rights of each one in soothing, wise explanations.

She refused one proposal of marriage.

When Lillian came into the house, and felt lost in it, unable to really enter into, to feel it, to participate, to care, as if it were all not present and warm but actually a family album, as if her son Paul did not come in and really take off his snow-covered boots, but it was a snapshot of Paul taking off his boots, as if her husband's face were a photograph too, and Adele was actually the painting of her above the piano...then Lillian rushed to the kitchen, unconsciously seeking Nanny's worries, Nanny's anxieties (Paul is too thin, and Adele lost her best friend in school) to convince herself of the poignant reality of this house and its occupants (her husband had forgotten his rubbers).

If the children had not been growing up (again according to Nanny's tabulations and calculations) Lillian would have thought herself back ten years! Her husband did not change.

Nanny was the only one who had felt the shock the day that Lillian decided to have her own room. And Lillian might not have changed the rooms over if it had not been for a cricket.

Lillian's husband had gone away on a trip. It was summer. Lillian felt deeply alone, and filled with anxiety. She could not understand the anxiety. Her first thought always was: Larry is happy. He is well. He looked very happy when he left. The children are well. Then what can be the matter with me? How can anything be the matter with me if they are well?

There were guests at the house. Among them was one who vaguely resembled Gerard, and the young man in her dreams, and the young man who appeared to her under anaesthetic. Always of the same family. But he was bold as a lover. He courted her swiftly, impetuously.

A cricket had lodged itself in one of the beams of her room. Perfectly silent until the young man came to visit her, until he caressed her. Then it burst into frenzied cricket song.

They laughed.

He came again the next night, and at the same moment the cricket sang again.

Always at the moment a cricket should sing.

The young man went away. Larry returned. Larry was happy to be with his wife.

But the cricket did not sing. Lillian wept. Lillian moved into a room of her own. Nanny was depressed and cross for a week.

When they sat together, alone, in the evenings, Larry did not appear to see her. When he talked about her he always talked about the Lillian of ten years ago; how she looked then, how she was, what she said. He delighted in reviving scenes out of the past, her behavior, her high temper and the troubles she got herself into. He often repeated these stories. And Lillian felt that she had known only one Larry, a Larry who had courted her and then remained as she had first known him. When she heard about the Lillian of ten years ago she felt no connection with her. But Larry was living with her, delighting in her presence. He reconstructed her out of his memory and sat her there every evening they had together.

One night they heard a commotion in the otherwise peaceful village. The police car passed and then the ambulance. Then the family doctor stopped his car before the gate. He asked for a drink. "My job is over," he said, "and I need a drink badly." Lillian gave him one, but at first he would not talk.

Later he explained: The man who rented the house next door was a young doctor, not a practicing one. His behavior and way of living had perplexed the neighbors. He received no one, allowed no one into the house. He was somber in mood, and attitude, and he was left alone. But people complained persistently of an unbearable odor. There were investigations. Finally it was discovered that his wife had died six months earlier, in California. He had brought her body back and he was living with it stretched on his bed. The doctor had seen her.

Lillian left the room. The odor of death, the image of death... everywhere.

No investigation would be made in her house. No change. Nanny was there.

But Lillian felt trapped without knowing what had trapped her.

Then she found Djuna. With Djuna she was alive. With Djuna her entire being burst into living, flowering cells. She could feel her own existence, the Lillian of today.

She spent much time with Djuna.

Paul felt his mother removed in some way. He noticed that she and his father had little to say to each other. He was anxious. Adele had nightmares that her mother was dying. Larry was concerned. Perhaps Lillian was not well. She ate little. He sent for the doctor. She objected to him violently. Nanny hovered, guarded, as if she scented danger. But nothing changed. Lillian waited. She always went first to the kitchen when she came home, as if it were the hearth itself, to warm himself. And then to each child's room, and then to Larry.

She could do nothing. Djuna's words illuminated her chaos, but changed nothing. What was it Djuna said: that life tended to crystallize into patterns which became traps and webs. That people tended to see each other in their first "state" or "form" and to adopt a rhythm in consequence. That they had greatest difficulty in seeing the transformations of the loved one, in seeing the becoming. If they did finally perceive the new self, they had the greatest difficulty nevertheless in changing the rhythm. The strong one was condemned to perpetual strength, the weak to perpetual weakness. The one who loved you best condemned you to a static role because he had adapted his being to the past self. If you attempted to change, warned Djuna, you would find a subtle, perverse opposition, and perhaps sabotage! Inwardly and outwardly, a pattern was a form which became a prison. And then we had to smash it. Mutation was difficult. Attempts at evasion were frequent, blind evasions, evasions from dead relationships, false relationships, false roles, and sometimes from the deeper self too, because of the great obstacle one encountered in affirming it. All our emotional history was that of the spider and the fly, with the added tragedy that the fly here collaborated in the weaving of the web. Crimes were frequent. People in desperation turned about and destroyed each other. No one could detect the cause or catch the criminal. There was no visible victim. It always had the appearance of suicide.

Lillian sensed the walls and locks. She did not even know she wanted to escape. She did not even know she was in rebellion. She did it with her body. Her body became ill from the friction, lacerations and daily duels with her beloved jailers. Her body became ill from the poisons of internal rebellion, the monotony of her prison, the greyness of its days, the poverty of the nourishment. She was in a fixed relationship and could not move forward.

Anxiety settled upon the house. Paul clung to his mother longer when they separated for short periods. Adele was less gay.

Larry was more silent.

Nanny began to weep noiselessly. Then she had a visitor. The same one she had sent away ten years earlier. The man was growing old. He wanted a home. He wanted Nanny. Nanny was growing old. He talked to her all evening, in the kitchen. Then one day Nanny cried without control. Lillian questioned her. She wanted to get married. But she hated to leave the family. The family! The sacred, united, complete family. In this big house, with so much work. And no one else to be had. And she wanted Lillian to protest, to cling to her—as the children did before, as Larry had done a few years back, each time the suitor had come again for his answer. But Lillian said quietly, "Nanny, it is time that you thought of yourself. You have lived for others all your life. Get married. I believe you should get married. He loves you. He waited for you such a long time. You deserve a home and life and protection and a rest. Get married."

And then Lillian walked into the dining room where the family was eating and she said: "Nanny is going to get married and leave us."

Paul then cried out: "This is the beginning of the end!" Larry looked up from his meal, for the first time struck with a clearer glimpse of what had been haunting the house.

Through the high building, the wind complained, playing a frenzied flute up and down the elevator shafts.

Lillian and Djuna opened the window and looked at the city covered with a mist. One could see only the lighted eyes of the buildings. One could hear only muffled sounds, the ducks from Central Park lake nagging loudly, the fog horns from the river which sounded at times like the mournful complaints of imprisoned ships not allowed to sail, at others like gay departures.

Lillian was sitting in the dark, speaking of her life, her voice charged with both laughter and tears.

In the dark a new being appears. A new being who has not the courage to face daylight. In the dark people dare to dream everything. And they dare to tell everything. In the dark there appeared a new Lillian.

There was just enough light from the city to show their faces chalk white, with shadows in the place of eyes and mouth, and an occasional gleam of white teeth. At first it was like two children sitting on a see-saw, because Lillian would talk about her life and her marriage and the disintegration of her home, and then Djuna would lean over to embrace her, overflowing with pity. Then Djuna would speak and Lillian would lean over and want to gather her in her arms with maternal compassion.

"I feel," said Lillian, "that I do everything wrong. I feel I do everything to bring about just what I fear. You will turn away from me too."

Lillian's unsatisfied hunger for life had evoked in Djuna another hunger. This hunger still hovered at times over the bright film of her eyes, shading them not with the violet shadows of either illness or sensual excess, of experience or fever, but with the pearl-grey shadow of denial, and Djuna said:

"I was born in the most utter poverty. My mother lying in bed with consumption, four brothers and sisters loudly claiming food and care, and I having to be the mother and nurse of them all. We were so hungry that we ate all the samples of food or medicines which were left at the house. I remember once we ate a whole box of chocolate-coated constipation pills. Father was a taxi driver but he spent the greatest part of what he made on drink along the way. As we lived among people who were all living as we were, without sufficient clothing, or heat or food, we knew no contrast and believed this was natural and general. But with me it was different. I suffered from other kinds of pangs. I was prone to the most excessive dreaming, of such intensity and realism that when I awakened I felt I lost an entire universe of legends, myths, figures and cities of such color that they made our room seem a thousand times more bare, the poverty of the table more acute. The disproportion was immense. And I'm not speaking merely of the banquets which were so obviously compensatory! Nor of the obvious way by which I filled my poor wardrobe. It was more than that. I saw in my dreams houses, forests, entire cities, and such a variety of personages that even today I wonder how a child, who had not even seen pictures, could invent such designs in textures, such colonnades, friezes, fabulous animals, statues, colors, as I did. And the activity! My dreams were so full of activity that at times I felt it was the dreams which exhausted me rather than all the washing, ironing, shopping, mending, sweeping, tending, nursing, dusting that I did. I remember I had to break soap boxes to burn in the fireplace. I used to scratch my hands and bruise my toes. Yet when my mother caressed me and said, you look tired, Djuna, I almost felt like confessing to her that what had tired me was my constant dreaming of a ship which insisted on sailing through a city, or my voyage in a chaise through the snow-covered steppes of Russia. And by the way, there was a lot of confusion of places and methods of travel in my dreams, as there must be in the dreams of the blind. Do you know what I think now? I think what tired me was the intensity of the pleasures I had together with the perfect awareness that such pleasure could not last and would be immediately followed by its opposite. Once out of my dreams, the only certitude I retained from these nocturnal expeditions was that pleasure could not possibly last. This conviction was strengthened by the fact that no matter how small a pleasure I wanted to take during the day it was followed by catastrophe. If I relaxed for one instant the watch over my sick mother to eat an orange all by myself in some abandoned lot, she would have a turn for the worse. Or if I spent some time looking at the pictures outside of the movie house one of my brothers or sisters would cut himself or burn his finger or get into a fight with another child. So I felt then that liberty must be paid for heavily. I learned a most severe accounting which was to consider pleasure as the jewel, a kind of stolen jewel for which one must be willing to pay vast sums in suffering and guilt. Even today, Lillian, when something very marvelous happens to me, when I attain love or ecstasy or a perfect moment, I expect it to be followed by pain."

Then Lillian leaned over and kissed Djuna warmly: "I want to protect you."

"We give each other courage."

The mist came into the room. Djuna thought: She's such a hurt woman. She is one who does not know what she suffers from, or why, or how to overcome it. She is all unconscious, motion, music. She is afraid to see, to analyze her nature. She thinks that nature just is and that nothing can be done about it. She would never have invented ships to conquer the sea, machines to create light where there was darkness. She would never have harnessed water power, electric power. She is like the primitive. She thinks it is all beyond her power. She accepts chaos. She suffers mutely...

"Djuna, tell me all that happened to you. I keep thinking about your hunger. I feel the pangs of it in my own stomach."

"My mother died," continued Djuna. "One of my brothers was hurt in an accident while playing in the street and crippled. Another was taken to the insane asylum. He harmed nobody. When the war started he began to eat flowers stolen from the florists. When he was arrested he said that he was eating flowers to bring peace to the world. That if everybody ate flowers peace would come to the world. My sister and I were put in an orphan asylum. I remember the day we were taken there. The night before I had a dream about a Chinese pagoda all in gold, filled with a marvelous odor. At the tip of the pagoda there was a mechanical bird who sang one little song repeatedly. I kept hearing this song and smelling the odor all the time and that seemed more real to me than the callous hands of the orphan asylum women when they changed me into a uniform. Oh, the greyness of those dresses! And if only the windows had been normal. But they were long and narrow, Lillian. Everything is changed when you look at it through long and narrow windows. It's as if the sky itself were compressed, limited. To me they were like the windows of a prison. The food was dark, and tasteless, like slime. The children were cruel to each other. No one visited us. And then there was the old watchman who made the rounds at night. He often lifted the corners of our bedcovers, and let his eyes rove and sometimes more than his eyes… He became the demon of the night for us little girls."

There was a silence, during which both Lillian and Djuna became children, listening to the watchman of the night become the demon of the night, the tutor of the forbidden, the initiator breaking the sheltered core of the child, breaking the innocence and staining the beds of adolescence.

"The satyr of the asylum," said Djuna, "who became also our jailer because when we grew older and wanted to slip out at night to go out with the boys, it was he who rattled the keys and prevented us. But for him we might have been free at times, but he watched us, and the women looked up to him for his fanaticism in keeping us from the street. The orphan asylum had a system which permitted families to adopt the orphans. But as it was known that the asylum supplied the sum of thirty-five dollars a month towards the feeding of the child, those who responded were most often those in need of the thirty-five dollars. Poor families, already burdened with many children, came forward to 'adopt' new ones. The orphans were allowed to enter these homes in which they found themselves doubly cheated. For at least in the asylum we had no illusion, no hope of love. But we did have illusions about the adoptions. We thought we would find a family. In most cases we did not even imagine that these families had children of their own. We expected to be a much wanted and only child! I was placed in one of them. The first thing that happened was that the other children were jealous of the intruder. And the spectacle of the love lavished on the legitimate children was terribly painful. It made me feel more abandoned, more hungry, more orphaned than ever. Every time a parent embraced his child I suffered so much that finally I ran away back to the asylum. And I was not the only one. And besides this emotional starvation we got even less to eat—the allowance being spent on the whole family. And now I lost my last treasure: the dreaming. For nothing in the dreams took the place of the human warmth I had witnessed. Now I felt utterly poor, because I could not create a human companion."

This hunger which had inhabited her entire being, which had thinned her blood, transpired through her bones, attacked the roots of her hair, given a fragility to her skin which was never to disappear entirely, had been so enormous that it had marked her whole being and her eyes with an indelible mark. Although her life changed and every want was filled later, this appearance of hunger remained. As if nothing could ever quite fill it. Her being had received no sun, no food, no air, no warmth, no love. It retained open pores of yearning and longing, mysterious spongy cells of absorption. The space between actuality, absolute deprivation, and the sumptuosity of her imagination could never be entirely covered. What she had created in the void, in the emptiness, in the bareness continued to shame all that was offered her, and her large, infinitely blue eyes continued to assert the immensity of her hunger.

This hunger of the eyes, skin, of the whole body and spirit, which made others criminals, robbers, rapers, barbarians, which caused wars, invasions, plundering and murder, in Djuna at the age of puberty alchemized into love.

Whatever was missing she became: she became mother, father, cousin, brother, friend, confidant, guide, companion to all.

This power of absorption, this sponge of receptivity which might have fed itself forever to fill the early want, she used to receive all communication of the need of others. The need and hunger became nourishment. Her breasts, which no poverty had been able to wither, were heavy with the milk of lucidity, the milk of devotion.

This hunger...became love.

While wearing the costume of utter femininity, the veils and the combs, the gloves and the perfumes, the muffs and the heels of femininity, she nevertheless disguised in herself an active lover of the world, the one who was actively roused by the object of his love, the one who was made strong as man is made strong in the center of his being by the softness of his love. Loving in men and women not their strength but their softness, not their fullness but their hunger, not their plenitude but their needs.

They had made contact then with the deepest aspect of themselves—Djuna with Lillian's emotional violence and her compassion for this force which destroyed her and hurled her against all obstacles, Lillian with Djuna's power of clarification. They needed each other. Djuna experienced deep in herself a pleasure each time Lillian exploded, for she herself kept her gestures, her feeling within an outer form, like an Oriental. When Lillian exploded it seemed to Djuna as if some of her violent feeling, so long contained within the forms, were released. Some of her own lightning, some of her own rebellions, some of her own angers. Djuna contained in herself a Lillian too, to whom she had never given a moment's freedom, and it made her strangely free when Lillian gave vent to her anger or rebellions. But after the havoc, when Lillian had bruised herself, or more seriously mutilated herself (war and explosion had their consequences) then Lillian needed Djuna. For the bitterness, the despair, the chaos submerged Lillian, drowned her. The hurt Lillian wanted to strike back and did so blindly, hurting herself all the more. And then Djuna was there, to remove the arrows implanted in Lillian, to cleanse them of their poison, to open the prison door, to open the trap door, to protect, to give transfusion of blood, and peace to the wounded.

But it was Lillian who was drowning, and it was Djuna who was able always at the last moment to save her, and in her moments of danger, Lillian knew only one thing: that she must possess Djuna.

It was as if someone had proclaimed: I need oxygen, and therefore I will lock some oxygen in my room and live on it.

So Lillian began her courtship.

She brought gifts. She pulled out perfume, and jewelry and clothes. She almost covered the bed with gifts. She wanted Djuna to put all the jewelry on, to smell all the perfumes at once, to wear all her clothes. Djuna was showered with gifts as in a fairy tale, but she could not find in them the fairy tale pleasure. She felt that to each gift was tied a little invisible cord or demand, of exactingness, of debt, of domination. She felt she could not wear all these things and walk away, freely. She felt that with the gifts, a golden spider wove a golden web of possession. Lillian was not only giving away objects, but golden threads woven out of her very own substance to fix and to hold. They were not the fairy tale gifts which Djuna had dreamed of receiving. (She had many dreams of receiving perfume, or receiving fur, or being given blue bottles, lamés, etc.) In the fairy tale the giver laid out the presents and then became invisible. In the fairy tales and in the dreams there was no debt, and there was no giver.

Lillian did not become invisible. Lillian became more and more present. Lillian became the mother who wanted to dress her child out of her own substance, Lillian became the lover who wanted to slip the shoes and slippers on the beloved's feet so she could contain these feet. The dresses were not chosen as Djuna's dresses, but as Lillian's choice and taste to cover Djuna.

The night of gifts, begun in gaiety and magnificence, began to thicken. Lillian had put too much of herself into the gifts. It was a lovely night, with the gifts scattered through the room like fragments of Miro's circus paintings, flickering and leaping, but not free. Djuna wanted to enjoy and she could not. She loved Lillian's generosity, Lillian's largeness, Lillian's opulence and magnificence, but she felt anxiety. She remembered as a child receiving gifts for Christmas, and among them a closed mysterious box gaily festooned with multicolored ribbons. She remembered that the mystery of this box affected her more than the open, exposed, familiar gifts of tea cups, dolls, etc. She opened the box and out of it jumped a grotesque devil who, propelled by taut springs, almost hit her face.

In these gifts, there is a demon somewhere; a demon who is hurting Lillian, and will hurt me, and I don't know where he is hiding. I haven't seen him yet, but he is here.

She thought of the old legends, of the knights who had to kill monsters before they could enjoy their love.

No demon here, thought Djuna, nothing but a woman drowning, who is clutching at me... I love her.

When Lillian dressed up in the evening in vivid colors with her ever tinkling jewelry, her face wildly alive, Djuna said to her, "You're made for a passionate life of some kind."

She looked like a white negress, a body made for rolling in natural undulations of pleasure and desire. Her vivid face, her avid mouth, her provocative, teasing glances proclaimed sensuality. She had rings under her eyes. She looked often as if she had just come from the arms of a lover. An energy smoked from her whole body.

But sensuality was paralyzed in her. When Djuna sought to show Lillian her face in the mirror, she found Lillian paralyzed with fear. She was impaled on a rigid pole of puritanism. One felt it, like a heavy silver chastity belt, around her soft, rounded body.

She bought a black lace gown like Djuna's. Then she wanted to own all the objects which carried Djuna's personality or spirit. She wanted to be clasped at the wrists by Djuna's bracelet watch, dressed in Djuna's kind of clothes.

(Djuna thought of the primitives eating the liver of the strong man of the tribe to acquire his strength, wearing the teeth of the elephant to acquire his durability, donning the lion's head and mane to appropriate his courage, gluing feathers on themselves to become as free as the bird.)

Lillian knew no mystery. Everything was open with her. Even the most ordinary mysteries of women she did not guard. She was open like a man, frank, direct. Her eyes shed lightning but no shadows.

One night Djuna and Lillian went to a night club together to watch the cancan. At such a moment Djuna forgot that she was a woman and looked at the women dancing with the eyes of an artist and the eyes of a man. She admired them, reveled in their beauty, in their seductions, in the interplay of black garters and black stockings and the snow-white frills of petticoats.

Lillian's face clouded. The storm gathered in her eyes. The lightning struck. She lashed out in anger: "If I were a man I would murder you."

Djuna was bewildered. Then Lillian's anger dissolved in lamentations: "Oh, the poor people, the poor people who love you. You love these women!"

She began to weep. Djuna put her arms around her and consoled her. The people around them looked baffled, as passers-by look up suddenly at an unexpected, freakish windstorm. Here it was, chaotically upsetting the universe, coming from right and left, great fury and velocity—and why?

Two women were looking at beautiful women dancing. One enjoyed it, and the other made a scene.

Lillian went home and wrote stuttering phrases on the back of a box of writing paper: Djuna, don't abandon me; if you abandon me, I am lost.

When Djuna came the next day, still angry from the inexplicable storm of the night before, she wanted to say: are you the woman I chose for a friend? Are you the egotistical, devouring child, all caprice and confusion who is always crossing my path? She could not say it, not before this chaotic helpless writing on the back of the box, a writing which could not stand alone, but wavered from left to right, from right to left, inclining, falling, spilling, retreating, ascending on the line as if for flight off the edge of the paper as if it were an airfield, or plummeting on the paper like a falling elevator.

If they met a couple along the street who were kissing, Lillian became equally unhinged.

If they talked about her children and Djuna said: I never liked real children, only the child in the grown-up, Lillian answered: you should have had children.

"But I lack the maternal feeling for children, Lillian, though I haven't lacked the maternal experience. There are plenty of children, abandoned children right in the so-called grown-ups. While you, well you are a real mother, you have a real maternal capacity. You are the mother type. I am not. I only like being the mistress. I don't even like being a wife."

Then Lillian's entire universe turned a somersault again, crashed, and Djuna was amazed to see the devastating results of an innocent phrase: "I am not a maternal woman," she said, as if it were an accusation. (Everything was an accusation.)

Then Djuna kissed her and said playfully: "Well, then, you're a *femme fatale!*"

But this was like fanning an already enormous flame. This aroused Lillian to despair: "No, no, I never destroyed or hurt anybody," she protested.

"You know, Lillian, someday I will sit down and write a little dictionary for you, a little Chinese dictionary. In it I will put down all the interpretations of what is said to you, the right interpretation, that is: the one that is not meant to injure, not meant to humiliate or accuse or doubt. And whenever something is said to you, you will look in my little dictionary to make sure, before you get desperate, that you have understood what is said to you."

The idea of the little Chinese dictionary made Lillian laugh. The storm passed.

But if they walked the streets together her obsession was to see who was looking at them or following them. In the shops she was obsessed about her plumpness and considered it not an attribute but a defect. In the movies it was emotionalism and tears. If they sat in a restaurant by a large window and saw the people passing it was denigration and dissection. The universe hinged and turned on her defeated self.

She was aggressive with people who waited on her, and then was hurt by their defensive abandon of her. When they did not wait on her she was personally injured, but could not see the injury she had inflicted by her demanding ways. Her commands bristled everyone's hair, raised obstacles and retaliations. As soon as she appeared she brought dissonance.

But she blamed the others, the world.

She could not bear to see lovers together, absorbed in each other.

She harassed the quiet men and lured them to an argument and she hated the aggressive men who held their own against her.

Her shame. She could not carry off gallantly a run in her stocking. She was overwhelmed by a lost button.

When Djuna was too swamped by other occupations or other people to pay attention to her, Lillian became ill. But she would not be ill at home surrounded by her family. She was ill alone, in a hotel room, so that Djuna ran in and out with medicines, with chicken soup, stayed with her day and night chained to her antics, and then Lillian clapped her hands and confessed: "I'm so happy! Now I've got you all to myself!"

The summer nights were passing outside like gay whores, with tinkles of cheap jewelry, opened and emollient like a vast bed. The summer nights were passing but not Lillian's tension with the world.

She read erotic memoirs avidly, she was obsessed with the lives and loves of others. But she herself could not yield, she was ashamed, she throttled her own nature, and all this desire, lust, became twisted inside of her and churned a poison of envy and jealousy. Whenever sensuality showed its flower head, Lillian would have liked to decapitate it, so it would cease troubling and haunting her.

At the same time she wanted to seduce the world, Djuna, everybody. She would want to be kissed on the lips and more warmly and then violently block herself. She thrived on this hysterical undercurrent without culmination. This throbbing sensual obsession and the blocking of it; this rapacious love without polarity, like a blind womb appetite; delighting in making the temperature rise and then clamping down the lid.

In her drowning she was like one constantly choking those around her, bringing them down with her into darkness.

Djuna felt caught in a sirocco.

She had lived once on a Spanish island and experienced exactly this impression.

The island had been calm, silvery and dormant until one morning when a strange wind began to blow from Africa, blowing in circles. It swept over the island charged with torpid warmth, charged with flower smells, with sandalwood and patchouli and incense, and turning in whirlpools, gathered up the nerves and swinging with them into whirlpools of dry enervating warmth and smells, reached no climax, no explosion. Blowing persistently, continuously, hour after hour, gathering every nerve in every human being, the nerves alone, and tangling them in this fatal waltz; drugging them and pulling them, and whirlpooling them, until the body shook with restlessness— all polarity and sense of gravity lost. Because of this insane waltz of the wind, its emollient warmth, its perfumes, the being lost its guidance, its clarity, its integrity. Hour after hour, all day and all night, the body was subjected to this insidious whirling rhythm, in which polarity was lost, and only the nerves and desires throbbed, tense and weary of movement—all in a void, with no respite, no climax, no great loosening as in other storms. A tension that gathered force but had no release. It abated not once in forty-eight hours, promising, arousing, caressing, destroying sleep, rest, repose, and then vanished without releasing, without culmination...

This violence which Djuna had loved so much! It had become a mere sirocco wind, burning and shriveling. This violence which Djuna had applauded, enjoyed, because she could not possess it in herself. It was now burning her, and their friendship. Because it was not attached to anything, it was not creating anything, it was a trap of negation.

"You will save me," said Lillian always, clinging.

Lillian was the large foundering ship, yes, and Djuna the small lifeboat. But now the big ship had been moored to the small lifeboat and was pitching too fast and furiously and the lifeboat was being swamped.

(She wants something of me that only a man can give her. But first of all she wants to become me, so that she can communicate with man. She has lost her ways of communicating with man. She is doing it through me!)

When they walked together, Lillian sometimes asked Djuna: "Walk in front of me, so I can see how you walk. You have such a sway of the hips!"

In front of Lillian walked Lillian's lost femininity, imprisoned in the male Lillian. Lillian's femininity imprisoned in the deepest wells of her being, loving Djuna, and knowing it must reach her own femininity at the bottom of the well by way of Djuna. By wearing Djuna's feminine exterior, swaying her hips, becoming Djuna.

As Djuna enjoyed Lillian's violence, Lillian enjoyed Djuna's feminine capitulations. The pleasure Djuna took in her capitulations to love, to desire. Lillian breathed out through Djuna. What took place in Djuna's being which Lillian could not reach, she at least reached by way of Djuna.

"The first time a boy hurt me," said Lillian to Djuna, "it was in school. I don't remember what he did. But I wept. And he laughed at me. Do you know what I did? I went home and dressed in my brother's suit. I tried to feel as the boy felt. Naturally as I put on the suit I felt I was putting on a costume of strength. It made me feel sure, as the boy was, confident, impudent. The mere fact of putting my hands in the pockets made me feel arrogant. I thought then that to be a boy meant one did not suffer. That it was being a girl that was responsible for the suffering. Later I felt the same way. I thought man had found a way out of suffering by objectivity. What the man called being reasonable. When my husband said: Lillian, let's be reasonable, it meant he had none of the feeling I had, that he could be objective. What a power! Then there was another thing. When I felt his great choking anguish I discovered one relief, and that was action. I felt like the women who had to sit and wait at home while there was a war going on. I felt if only I could join the war, participate, I wouldn't feel the anguish and the fear. All through the last war as a child I felt: if only they would let me be Joan of Arc. Joan of Arc wore a suit of armor, she sat on a horse, she fought side by side with the men. She must have gained their strength. Then it was the same way about men. At a dance, as a girl, the moment of waiting before they asked me seemed intolerable, the suspense, and the insecurity; perhaps they were not going to ask me! So I rushed forward, to cut the suspense. I rushed. All my nature became rushed, propelled by the anxiety, merely to cut through all the moment of anxious uncertainty."

Djuna looked tenderly at her, not the strong Lillian, the overwhelming Lillian, the aggressive Lillian, but the hidden, secret, frightened Lillian who had created such a hard armor and disguise around her weakness.

Djuna saw the Lillian hidden in her coat of armor, and all of Lillian's armor lay broken around her, like cruel pieces of mail which had wounded her more than they had protected her from the enemy. The mail had melted, and revealed the bruised feminine flesh. At the first knowledge of the weakness Lillian had picked up the mail, wrapped herself in it and had taken up a lance. The lance! The man's lance. Uncertainty resolved, relieved by the activity of attack!

The body of Lillian changed as she talked, the fast coming words accelerating the dismantling. She was taking off the shell, the covering, the defenses, the coat of mail, the activity.

Suddenly Lillian laughed. In the middle of tears, she laughed: "I'm remembering a very comical incident. I was about sixteen. There was a boy in love with me. Shyly, quietly in love. We were in the same school but he lived quite far away. We all used bicycles. One day we were going to be separated for a week by the holidays. He suggested we both bicycle together towards a meeting place between the two towns. The week of separation seemed too unbearable. So it was agreed: at a certain hour we would leave the house together and meet half way."

Lillian started off. At first at a normal pace. She knew the rhythm of the boy. A rather easy, relaxed rhythm. Never rushed. Never precipitate. She at first adopted his rhythm. Dreaming of him, of his slow smile, of his shy worship, of his expression of this worship, which consisted mainly in waiting for her here, there. Waiting. Not advancing, inviting, but waiting. Watching her pass by.

She pedaled slowly, dreamily. Then slowly her pleasure and tranquility turned to anguish: suppose he did not come? Suppose she arrived before him? Could she bear the sight of the desolate place of their meeting, the failed meeting? The exaltation that had been increasing in her, like some powerful motor, what could she do with this exaltation if she arrived alone, and the meeting failed? The fear affected her in two directions. She could stop right there, and turn back, and not face the possibility of disappointment, or she could rush forward and accelerate the moment of painful suspense, and she chose the second. Her lack of confidence in life, in realization, in the fulfillment of her desires, in the outcome of a dream, in the possibility of reality corresponding to her fantasy, speeded her bicycle with the incredible speed of anxiety, a speed beyond the human body, beyond human endurance.

She arrived before him. Her fear was justified! She could not measure what the anxiety had done to her speed, the acceleration which had broken the equality of rhythm. She arrived as she had feared, at a desolate spot on the road, and the boy had become this invisible image which taunts the dreamer, a mirage that could not be made real. It had become reality eluding the dreamer, the wish unfulfilled.

The boy may have arrived later. He may have fallen asleep and not come at all. He may have had a tire puncture. Nothing mattered. Nothing could prevent her from feeling that she was not Juliet waiting on the balcony, but Romeo who had to leap across space to join her. She had leaped, she had acted Romeo, and when woman leaped she leaped into a void.

Later it was not the drama of two bicycles, of a road, of two separated towns; later it was a darkened room, and a man and woman pursuing pleasure and fusion.

At first she lay passive dreaming of the pleasure that would come out of the darkness, to dissolve and invade her. But it was not pleasure which came out of the darkness to clasp her. It was anxiety. Anxiety made confused gestures in the dark, crosscurrents of forces, short circuits, and no pleasure. A depression, a broken rhythm, a feeling such as men must have after they have taken a whore.

Out of the prone figure of the woman, apparently passive, apparently receptive, there rose a taut and anxious shadow, the shadow of the woman bicycling too fast; who, to relieve her insecurity, plunges forward as the desperado does and is defeated because this aggressiveness cannot meet its mate and unite with it. A part of the woman has not participated in this marriage, has not been taken. But was it a part of the woman, or the shadow of anxiety, which dressed itself in man's clothes and assumed man's active role to quiet its anguish? Wasn't it the woman who dressed as a man and pedaled too fast?

Jay. The table at which he sat was stained with wine. His blue eyes were inscrutable like those of a Chinese sage. He ended all his phrases in a kind of hum, as if he put his foot on the pedal of his voice and created an echo. In this way none of his phrases ended abruptly.

Sitting at the bar he immediately created a climate, a tropical day. In spite of the tension in her, Lillian felt it. Sitting at a bar with his voice rolling over, he dissolved and liquefied the hard click of silver on plates, the icy dissonances of glasses, the brittle sound of money thrown on the counter.

He was tall but he carried his tallness slackly and easily, as easily as his coat and hat, as if all of it could be discarded and sloughed off at any moment when he needed lightness or nimbleness. His body large, shaggy, as if never definitely chiseled, never quite ultimately finished, was as casually his as his passing moods and varying fancies and fortunes.

He opened his soft animal mouth a little, as if in expectancy of a drink. But instead, he said (as if he had absorbed Lillian's face and voice in place of the drink), "I'm happy. I'm too happy." Then he began to laugh, to laugh, to laugh, with his head shaking like a bear, shaking from right to left as if it were too heavy a head. "I can't help it. I can't help laughing. I'm too happy. Last night I spent the night here. It was Christmas and I didn't have the money for a hotel room. And the night before I slept at a movie house. They overlooked me, didn't sweep where I lay. In the morning I played the movie piano. In walked the furious manager, then he listened, then he gave me a contract starting this evening. Christ, Lillian, I never thought Christmas would bring me anything, yet it brought you."

How gently he had walked into her life, how quietly he seemed to be living, while all the time he was drawing bitter caricatures on the bar table, on the backs of envelopes. Drawing bums, drunks, derelicts.

"So you're a pianist...that's what I should have been. I'm not bad, but I would never work hard enough. I wanted also to be a painter. I might have been a writer too, if I had worked enough. I did a bit of acting too, at one time. As it is, I guess I'm the last man on earth. Why did you single me out?"

This man who would not be distinguished in a crowd, who could pass through it like an ordinary man, so quiet, so absorbed, with his hat on one side, his steps dragging a little, like a lazy devil enjoying everything, why did she see him hungry, thirsty, abandoned?

Behind this Jay, with his southern roguishness, perpetually calling for drinks, why did she see a lost man?

He sat like a workman before his drinks, he talked like a cart driver to the whores at the bar; they were all at ease with him. His presence took all the straining and willing out of Lillian. He was like the south wind: blowing when he came, melting and softening, bearing joy and abundance.

When they met, and she saw him walking towards her, she felt he would never stop walking towards her and into her very being: he would walk right into her being with his soft lazy walk and purring voice and his mouth slightly open.

She could not hear his voice. His voice rumbled over the surface of her skin, like another caress. She had no power against his voice. It came straight from him into her. She could stuff her ears and still it would find its way into her blood and make it rise.

All things were born anew when her dress fell on the floor of his room.

He said: "I feel humble, Lillian, but it is all so good, so good." He gave to the word good a mellowness which made the whole room glow, which gave a warmer color to the bare window, to the woolen shirt hung on a peg, to the single glass out of which they drank together.

Behind the yellow curtain the sun seeped in: everything was the color of a tropical afternoon.

The small room was like a deep-set alcove. Warm mist and warm blood; the high drunkenness which made Jay flushed and heavy blooded. His sensual features expanded.

"As soon as you come, I'm jubilant." And he did somersaults on the bed, two or three of them.

"This is fine wine, Lillian. Let's drink to my failure. There's no doubt about it, no doubt whatever that I'm a failure."

"I won't let you be a failure," said Lillian.

"You say: I want, as if that made things happen."

"It does."

"I don't know what I expect of you. I expect miracles," He looked up at her slyly, then mockingly, then gravely again. "I have no illusions," he said.

Then he sat down with his heavy shoulders bowed, and his head bowed, but Lillian caught that swift, passing flash, a moment's hope, the lightning passage of a spark of faith left in his indifference to his fate. She clung to this.

Jay—gnome and sprite and faun, and playboy of the mother-bound world. Brightly gifted, he painted while he enjoyed the painting; the accidental marvels of colors, the pleasant shock of apparitions made in a game with paint. He stopped painting where the effort began, the need for discipline or travail. He danced while he was allowed to improvise, to surprise himself and others, to stretch, laugh, and court and be courted; but stopped if there were studying, developing or disciplining or effort or repetition involved. He acted, he acted loosely, flowingly, emotionally, while nothing more difficult was demanded of him, but he evaded rehearsals, fatigue, strain, effort. He pursued no friend, he took what came.

He gave himself to the present moment. To be with the friend, to drink with the friend, to talk with the friend, he forgot what was due the next day, and if it were something which demanded time, or energy, he could not meet it. He had not provided for it. He was asleep when he should have been awake, and tired when his energy was required, and absent when his presence was summoned. The merest expectation from a friend, the most trivial obligation, sent him running in the opposite direction. He came to the friend while there was pleasure to be had. He left as soon as the pleasure vanished and reality began. An accident, an illness, poverty, a quarrel—he was never there for them.

It was as if he smelled the climate: was it good? Was there the odor of pleasure, the colors of pleasure? Expansion, forgetfulness, abandon, enjoyment? Then he stayed. Difficulties? Then he vanished.

Lillian and Jay.

It was a merciless winter day. The wind persecuted them around the corners of the street. The snow slid into their collars. They could not talk to each other. They took a taxi.

The windows of the taxi had frosted, so they seemed completely shut off from the rest of the world. It was small and dark and warm. Jay buried his face in her fur. He made himself small. He had a way of becoming so passive and soft that he seemed to lose his height and weight. He did this now, his face in her fur, and she felt as if she were the darkness, the smallness of the taxi, and were hiding him, protecting him from the elements. Here the cold could not reach him, the snow, the wind, the daylight. He sheltered himself, she carried his head on her breast, she carried his body become limp, his hands nestling in her pocket. She was the fur, the pocket, the warmth that sheltered him. She felt immense, and strong, and illimitable, the boundless mother opening her arms and her wings, flying to carry him somewhere; she his shelter and refuge, his secret hiding place, his tent, his sky, his blanket.

The soundproof mother, the shockproof mother of man!

This passion warmer, stronger than the other passion, annihilating desire and becoming the desire, a boundless passion to surround, envelop, sustain, strengthen, uphold, to answer all needs. He closed his eyes. He almost slept in her warmth and furriness. He caressed the fur, he feared no claws, he abandoned himself, and the waves of passion inspired by his abandon intoxicated her.

He usually wore colored shirts to suit his fancy. Once he wore a white one, because it had been given to him. It did not suit him. Whiteness and blackness did not suit him. Only the intermediate colors.

Lillian was standing near him and they had just been discussing their life together. Jay had admitted that he would not work. He could not bear repetition, he could not bear a "boss," he could not bear regular hours. He could not bear the seriousness.

"Then you will have to be a hobo."

"I'll be a hobo, then."

"A hobo has no wife," said Lillian.

"No," he said. And added nothing: If she became part of the effort, he would not cling to her either.

"I will have to work, then," she said. "One of us has to work."

He said nothing.

Lillian was doubly disturbed by the unfamiliarity of the scene, the portentousness of it, and by the familiarity of the white shirt. The white shirt disturbed her more than his words. And then she knew. The white shirt reminded her of her husband. Just before he put on his coat she had always seen him and obscurely felt: how straight and rigid he stands in his white shirt. Black and white. Definite and starched, and always the same. But there it was. She was not sure she had liked the white shirt. From it came authority, a firm guidance, a firm construction. And now she was again facing a white shirt but with a strange feeling that there was nothing in it: no rigidity, no straight shoulders, no man. If she approached she would feel something fragile, soft and wavering: the shirt was not upheld by the body of the man. If she broke suddenly at the idea of assuming the responsibility, if she broke against this shirt it would collapse, turn to sand, trickle sand and soft laughter and elusive flickering love.

Against this white shirt of the husband she had lain her head once and heard a strong heart beat evenly, and now it was as if it were empty, and she were in a dream of falling down soft sand dunes to softer and more sliding shifty sand dunes... Her head turned.

She kept herself on this new equilibrium by a great effort, fearing to touch the white shirt of weakness and to feel the yielding, the softness and the sand.

When she sewed on buttons for him she was sewing not only buttons but also sewing together the sparse, disconnected fragments of his ideas, of his inventions, of his unfinished dreams. She was weaving and sewing and mending because he carried in himself no thread of connection, no knowledge of mending, no thread of continuity or repair. If he allowed a word to pass that was poisoned like a primitive arrow, he never sought the counter-poison, he never measured its fatal consequences. She was sewing on a button and the broken pieces of his waywardness; sewing a button and his words too loosely strung; sewing their days together to make a tapestry; their words together, their moods together, which he dispersed and tore. As he tore his clothes with his precipitations towards his wishes, his wanderings, his rambles, his peripheral journeys. She was sewing together the little proofs of his devotion out of which to make a garment for her tattered love and faith. He cut into the faith with negligent scissors, and she mended and sewed and rewove and patched. He wasted, and threw away, and could not evaluate or preserve, or contain, or keep his treasures. Like his ever torn pockets, everything slipped through and was lost, as he lost gifts, mementos—all the objects from the past. She sewed his pockets that he might keep some of their days together, hold together the key to the house, to their room, to their bed. She sewed the sleeve so he could reach out his arm and hold her, when loneliness dissolved her. She sewed the lining so that the warmth would not seep out of their days together, the soft inner skin of their relationship.

He always admitted and conceded to his own wishes first, before she admitted hers. Because he was sleepy, she had to become the panoply on which he rested. Her love must fan him if he were warm and be the fire if he were cold. In illness he required day and night nursing, one for the illness, the other for the pleasure he took in her attentiveness.

His helplessness made him the *"homme fatal"* for such a woman. He reached without sureness or nimbleness for the cup, for the food. Her hand flew to finish off the uncertain gesture, to supply the missing object. His hunger for anything metamorphosed her into an Aladdin's lamp: even his dreams must be fulfilled.

Towards the greater obstacles he assumed a definitely noncombatant attitude. Rather than claim his due, or face an angry landlord, or obtain a rightful privilege, his first impulse was to surrender. Move out of the house that could not be repaired, move out of the country if his papers were not in order, move out of a woman's way if another man stalked too near. Retreat, surrender.

At times Lillian remembered her husband, and now that he was no longer the husband she could see that he had been, as much as the other men she liked; handsome and desirable, and she could not understand why he had never been able to enter her being and her feelings as a lover. She had truly liked every aspect of him except the aspect of lover. When she saw him, with the clarity of distance and separation, she saw him quite outside of herself. He stood erect, and self-sufficient, and manly. He always retained his normal male largeness and upstanding protectiveness.

But Jay...came towards her almost as a man who limps and whom one instinctively wishes to sustain. He came as the man who did not see very well, slightly awkward, slightly stumbling. In this helplessness, in spite of his actual stature (he was the same height as her husband) he gave the air of being smaller, more fragile, more vulnerable. It was this fear in the man, who seemed inadequate in regard to life, trapped in it, the victim of it, which somehow affected her. In a smaller, weaker dimension he seemed to reach the right proportion for his being to enter into hers. He entered by the route of her compassion. She opened as the refuge opens; not conscious that it was a man who entered (man of whom she had a certain suspicion) but a child in need. Because he knocked as a beggar begging for a retreat, as a victim seeking solace, as a weakling seeking sustenance, she opened the door without suspicion.

It was in her frenzy to shelter, cover, defend him that she laid her strength over his head like an enormous starry roof, and the stretching immensity of the boundless mother was substituted for the normal image of the man covering the woman.

Jay came and he had a cold. And though he at first pretended it was of no importance, he slowly melted entirely into her, became soft and tender, waiting to be pampered, exaggerating his cough. And they wandered through the city like two lazy southerners, he said, like two convalescents. And she pampered him laughingly, ignoring time, eating when they were hungry, and seeing a radium sunlight lighting up the rain, seeing only the shimmer of the wet streets and not the greyness. He confessed that he craved a phonograph, and they shopped together and brought it back in a taxi. They slept soundly inside the warmth of this closeness, in the luxury of their contentment. It was Jay who touched everything with the magic of his contentment. It was Jay who said: isn't this ham good, isn't this salad good, isn't this wine good. Everything was good and savory, palatable and expansive.

He gave her the savor of the present, and let her care for the morrow.

This moment of utter and absolute tasting of food, of color, this moment of human breathing. No fragment detached, errant, disconnected or lost.

Because as Jay gathered the food on the table, the phonograph to his room, he gathered her into the present moment.

His taking her was not to take her or master her. He was the lover inside of the woman, as the child is inside of the woman. His caresses were as if he yearned and craved to be taken in not only as a lover; not merely to satisfy his desire but to remain within her. And her yearning answered this, by her desire to be filled. She never felt him outside of herself. Her husband had stood outside of her, and had come to visit her as a man, sensually. But he had not lodged himself as Jay had done, by reposing in her, by losing himself in her, by melting within her, with such feeling of physical intermingling as she had had with her child. Her husband had come to be renewed, to emerge again, to leave her and go to his male activities, to his struggles with the world.

The maternal and the feminine cravings were all confused in her, and all she felt was that it was through this softening and through this maternal yieldingness that Jay had penetrated where she had not allowed her husband's manliness to enter, only to visit her.

He liked prostitutes. "Because one does not have to make love to them, one does not have to write them beautiful letters." He liked them, and he liked to tell Lillian how much he liked them. He had to share all this with Lillian. He could not conceal any part of it from her, even if it hurt her. He could retain and hold nothing back from her. She was his confessor and his companion, his collaborator and his guardian angel. He did not see her weep when he launched into descriptions. At this moment he treated her as if she were a man (or the mother). As if the spectacle of his life could amuse her. "I even think if you had seen me that time, you could have enjoyed it."

He liked her to assume the burden of their life together, its material basis. Yet when she came to him, she must be all ready to discard this mantle of responsibilities, and become a child with him. His sense of humor took wayward forms.

His favorite prank: something that could be thrown away, which others valued; something that could be broken which others preserved. Traditions, habits, possessions. His greatest enjoyment was in demolition.

One of his most joyous experiences had been when a neighbor pianist who lived on the same quiet little street with him many years ago had been obliged to visit his mother at the hospital on the same day as the piano house had promised him an exchange of pianos. The man had been looking forward to this for many months. He begged Jay to attend to this. It was a complicated affair, getting the old piano out and the new one in. It was to be done by two different houses. One, a moving man, was to take the old piano out, then the piano house was to deliver the new. Jay had laughed it all off, and walked out unconcernedly, never remembering the promise he made. When he came home he found the two pianos in the street, before the entrance of the house, and the rain pouring down on them. The sight of the two pianos in the rain sent him into an absolute state of gaiety. "It was the most surrealistic sight I have ever seen." His laughter was so contagious that Lillian laughed with him, at the same time as she felt, somehow, a kind of pain at the image of pianos drenched in rain, and a pain even for the unknown pianist's feeling on his return home.

He seized only upon the comedy of the events.

At times Lillian asked herself: what will he make of me some day, when will he hurt me? And what if he does: I will try to love him gaily, more easily and loosely. To endure space and distance and betrayals. My courage is born today. Here lies Jay, breathing into my hair, over my neck. No hurt will come from me. No judgment. No woman ever judged the life stirring within her womb. I am too close to you. I will laugh with you even if it is against me.

Against me. Now the pain about the pianos left out in the rain suddenly touched her personally, and she understood why she had not been able to laugh freely. Those pianos were not only those of Jay's friend in the past, but her own too, since she had given up playing in order to work for Jay's support. She had surrendered any hope of becoming a concert pianist to attend better to their immediate needs. Jay's mockery wounded her, for it exposed his insensitiveness to anyone's loss, and to her loss too, his incapacity to feel for others, to understand that with the loss of her pianist self she had lost a very large part of herself, annihilated an entire portion of her personality, sacrificed it to him.

It was her piano Jay had left out in the rain, to be ruined...

He was wearing bedroom slippers and he was painting, with a bottle of red wine beside him. Circles of red wine on the floor. Stains. The edge of the table was burnt by cigarette stubs.

He didn't care. He said that what he had painted today was not as good as yesterday, but he didn't care. He was enjoying it just the same. He wasn't worrying about art. Everything was good, hang perfection, and he was out of cigarettes and if she would give him one he might finish that watercolor. She had come to interrupt him, that was good too, that was life; life was more important than any painting, let the interruptions come, specially in the form of a woman; let people walk in, it was good, to paint was good, not to paint was just as good, and eating and love making were even better, and now he was finished and he was hungry, and he wished they might go to the movies, good or bad...

The room was black. Jay was asleep in her arms, now, heavily asleep. She heard the organ grinder grinding his music. It was Saturday night. Always a holiday with him, always Saturday night with the crowds laughing and shouting and the organ grinder playing.

"According to the Chinese," said Jay, awakening, "there was a realm between heaven and earth...this must be it."

Tornadoes of desire and exquisite calms. She felt heavy and burnt.

"I want to keep you under lock and key, Lillian."

Suddenly he leaped up with a whiplike alacrity and exuberance and began to talk about his childhood, about his life in the streets, about the women he had loved and ditched, and the women who had ditched and bitched him, as he put it. He seemed to remember everything at once, as though it was a ball inside of him which unraveled of itself, and as it unraveled made new balls which he would unravel again another day. Had he actually done all these things he was relating to Lillian with such kaleidoscopic fury and passion? Had he really killed a boy in school with a snow ball? Had he really struck his first wife down when she was with child? Had he really butted his head against a wall in sudden anger because the woman he loved had rejected him? Had he really taken abortions and thrown them off the ferry boat in order to pick up a little extra change? Had he really stolen silver from a blind news vendor?

All the layers of his past he unraveled and laid before her, his masks, his buffooneries, and she saw him pretending, driven by obscure revenges, by fears, by weaknesses.

She saw him in the past and in the world, another man from the one she knew. And like all women in love she discarded this man of the past, holding others responsible for his behavior; and thinking: before me he sheds all his poses and defenses. The legend of hardness and callousness she did not believe. She saw him innocent, as we always see the loved one, innocent and even a victim.

She felt that she knew which was the rind and which the core of the man. "You always know," he said, "what is to be laughed away."

Then he rolled over and fell asleep. No noise, no care, no work undone, no imperfection unmastered, no love scene unresumed, no problem unsolved, ever kept him awake. He could roll over and forget. He could roll over with such grand indifference and let everything wait. When he rolled over the day ended. Nothing could be carried over into the next day. The next day would be absolutely new and clean. He just rolled over and extinguished everything. Just rolling over.

Djuna and Jay. For Djuna Jay does not look nonchalant but rather intent and listening, as if in quest of some revelation, as if he were questioning for the first time.

"I've lived so blindly... No time to think much. Tons and tons of experience. Lillian always creating trouble, misery, changes, flights, dramas. No time to digest anything. And then she says I die when she leaves, that pain and war are good for me."

Djuna notices that although he is only forty years old, his hair is greying at the temple.

"Your eyes are full of wonder," he said, "as if you expected a miracle every day. I can't let you go now. I want to go places with you, obscure little places, just to be able to say: here I came with Djuna. I'm insatiable, you know. I'll ask you for the impossible. What it is, I don't know. You'll tell me, probably. You're quicker than I am. And you're the first woman with whom I feel I can be absolutely sincere. You make me happy because I can talk with you. I feel at ease with you. This is a little drunken, but you know what I mean. You always seem to know what I mean."

"You change from a wise old man to a savage. You're both timid and cruel too, aren't you?"

"There is something here it is impossible for Lillian to understand, or to break either. I feel we are friends. Don't you see? Friends. Christ, have a man and woman ever been friends, beyond love and beyond desire, and beyond everything, friends? Well, this is what I feel with you."

She hated the gaiety with which she received these words, for that condemnation of her body to be the pale watcher, the understanding one upon whom others laid their burdens, laying their heads on her lap to sleep, to be lulled from others' wounds. And even as she hated her own goodness, she heard herself say quietly, out of the very core of this sense of justice: "The destroyers do not always destroy, Jay."

"You see more, you just see more, and what you see is there all right. You get at the core of everything."

And now she was caught between them, to be the witch of words, a silent swift shadow darkened by uncanny knowledge, forgetting herself, her human needs, in the unfolding of this choking blind relationship: Lillian and Jay lacerating each other because of their different needs.

Pale beauty of the watcher shining in the dark.

Both of them now, Jay and Lillian, entered Djuna's life by gusts, and left by gusts, as they lived.

She sat for hours afterwards sailing her lingering mind like a slow river boat down the feelings they had dispensed with prodigality.

"In my case," said Jay, alone with her, "what's difficult is to keep any image of myself clear. I have never thought about myself much. The first time I saw myself full length, as it were, was in you. I have grown used to considering your image of me as the correct one. Probably because it makes me feel good. I was like a wheel without a hub."

"And I'm the hub, now," said Djuna, laughing.

Jay was lying on the couch in the parlor, and she had left him to dress for an evening party. When she was dressed she opened the door and then stood before her long mirror perfuming herself.

The window was open on the garden and he said: "This is like a setting for Pelleas and Melisande. It is all a dream."

The perfume made a silky sound as she squirted it with the atomizer, touching her ear lobes, her neck. "Your dress is green like a princess," he said, "I could swear it is a green I have never seen before and will never see again. I could swear the garden is made of cardboard, that the trembling of the light behind you comes from the footlights, that the sounds are music. You are almost transparent there, like the mist of perfume you are throwing on yourself. Throw more perfume on yourself, like a fixative on a water color. Let me have the atomizer. Let me put perfume all over you so that you won't disappear and fade like a water color."

She moved towards him and sat on the edge of the couch: "You don't quite believe in me as a woman," she said, with an immense distress quite out of proportion to his fancy.

"This is a setting for Pelleas and Melisande," he said, "and I know that when you leave me for that dinner I will never see you again. Those incidents last at the most three hours, and the echoes of the music maybe a day. No more."

The color of the day, the color of Byzantine paintings, that gold which did not have the firm surface of lacquer, that gold made of a fine powder easily decomposed by time, a soft powdery gold which seemed on the verge of decomposing, as if each grain of dust, held together only by atoms, was ever ready to fall apart like a mist of perfume; that gold so thin in substance that it allowed one to divine the canvas behind it, the space in the painting, the presence of reality behind its thinness, the fibrous space lying behind the illusion, the absence of color and depth, the condition of emptiness and blackness underneath the gold powder. This gold powder which had fallen now on the garden, on each leaf of the trees, which was flowering inside the room, on her black hair, on the skin of his wrists, on his frayed suit sleeve, on the green carpet, on her green dress, on the bottle of perfume, on his voice, on her anxiety—the very breath of living, the very breath he and she took in to live and breathed out to live—that very breath could mow and blow it all down.

The essence, the human essence always evaporating where the dream installs itself.

The air of that summer day, when the wind itself had suspended its breathing, hung between the window and garden; the air itself could displace a leaf, could displace a word, and a displaced leaf or word might change the whole aspect of the day.

The essence, the human essence always evaporating where the dream installed itself and presided.

Every time he said he had been out the night before with friends and that he had met a woman, there was a suspense in Lillian's being, a moment of fear that he might add: I met the woman who will replace you. This moment was repeated for many years with the same suspense, the same sense of the fragility of love, without bringing any change in his love. A kind of superstition haunted her, running crosscurrent to the strength of the ties binding them, a sense of menace. At first because the love was all expansion and did not show its roots; and later, when the roots were apparent, because she expected a natural fading and death.

This fear appeared at the peak of their deepest moments, a precipice all around their ascensions. This fear appeared through the days of their tranquility, as a sign of death rather than a sign of natural repose. It marked every moment of silence with the seal of a fatal secret. The greater the circle spanned by the attachment, the larger she saw the fissure through which human beings fall again into solitude.

The woman who personified this danger never appeared. His description gave no clues. Jay made swift portraits which he seemed to forget the next day. He was a man of many friends. His very ebullience created a warm passage but an onward flowing one, forming no grooves, fixing no image permanently. His enthusiasms were quickly burned out, sometimes in one evening. She never sought out these passing images.

Now and then he said with great simplicity: "You are the only one. You are the only one."

And then one day he said: "The other day I met a woman you would like. I was sorry you were not there. She is coming with friends this evening. Do you want to stay? You will see. She has the most extraordinary eyes."

"She has extraordinary eyes? I'll stay. I want to know her."

(Perhaps if I run fast enough ahead of the present I will outdistance the shock. What is the difference between fear and intuition? How clearly I have seen what I imagine, as clearly as a vision. What is it I feel now, fear or premonition?)

Helen's knock on the door was vigorous, like an attack. She was very big and wore a severely tailored suit. She looked like a statue, but a statue with haunted eyes, inhuman eyes not made for weeping, full of animal glow. And the rest of her body a statue pinned down to its base, immobilized by a fear. She had the immobility of a Medusa waiting to transfix others into stone: hypnotic and cold, attracting others to her mineral glow.

She had two voices, one which fell deep like the voice of a man, and another light and innocent. Two women disputing inside of her.

She aroused a feeling in Lillian which was not human. She felt she was looking at a painting in which there was an infinity of violent blue. A white statue with lascivious Medusa hair. Not a woman but a legend with enormous space around her.

Her eyes were begging for an answer to an enigma. The pupils seemed to want to separate from the whites of the eyes.

Lillian felt no longer any jealousy, but a curiosity as in a dream. She did not feel any danger or fear in the meeting, only an enormous blue space in which a woman stood waiting. This space and grandeur around Helen drew Lillian to her.

Helen was describing a dream she often had of being carried away by a Centaur, and Lillian could see the Centaur holding Helen's head, the head of a woman in a myth. People in myths were larger than human beings.

Helen's dreams took place in an enormous desert where she was lost among the prisons. She was tearing her hands to get free. The columns of these prisons were human beings all bound in bandages. Her own draperies were of sackcloth, the woolen robes of punishment.

And then came her questions to Lillian: "Why am I not free? I ran away from my husband and my two little girls many years ago. I did not know it then, but I didn't want to be a mother, the mother of children. I wanted to be the mother of creations and dreams, the mother of artists, the muse and the mistress. In my marriage I was buried alive. My husband was a man without courage for life. We lived as if he were a cripple, and I a nurse. His presence killed the life in me so completely that I could hardly feel the birth of my children. I became afraid of nature, of being swallowed by the mountains, stifled by the forest, absorbed by the sea. I rebelled so violently against my married life that in one day I destroyed everything and ran away, abandoning my children, my home and my native country. But I never attained the life I had struggled to reach. My escape brought me no liberation. Every night I dream the same dream of prisons and struggles to escape. It is as if only my body escaped, and not my feelings. My feelings were left over there like roots dangling when you tear a plant too violently. Violence means nothing. And it does not free one. Part of my being remained with my children, imprisoned in the past. Now I have to liberate myself wholly, body and soul, and I don't know how. The violent gestures I make only tighten the knot of resistance around me. How can one liquidate the past? Guilt and regrets can't be shed like an old coat."

Then she saw that Lillian was affected by her story and she added: "I am grateful to Jay for having met you."

Only then Lillian remembered her painful secret. For a moment she wanted to lay her head on Helen's shoulder and confess to her: "I only came because I was afraid of you. I came because I thought you were going to take Jay away from me." But now that Helen had revealed her innermost dreams and pains, Lillian felt: perhaps she needs me more than she needs Jay. For he cannot console. He can only make her laugh.

At the same time she thought that this was equally effective. And she remembered how much Jay liked audacity in women, how some feminine part of him liked to yield, liked to be chosen, courted. Deep down he was timid, and he liked audacity in women. Helen could be given the key to his being, if Lillian told her this. If Lillian advised her to take the first step, because he was a being perpetually waiting to be ignited, never set off by himself, always seeking in women the explosion which swept him along.

All around her there were signs, signs of danger and loss. Without knowing consciously what she was doing, Lillian began to assume the role she feared Jay might assume. She became like a lover. She was full of attentiveness and thoughtfulness. She divined Helen's needs uncannily. She telephoned her at the moment Helen felt the deepest loneliness. She said the gallant words Helen wanted to hear. She gave Helen such faith as lovers give. She gave to the friendship an atmosphere of courtship which accomplished the same miracles as love. Helen began to feel enthusiasm and hunger again. She forgot her illness to take up painting, her singing, and writing. She recreated, redecorated the place she was living in. She displayed art in her dressing, care and fantasy. She ceased to feel alone.

On a magnificent day of sun and warmth Lillian said to her: "If I were a man, I would make love to you."

Whether she said this to help Helen bloom like a flower in warmth and fervor, or to take the place of Jay and enact the courtship she had imagined, which she felt she had perhaps deprived Helen of, she did not know.

But Helen felt as rich as a woman with a new love.

At times when Lillian rang Helen's bell, she imagined Jay ringing it. And she tried to divine what Jay might feel at the sight of Helen's face. Every time she fully conceded that Helen was beautiful. She asked herself whether she was enhancing Helen's beauty with her own capacity for admiration. But then Jay too had this capacity for exalting all that he admired.

Lillian imagined him coming and looking at the paintings. He would like the blue walls. It was true he would not like her obsessions with disease, her fear of cancer. But then he would laugh at them, and his laughter might dispel her fears.

In Helen's bathroom, where she went to powder and comb her hair, she felt a greater anguish, because there she was nearer to the intimacy of Helen's life. Lillian looked at her kimono, her bedroom slippers, her creams and medicines as if trying to divine with what feelings Jay might look at them. She remembered how much he liked to go behind the scenes of people's lives. He liked to rummage among intimate belongings and dispel illusions. It was his passion. He would come out triumphantly with a jar: and this, what is this for? as if women were always seeking to delude him. He doubted the most simple things. He had often pulled at her eyelashes to make certain they were not artificial.

What would he feel in Helen's bathroom? Would he feel tenderness for her bedroom slippers? Why were there objects which inspired tenderness and others none? Helen's slippers did not inspire tenderness. Nothing about her inspired tenderness. But it might inspire desire, passion, anything else— even if she remained outside of one, like a sculpture, a painting, a form, not something which penetrated and enveloped one. But inhuman figures could inspire passion. Even if she were the statue in a Chirico painting, unable to mingle with human beings, even if she could not be impregnated by others or live inside of another all tangled in threads of blood and emotion.

When they went out together Lillian always expected the coincidence which would bring the three of them together to the same concert, the same exhibit, the same play, But it never happened. They always missed each other. All winter long the coincidences of city life did not bring the three of them together. Lillian began to think that this meeting was not destined, that it was not she who was keeping them apart.

Helen's eyes grew greener and sank more and more into the myth. She could not feel. And Lillian felt as if she were keeping from her the man who might bring her back to life. Felt almost as if she were burying her alive by not giving her Jay.

Perhaps Lillian was imagining too much.

Meanwhile Helen's need of Lillian grew immense. She was not contented with Lillian's occasional visits. She wanted to fill the entire void of her life with Lillian. She wanted Lillian to stay over night when she was lonely. The burden grew heavier and heavier.

Lillian became frightened. In wanting to amuse and draw Helen away from her first interest in Jay, she had surpassed herself and become this interest.

Helen dramatized the smallest incident, suffered from insomnia, said her bedroom was haunted at night, sent for Lillian on every possible occasion.

Lillian was punished for playing the lover. Now she must be the husband, too. Helen had forgotten Jay but the exchange had left Lillian as a hostage.

Not knowing how to lighten the burden she said one day: "You ought to travel again. This city cannot be good for you. A place where you have been lonely and unhappy for so long must be the wrong place."

That very night there was a fire in Helen's house, in the apartment next to hers. She interpreted this as a sign that Lillian's intuitions for her were wise. She decided to travel again.

They parted at the corner of a street, gaily, as if for a short separation. Gaily, with green eyes flashing at one another. They lost each other's address. It all dissolved very quickly, like a dream.

And then Lillian felt free again. Once again she had worn the warrior armor to protect a core of love. Once again she had worn the man's costume.

Jay had not made her woman, but the husband and mother of his weakness.

Lillian confessed to Jay that she was pregnant. He said: "We must find the money for an abortion." He looked irritated. She waited. She thought he might slowly evince interest in the possibility of a child. He revealed only an increased irritation. It disturbed his plans, his enjoyment. The mere idea of a child was an intrusion. He let her go alone to the doctor. He expressed resentment. And then she understood.

She sat alone one day in their darkened room. She talked to the child inside of her.

"My little one not born yet, I feel your small feet kicking against my womb. My little one not born yet, it is very dark in the room you and I are sitting in, just as dark as it must be for you inside of me, but it must be sweeter for you to be lying in the warmth than it is for me to be seeking in this dark room the joy of not knowing, not feeling, not seeing; the joy of lying still in utter warmth and this darkness. All of us forever seeking this warmth and this darkness, this being alive without pain, this being alive without anxiety, fear or loneliness. You are impatient to live, you kick with your small feet, but you ought to die. You ought to die in warmth and darkness because you are a child without a father. You will not find on earth this father as large as the sky, big enough to hold your whole being and your fears, larger than house or church. You will not find a father who will lull you and cover you with his greatness and his warmth. It would be better if you died inside of me, quietly, in the warmth and in the darkness."

Did the child hear her? At six months she had a miscarriage and lost it.

Lillian was giving a concert in a private home which was like a temple of treasures. Paintings and people had been collected with expert and exquisite taste. There was a concentration of beautiful women so that one was reminded of a hothouse exhibit.

The floor was so highly polished there were two Lillians, two white pianos, two audiences.

The piano under her strong hands became small like a child's piano. She overwhelmed it, she tormented it, crushed it. She played with all her intensity, as if the piano must be possessed or possess her.

The women in the audience shivered before this *corps à corps*.

Lillian was pushing her vigor into the piano. Her face was full of vehemence and possessiveness. She turned her face upwards as if to direct the music upwards, but the music would not rise, volatilize itself. It was too heavily charged with passion.

She was not playing to throw music into the blue space, but to reach some climax, some impossible union with the piano, to reach that which men and women could reach together. A moment of pleasure, a moment of fusion. The passion and the blood in her rushed against the ivory notes and overloaded them. She pounded the coffer of the piano as she wanted her own body pounded and shattered. And the pain on her face was that of one who reached neither sainthood nor pleasure. No music rose and passed out of the window, but a sensual cry, heavy with unspent forces...

Lillian storming against her piano, using the music to tell all how she wanted to be stormed with equal strength and fervor.

This tidal power was still in her when the women moved towards her to tell her it was wonderful. She rose from the piano as if she would engulf them, the smaller women; she embraced them with all the fervor of unspent intensity that had not reached a climax—which the music, like too delicate a vessel, the piano with too delicate a frame, had not been able to contain.

It was while Lillian was struggling to tear from the piano what the piano could not possibly give her that Djuna's attention was wafted towards the window.

In the golden salon, with the crystal lamps, the tapestries and the paintings there were immense bay windows, and Djuna's chair had been placed in one of the recesses, so that she sat on the borderline between the perfumed crowd and the silent, static garden.

It was late in the afternoon, the music had fallen back upon the people like a heavy storm cloud which could not be dispersed to lighten and lift them, the air was growing heavy, when her eyes caught the garden as if in a secret exposure. As everyone was looking at Lillian, Djuna's sudden glance seemed to have caught the garden unaware, in a dissolution of peace and greens. A light rain had washed the faces of the leaves, the knots in the tree trunks stared with aged eyes, the grass was drinking, there was a sensual humidity as if leaves, trees, grass and wind were all in a state of caress.

The garden had an air of nudity.

Djuna let her eyes melt into the garden. The garden had an air of nudity, of efflorescence, of abundance, of plenitude.

The salon was gilded, the people were costumed for false roles, the lights and the faces were attenuated, the gestures were starched—all but Lillian whose nature had not been stylized, compressed or gilded, and whose nature was warring with a piano.

Music did not open doors.

Nature flowered, caressed, spilled, relaxed, slept.

In the gilded frames, the ancestors were mummified forever, and descendants took the same poses. The women were candied in perfume, conserved in cosmetics, the men preserved in their elegance. All the violence of naked truths had evaporated, volatilized within gold frames.

And then, as Djuna's eyes followed the path carpeted with detached leaves, her eyes encountered for the first time three full-length mirrors placed among the bushes and flowers as casually as in a boudoir. Three mirrors.

The eyes of the people inside could not bear the nudity of the garden, its exposure. The eyes of the people had needed the mirrors, delighted in the fragility of reflections. All the truth of the garden, the moisture, and the worms, the insects and the roots, the running sap and the rotting bark, had all to be reflected in the mirrors.

Lillian was playing among vast mirrors. Lillian's violence was attenuated by her reflection in the mirrors.

The garden in the mirror was polished with the mist of perfection. Art and artifice had breathed upon the garden and the garden had breathed upon the mirror, and all the danger of truth and revelation had been exorcised.

Under the house and under the garden there were subterranean passages and if no one heard the premonitory rumblings before the explosion, it would all erupt in the form of war and revolution.

The humiliated, the defeated, the oppressed, the enslaved. Woman's misused and twisted strength...

Notes

Text: *Ladders to Fire* (Denver: Alan Swallow, 1966).

Someone—presumably Nin—made textual changes to "Lillian and Djuna" for its inclusion, as "This Hunger," in *Ladders to Fire* (London: Peter Owen, 1963). Although Alan Swallow used a facsimile of the 1946 Dutton edition of the novel (exclusive of "Stella") when preparing to publish it in 1966, he incorporated the textual changes made to the 1963 edition by setting new lines of type in the facsimile.

⟍ PROLOGUE TO *LADDERS TO FIRE* ⟎

(1946)

Context

For *This Hunger* (1945), Nin composed a prologue that she revised and used as the prologue to *Ladders to Fire* (1946). In it, she emphasizes that this novel represents "woman at war with herself," a "negative pole," implying that in time she will depict tranquility, a positive pole, as she does at the conclusion of the final volume of the continuous novel, *Seduction of the Minotaur* (1961).

◆ ◆ ◆ ◆

I have to begin where everything begins, in the blindness and in the shadows. I have to begin the story of women's development where all things begin: in nature, at the roots. It is necessary to return to the origin of confusion, which is woman's struggle to understand her own nature. Man struggled with nature, fought the elements with his objectivity, his inventions, and mastered them. Woman has not been able to organize her own nature, her simoons, her tornadoes, her obscurantisms, because she lacked the eye of consciousness. She was nature. Man did not help her in this because his interpretations, whether psychological, or intellectual, or artistic, did not seize her. And she could not speak for herself.

Today marvelous women speak for themselves in terms of heroic action, integrating the woman, mother, wife, inharmonious relation to history, to larger worlds of art and science. But many more, when entering action or creation, followed man's patterns and could not carry along or integrate within them the feminine part of themselves. Action and creation, for woman, was man—or an imitation of man. In this imitation of man she lost contact with her nature and her relation to man.

Man appears only partially in this volume, because for the woman at war with herself, he can only appear thus, not as an entity. Woman at war with herself, has not yet been related to man, only to the child in man, being capable only of maternity.

This novel deals with the negative pole, the pole of confused and twisted nature.

The mirrors in the garden are the mirrors women must look into before they can go further. This is only the story of the mirrors and nature in opposition, and in the mirrors is only what woman dares to see...so far an incomplete woman.

Notes

Text: *Ladders to Fire* (New York: Dutton, 1946), [7].

"Mirrors in the garden" refers to an image in "Lillian and Djuna" ("This Hunger").

⊂⊰ PROLOGUE TO *LADDERS TO FIRE* ⊱⊃

(1963)

Context

In a later edition of *Ladders to Fire*, Nin characterizes her first five novels as a *roman-fleuve*.

◆ ◆ ◆ ◆

My original concept was a *Roman Fleuve*, a series of novels on various aspects of relationships, portraying four women in a continuous symphony of experience. All the characters are presented fully in the first volume, *Ladders to Fire*. They are developed later in the succeeding volumes, *Children of the Albatross*, *The Four-Chambered Heart*, *A Spy in the House of Love*, and *Seduction of the Minotaur*.

The complete series has been published in America under the title of *Cities of the Interior*.

As each book came out, however, it was reviewed as if it were an independent novel. Naturally the interrelations and interdependence of the total design were lost and obscured. Cross references and allusions lost their cumulative effect and some characters seemed to appear out of nowhere.

For an indication of the intention of my novel I refer you to a critique by Oliver Evans which appeared in the review *Prairie Schooner* in the Autumn of 1962.

"Her technique has for its object not so much the telling of a story as the direct revelation of experience, and her use of rhythmical language has the same object, as a kind of catalyst which induces in the hearer a state of proper receptivity...she really has succeeded in introducing a new dimension in fiction...no one to my knowledge, has searched so relentlessly and with such artistic effects into the ultimate sources of character, or has concerned himself so exclusively and so successfully with the nuance of emotional relationships, the myriad subtle influences and all constantly changing— which human beings, consciously or unconsciously, exert upon one another."

Notes

Text: *Ladders to Fire* (London: Peter Owen, 1963), [5]-[6].

❦ PREFACE TO *CITIES OF THE INTERIOR* ❧

(1974)

Context

In the preface to *Cities of the Interior*, Nin recounts the publishing history of the novels that constitute her *roman-fleuve*.

◆ ◆ ◆ ◆

The story of *Cities of the Interior* has never been told, and it is time to clear up misunderstandings. I have never planned my novels ahead. I have always improvised on a theme. My only preconception was that it was to be a study of women. The first book turned out to be *Ladders to Fire*. All the women I was to write about appeared in it, including Stella, whom I later dropped because she seemed so complete in herself rather than related to the other women. (*Stella*, with two other novelettes, *Winter of Artifice* and *The Voice*, was later published under the title *Winter of Artifice* by Alan Swallow.)

When *Ladders to Fire* was accepted by E. P. Dutton, I explained that it was part of a larger design, and that other novels would follow and round out the characters. The editors were aghast. They said the American public would never read a novel which threatened to continue, a *"roman fleuve"* as it is called in France. In 1946 the book was published as an independent novel, and nothing was said about development and continuity. For that reason, I did not develop a method of linking the various narratives.

I began the next novel, *Children of the Albatross*, as if it were a new story. Though the same characters appeared, the theme was altogether different. Dutton's nervousness was dissipated. *Children of the Albatross* was published a year after *Ladders to Fire*, but the link had to be made by the reader (or the critics), and naturally it was not.

Then Dutton planned to wait four years before publishing the third novel, *The Four-Chambered Heart*, and I feared the continuity would be lost in the waiting, so I gave it to Duell, Sloan and Pearce. But it was still to take three years after *Children of the Albatross* appeared before *The Four-Chambered Heart* was published. Much was lost by never stressing the continuity and interrelatedness of the novels. Unlike Durrell's *Quartet*, which was openly described as a unity, my novels (in a much earlier period) appeared without explanation. Duell, Sloan and Pearce turned down the fourth book, *A Spy in the House of Love*. It was finally done by British Book Centre four years after

The Four-Chambered Heart saw print. The continuity was totally erased by then.

Finally, I published *Solar Barque* myself, making it a small book with interesting drawings by Peter Loomer, age 11. It focused on an episode of Lillian's life. At the time I thought it contained all I wished to say, but like a piece of music which continues to haunt one, the theme continued to develop in my head, and I took it up again and carried it to completion.

Now there was a problem for my new and loyal publisher, Alan Swallow. Should we reprint *Solar Barque* with the new material? No one would notice then that it had been added to, and the reviewers would not review the same title twice. Swallow decided to make a new book with a new title: *Seduction of the Minotaur*. Some reviewers complained bitterly because they had already read the first part. Generosity was not exactly rampant, and again I could not come forward to explain how I worked. It might have compounded the difficulties.

When all the novels went out of print, and people wrote me asking for them, I published them together under the title *Cities of the Interior* (1959), and for the first time the continuity was established. This is the book which The Swallow Press is publishing now, with the addition of the second part of *Solar Barque* included in *Seduction of the Minotaur*.

Now that the links between the novels are made clear, I hope the journey through the *Cities of the Interior* will be deeper and less difficult.

Notes

Text: *Cities of the Interior* (Chicago: Swallow Press, 1974), vii-ix.

Nin refers to Lawrence Durrell's *Alexandria Quartet*. Peter Loomer (1943-1964) was the son of Nin's friend Renate Druks (1921-2007).

෬ "STELLA" ෬

(1945)

Context

Nin experimented with the placement of the novella "Stella"—in *This Hunger* (1945), in *Ladders to Fire* (1946), and finally in *Winter of Artifice* (1961).

♦ ♦ ♦ ♦

Stella sat in a small, dark room and watched her own figure acting on the screen. Stella watched her "double" moving in the light, and she did not recognize her. She almost hated her. Her first reaction was one of revolt, of rejection. This image was not she. She repudiated it. It was a work of artifice, of lighting, of stage setting.

The shock she felt could not be explained by the obvious difference between her daily self to which she purposely brought no enhancement and the screen image which was illuminated. It was not only that the eyes were enlarged and deepened, that the long eyelashes played like some Oriental latticework around them and intensified the interior light. The shock came from some violent contrast between Stella's image of herself and the projected self she could not recognize at all. To begin with, she had always seen herself in her own interior mirror, as a child woman, too small. And then this little bag of poison she carried within, the poison of melancholy and dissatisfaction she always felt must be apparent in her coloring, must produce a grey tone, or brown (the colors she wore in preference to others, the sackcloth robes of punishment). And the paralyzing fears, fear of love, fear of people coming too near (nearness brings wounds), invading her—her tensions and stage frights in the face of love... The first kiss for example, that first kiss which was to transport her, dissolve her, which was to swing her upward into the only paradise on earth...that first kiss of which she had been so frightened that at the moment of the miracle, out of panic, nerves, from her delicately shaped stomach came dark rumbling like some long-sleeping volcano becoming active.

Whereas the image on the screen was completely washed of the coloring and tones of sadness. It was imponderably light, and moved always with such a flowering of gestures that it was like the bloom and flowering of nature. This figure moved with ease, with illimitableness towards others, in a dissolution of feeling. The eyes opened and all the marvels of love, all its tonalities and nuances and multiplicities poured out as for a feast. The body danced a dance of receptivity and response. The hair undulated and swung as if it had breathing pores of its own, its own currents of life and electricity, and the hands preceded the gesture of the body like some slender orchestra leader's baton unleashing a symphony.

This was not the grey-faced child who had run away from home to become an actress, who had known hunger and limitations and obstacles, who had not yet given herself as she was giving herself on the screen...

And the second shock was the response of the people.

They loved her.

Sitting next to her, they did not see her, intent on loving the woman on the screen.

Because she was giving to many what most gave to the loved one. A voice altered by love, desire, the lips forming a smile of open tenderness. They were permitted to witness the exposure of being in a moment of high feeling, of tenderness, indulgence, dreaming, abandon, sleepiness, mischievousness, which was only uncovered in moments of love and intimacy.

They received these treasures of a caressing glance, a unique tonality and voice, an intimate gesture by which we are enchanted and drawn to the one we love. This openness they were sharing was the miraculous openness and revelation which took place only in love, and it caused a current of love to flow between the audience and the woman on the screen, a current of gratitude... Then this response moved like a searchlight and found her, smaller, less luminous, less open, poorer, and like some diminished image of the other, but it flowed around her, identified her. The audience came near her, touched her, asked for her signature. And she hung her head, drooped, could not accept the worship. The woman on the screen was a stranger to her. She did not see any analogy, she saw only the violent contrast which only reinforced her conviction that the screen image was illusory, artificial, artful. She was a deceiver, a pretender. The woman on the screen went continually forward, carried by her story, led by the plot loaned to her. But Stella, Stella herself was blocked over and over again by inner obstacles.

What Stella had seen on the screen, the figure of which she had been so instantaneously jealous, was the free Stella. What did not appear on the screen was the shadow of Stella, her demons, doubt and fear. And Stella was jealous. She was not only jealous of a more beautiful woman, but of a free woman. She marveled at her own movements, their flow and ease. She marveled at the passionate giving that came like a flood from her eyes, melting everyone, an act of osmosis.

And it was to this woman men wrote letters and this woman they fell in love with, courted.

They courted the face on the screen, the face of translucence, the face of wax on which men found it possible to imprint the image of their fantasy.

No metallic eyes or eyes of crystal as in other women, but liquid, throwing a mist dew and vapor. No definite smile but a hovering, evanescent, uncapturable smile which set off all pursuits. An air of the unformed, waiting to be formed, an air of eluding, waiting to be crystallized, an air of evasion, waiting to be catalyzed. Indefinite contours, a wavering voice capable of all tonalities, tapering to a whisper, an air of flight waiting to be captured, an air of turning corners perpetually and vanishing, some quality of matter that calls for an imprint, a carving, this essence of the feminine on which men could impose any desire, which awaited fecundation, which invited, lured, appealed, drew, ensorcelled by its seeming incompleteness, its hazy mysteries, its rounded edges.

The screen Stella with her transparent wax face, changing and changeable, promising to meet any desire, to mould itself, to respond, to invent if necessary...so that the dream of man like some sharp instrument knew the moment had come to imprint his most secret image... The image of Stella mobile, receiving the wish, the desire, the image imposed upon it.

She bought a very large, very spacious Movie Star bed of white satin.

It was not the bed of her childhood, which was particularly small because her father had said she was a pixie and she would never grow taller.

It was not the student bed on which she had slept during the years of poverty before she became a well-known actress.

It was the bed she had dreamed and placed in a setting of grandeur, it was the bed that her screen self had often been placed in, very wide and very sumptuous and not like her at all. And together with the bed she had dreamed a room of mirrors, and very large perfume bottles and a closet full of hats and rows of shoes, and the white rug and setting of a famous screen actress, altogether as it had been dreamed by so many women. And finally she had them all, and she lived among them without feeling that they belonged to her, that she had the stature and the assurance they demanded. The large bed...she slept in it as if she were sleeping in a screen story. Uneasily. And not until she found a way of slipping her small body away from the splendor, satin, space, did she sleep well: by covering her head.

And when she covered her head she was back in the small bed of her childhood, back in the small space of the little girl who was afraid.

The hats, properly perched on stands as in all women's dreams of an actress wardrobe, were never taken down. They required such audacity. They demanded that a role be played to its maximum perfection. So each time she had reached into the joyous hat exhibit, looked at the treasured hats, she took again the little skull cap, the unobtrusive page and choir-boy cap.

The moment when her small hand hesitated, lavishing even a caress over the arrogant feather, the challenged upward tilts, the regal velvets, the labyrinthian veils, the assertive gallant ribbons, the plumage and decorations of triumph, was it doubt which reached for the tiny skull cap of the priest, choir boy and scholar?

Was it doubt which threw a suspicious glance over the shoes she had collected for their courage, shoes intended to walk the most entrancing and dangerous paths? Shoes of assurance and daring exploration, shoes for new situations, new steps, new places. All shined and polished for variety and change and adventure, and then each day rebuked, left like museum pieces on their shelves while she took the familiar and slightly worn ones that would not impose on her feet too large a role, too great an undertaking, shoes for the familiar route to the studio, to the people she knew well, to the places which held no surprises...

Once when Stella was on the stage acting a love scene, which was taking place after a scene in a snowstorm, one of the flakes of artificial snow remained on the wing of her small and delicate nose. And then, during the exalted scene, the woman of warm snow whose voice and body seemed to melt into one's hands, the dream of osmosis, the dream of every lover, to find a substance that will confound with yours, dissolve, and yield and incorporate and become indissoluble—all during this scene there lay the snowflake catching the light and flashing signals of gently humorous inappropriateness and misplacement. The snowflake gave the scene an imperfection which touched the heart and brought all the feelings of the watchers to converge and rest upon that infinitely moving absurdity of the misplaced snowflake.

If Stella had known it she would have been crushed. The lightest of her defects, weighing no more than a snowflake, which touched the human heart as only fallibility can touch it, aroused Stella's self-condemnation and weighed down upon her soul with the oppressive weight of all perfectionism.

At times the woman on the screen and the woman she was every day encountered and fused together. And those were the moments when the impetus took its flight in full opulence and reached plenitude. They were so rare that she considered them peaks inaccessible to daily living, impossible to attain continuously.

But what killed them was not the altitude, the rarefied intensity of them. What killed them for her was that they remained unanswerable. It was a moment human beings did not feel together or in rhythm. It was a moment to be felt alone. It was the solitude that was unbearable.

Whenever she moved forward she fell into an abysm.

She remembered a day spent in full freedom by the sea with Bruno. He had fallen asleep late and she had slipped away for a swim. All through the swimming she had the impression of swimming into an ocean of feeling— because of Bruno she would no longer move separately from this great moving body of feeling undulating with her which made of her emotions an illimitable symphonic joy. She had the marvelous sensation of being a part of a vaster world and moving with it because of moving in rhythm with another being.

The joy of this was so intense that when she saw him approaching she ran towards him wildly, joyously. Coming near him like a ballet dancer she took a leap towards him; and he, frightened by her vehemence, and fearing that she would crash against him, instinctively became absolutely rigid, and she felt herself embracing a statue. Without hurt to her body, but with immeasurable hurt to her feelings.

Bruno had never seen her on the screen. He had seen her for the first time at a pompous reception where she moved among the other women like a dancer among pedestrians and distinguished herself by her mobility, by her voice which trembled and wavered, by her little nose which wrinkled when she smiled; her lips which shivered, the foreign accent which gave a hesitancy to her phrases as if she were about to make a portentous revelation, and by her hands which vibrated in the air.

He saw her in reality, yet he did not see Stella but the dream of Stella. He loved instantly a woman without fear, without doubt, and his nature, which had never taken flight, could now do so with her. He saw her in flight. He did not sense that a nature such as hers could be paralyzed, frozen with fear, could retreat, could regress, negate, and then in extreme fear, could also turn about and destroy.

For Stella this love had been born under the zodiacal sign of doubt. For Bruno, under the sign of faith.

In a setting of opulence, a setting of such elegance that it had required the wearing of one of the museum hats, the one with the regal feather, from two opposite worlds they came: Stella consumed with a hunger for love, and Bruno by the emptiness of his life.

As Stella appeared among the women, what struck Bruno was that he was seeing for the first time an animated woman. He felt caught in her current, carried. Her rhythm was contagious. He felt instantaneous obedience to her movement.

At the same time he felt wounded. Her eyes had pierced some region of his being no eyes had ever touched before. The vulnerable Bruno was captured; his moods and feelings henceforth determined, woven into hers. From the first moment they looked at each other it was determined that all she said would hurt him but that she could instantly heal him by moving one inch nearer to him. Then the hurt was instantly healed by the odor of her hair or the light touch of her hand on him.

An acute sense of distance was immediately established, such as Bruno had never known before to exist between men and women. A slight contradiction (and she loved contradiction) separated him from her and he suffered. And this suffering could only be abated by her presence and would be renewed as soon as they separated.

Bruno was discovering that he was not complete or autonomous.

Nor did Stella promise him completeness, nearness. She had the changing quality of dream. She obeyed her own oscillations. What came into being between them was not a marriage but an interplay where nothing was ever fixed. No planetary tensions, chartered and mapped and measured.

Her movements were of absolute abandon, yieldingness, and then at the smallest sign of lethargy or neglect, complete withdrawal and he had to begin courtship anew. Every day she could be won again and lost again. And the reason for her flights and departures, her breaks from him, were obscure and mysterious to him.

One night when they had been separated for many days, she received a telegram that he would visit her for a whole night. For her this whole night was as long, as portentous, as deep as a whole existence. She dwelt on every detail of it, she improvised upon it, she constructed and imagined and lived in it completely for many days. This was to be their marriage.

Her eyes overflowed with expectancy as she met him. Then she noticed that he had come without a valise. She did not seek the cause. She was struck by this as a betrayal of their love. Her being closed with an anguish inexplicable to him (an anguish over the possibility of a break, a separation, made her consider every small break, every small separation like a premonition of an ultimate one).

He spent his time in a struggle to reassure her, to reconquer her, to renew her faith, and she in resisting. She considered the demands of reality as something to be entirely crushed in favor of love, that obedience to reality meant a weakness in love.

Reality was the dragon that must be killed by the lover each time anew. And she was blind to her own crime against love, corroding it with the acid of her own doubt.

But a greater obstacle she had yet to encounter.

At the first meeting the dream of their encounter eclipsed the surrounding regions of their lives and isolated them together as inside a cocoon of silk and sensation. It gave them the illusion that each was the center of the other's existence.

No matter how exigent was the demand made upon Stella by her screen work, she always overthrew every obstacle in favor of love. She broke contracts easily, sailed at a moment's notice, and no pursuit of fame could interfere with the course of love. This willingness to sacrifice external achievements or success to love was typically feminine but she expected Bruno to behave in the same manner.

But he was a person who could only swim in the ocean of love if his moorings were maintained, the long established moorings of marriage and children. The stately house of permanency and continuity that was his home, built around his role in the world, built on peace and faith, with the smile of his wife which had become for him the smile of his mother—this edifice made out of the other components of his nature, his need for a haven, for children who were as his brothers had been, for a wife who was that which his mother had been. He could not throw over all these creations and possessions of his day for a night's dream, and Stella was that night's dream, all impermanency, vanishing and returning only with the night.

She, the homeless one, could not respect that which he respected. He, by respecting the established, felt free of guilt. He was paying his debt of honor and he was free, free to adore her, free to dream her. This did not appease her. Nor the simplicity with which he explained that he could not tear from its foundation the human home, with the children and the wife whom he protected. He could only love and live in peace if he fulfilled his promises to what he had created.

It was not that Stella wanted the wife's role or place. She knew deep down how unfitted she was for this role and to that side of his nature. It was merely that she could not share a love without the feeling that into this region of Bruno's being she did not care to enter, that there lay there a danger of death to their relationship. For her, any opening, any unconquered region contained the hidden enemy, the seed of death, the possible destroyer. Only absolute possession calmed her fear.

He was at peace with his conscience and therefore he feared no punishment for the joys she gave him. It was a condition of his nature. Because he had not destroyed or displaced, he felt he would not be destroyed or displaced and he could give his faith and joy to the dream. Her anguish and fears were inexplicable to him. For him there was no enemy ready to spring at her from the calm of his house.

If a telephone call or some emergency at home tore him away from her, for her it was abandon, and the end of love. If the time were shortened it signified a diminishing of love. If a choice were to be made she felt that he would choose his wife and children against her. None of these fatalistic signs were visible to him.

This hotel room was for him the symbol of the freedom of their love, the voyage, the exploration, the unknown, the restlessness that could be shared together; the surprises, the marvelously formless and bodiless and houseless freedom of this world created by two people in a hotel room. It was outside of the known, the familiar, and built only out of intensity, the present, with the great exalted beauty of the changing, the fluctuating, the dangerous and unmoored...

Would she destroy this world created only on the fragrance of a voice, enhanced by intermittent disappearances? The privilege of traveling further into space and wonder because free of ballast? This marvelous world patterned only according to the irregularities of a dream, with its dark abysms in between, its change and flow and capriciousness?

Bruno clung desperately to the beauty, to the preciousness of this essence, pure because it was an essence. And for him even less threatened by death than his first love had been by the development of daily life. (For at a certain moment the face of his wife was no longer the face of a dream but became the face of his mother. At the same moment as the dream died, his home became the human and dreamless home of his boyhood, his children became the playmates of his adolescence.)

And Stella, when he explained this, knew the truth of it, yet she was the victim of a stronger demon, a demon of doubt blindly seeking visible proofs, the proofs of the love in reality which would most effectively destroy the dream. For passion usually has the instinctive wisdom to evade the test of human life together which is only possible to love. For Stella, because of her doubt, so desperately in need of reassurance, if he surrendered all to her it would mean that he was giving all his total love to their dream, whereas to him surrendering all meant giving Stella a lesser self (since passion was the love of the dreamed self and not the reality).

There was in this hotel room stronger proof of the strength of the dream, and Stella demanded proofs of its human reality and in so doing exposed its incompleteness, and hastened its end (Pandora's box).

Stella! he always cried out as he entered, enveloping her in the fervor of his voice.

Stella! he repeated, to express how she filled his being and overflowed within him to fill the room with this name which filled him.

He had a way of saying it which was like crowning her the favorite. He made of each encounter such a rounded, complete experience, charged with the violence of a great hunger. Not having seen her upon awakening, not having helped to free her of the cocoon web of the night, not having shared her first contact with daylight, her first meal, the inception of her moods for that day, the first intentions and plans for action, he felt all the more impelled to catch her at the moment of the climax, to join her at the culmination. The lost, missed moments of life together, the lost, missed gestures, were thrown in desperation to feed the bonfire known only to foreshortened lives.

Because of all this that was lost around the love, the hotel room became the island, the poem and the paradise, because of all that was torn away, and sunk away.

The miracle of intensification.

Yet Stella asked, mutely, with every gasp of doubt and anguish: Let us live together (as if human life would give a certitude!). And he answered, mutely, with every act of faith: Let us dream together!

He arrived each day with new eyes. Undimmed by familiarity. New eyes for the woman he had not seen enough. New, intense, deeply seeing eyes, seeing her in her entirety each time like a new person.

As he did not see the process of her walking towards their island, dressing for it, resting for it, fighting off the inundation and demands of other people to reach him, her presence seemed like an apparition, and he had to repossess her, because apparitions tend to disappear as they come, by routes unknown, into countries unknown.

There was between them this knowledge of the missing dimension and the need to recapture the lost terrain, to play the emotional detective for the lost fragments of the selves which had lived alone, as separate pieces, in a great effort to bring them all together into one again.

At his wrists the hair showed brilliant gold.

Hers dark and straight, and his curled, so that at times it seemed it was his hair which enveloped her, it was his desire which had the feminine sinuosities to espouse and cling, while hers was rigid.

It was he who surrounded and enveloped her, as his curled hair wound around the straightness of hers, and how sweet this had been in her distress and her chaos. She touched his wrists always in wonder; as if to ascertain his presence, because the joyousness of his coloring delighted her, because the smoothness of his movements was a preliminary to their accord and rhythms. Their movements toward each other were symphonic and preordained her divination of his moods and his of hers synchronized their movements like those of a dance. There were days when she felt small and weak, and he then increased his stature to receive and shelter her, and his arms and body seemed a fortress, and there were days when he was in need of her strength, days when their mouths transmitted all the fevers and hungers, days when frenzy called for an abandon of the whole body. Days when the caresses were a drug, or a symphony, or small secret duets and duels, or vast complex veilings which neither could entirely tear apart, and there were secrets, and resistances, and frenzies, and again dissolutions from which it seemed as if neither could ever return to the possession of his independence.

There was always this mingling of hairs, which later in the bath she would tenderly separate from hers, laying the tendrils before her like the signs of the calendar of their love, the unwitherable flowers of their caresses.

While he was there, melted, by his eyes, his voice, sheltered in his tallness, encompassed by his attentiveness, she was joyous. But when he was gone, and so entirely gone that she was forbidden to write him or telephone him, that she had in reality no way to reach him, touch him, call him back, then she became possessed again with this frenzy against barriers, against limitations, against forbidden regions. To have touched the point of fire in him was not enough. To be his secret dream, his secret passion. She must ravage and conquer the absolute, for the sake of love. Not knowing that she was at this moment the enemy of love, its executioner.

Once he stood about to depart and she asked him: can't you stay for the whole night? And he shook his head sadly, his blue eyes no longer joyous, but blurred. This firmness with which she thought he was defending the rights of his wife, and with which in reality he only defended the equilibrium of his scrupulous soul, appeared to her like a flaw in the love.

If Stella felt an obstacle placed before one of her wishes such as her wish that Bruno should stay the whole night with her when it was utterly impossible for him to do so, this obstacle, no matter of what nature, became the symbol of a battle she must win or else consider herself destroyed.

She did not pause to ask herself the reasons for the refusal, or to consider the validity of these reasons, the claims to which others may have had a right. The refusal represented for her the failure to obtain a proof of love. The removal of this obstacle became a matter of life and death, because for her it balanced success or failure, abandon or treachery, triumph or power.

The small refusal, based on an altogether separate reason, unrelated to Stella, became the very symbol of her inner sense of frustration, and the effort to overcome it the very symbol of her salvation.

If she could bend the will and decision of Bruno, it meant that Bruno loved her. If not, it meant Bruno did not love her. The test was as devoid of real meaning as the tearing of leaves on a flower done by superstitious lovers who place their destiny in the mathematics of coincidence or accident.

And Stella, regardless of the cause, became suddenly blind to the feelings of everyone else as only sick people can become blind. She became completely isolated in this purely personal drama of a refusal she could not accept and could not see in any other light but that of a personal offense to her. A love that could not overcome all obstacles (as in the myths and legends of romantic ages) was not a love at all.

(This small favor she demanded took on the proportions of the ancient holocausts demanded by the mystics as proofs of devotion.)

She had reached the exaggeration, known to the emotionally unstable, of considering every small act as an absolute proof of love or hatred, and demanding of the faithful an absolute surrender. In every small act of yielding Stella accumulated defenses against the inundating flood of doubts. The doubt devoured her faster than she could gather external proofs of reassurance, and so the love given her was not a free love but a love that must accumulate votive offerings like those made by the primitives to their jealous gods. There must be every day the renewal of candles, foods and precious gifts, incense and sacrifice and if necessary (and it was always necessary to the neurotic) the sacrifice of human life. Every human being who fell under her spell became not the lover, but the day and night nurse to this sickness, this unfillable longing, this ravenous devourer of human happiness.

You won't stay all night?

The muted, inarticulate despair these few words contained. The unheard, unnoticed, unregistered cry of loneliness which arises from human beings. And not a loneliness which could be appeased with one night, or with a thousand nights, or with a lifetime, or with a marriage. A loneliness that human beings could not fill. For it came from her separation from human beings. She felt her separation from human beings and believed the lover alone could destroy it.

The doubt and fear which accompanied this question made her stand apart like some unbending god of ancient rituals watching for this accumulation of proofs, the faithful offering food, blood and their very lives. And still the doubt was there for these were but external proofs and they proved nothing. They could not give her back her faith.

The word penetrated Stella's being as if someone had uttered for the first time the name of her enemy, until then unknown to her.

Doubt. She turned this word in the palm of her dreaming hands, like some tiny hieroglyph with meaning on four sides.

From some little tunnel of obscure sensations there came almost imperceptible signs of agitation.

She packed hurriedly, crushing the hat with the feather, breaking his presents.

Driving fast in her very large, too large, her movie star car, driving fast, too fast away from pain, the water obscured her vision of the road and she set the wipers in motion. But it was not rain that clouded the windows.

In her movie star apartment there was a small turning stairway like that of a lighthouse leading to her bedroom, which was watched by a tall window of square glass bricks. These shone like a quartz cave at night. It was the prism which threw her vision back into seclusion again, into the wall of the self.

It was the window of the solitary cell of the neurotic.

One night when Bruno had written her that he would telephone her that night (he had been banished once again, and once again had tried to reconquer her) because he sensed that his voice might accomplish what his note failed to do, at the moment when she knew he would telephone, she installed a long concerto on the phonograph and climbed the little stairway and sat on the step.

No sooner did the concerto begin to spin than the telephone rung imperatively.

Stella allowed the music to produce its counter-witchcraft. Against the mechanical demand of the telephone, the music spiraled upward like a mystical skyscraper, and triumphed. The telephone was silenced.

But this was only the first bout. She climbed another step of the stairway and sat under the quartz window, wondering if the music would help her ascension away from the warmth of Bruno's voice.

In the music there was a parallel to the conflict which disturbed her. Within the concerto too the feminine and the masculine elements were interacting. The trombone, with its assertions, and the flute, with its sinuosities. In this transparent battle the trombone, in Stella's ears and perhaps because of her mood, had a tone of defiance which was almost grotesque. In her present mood the masculine instrument would appear as a caricature!

And as for the flute, it was so easily victimized and overpowered. But it triumphed ultimately because it left an echo. Long after the trombone had had its say, the flute continued its mischievous, insistent tremolos.

The telephone rang again. Stella moved a step farther up the stairs. She needed the stairs, the window, the concerto, to help her reach an inaccessible region where the phone might ring as any mechanical instrument, without reverberating in her being. If the ringing of the telephone had caused the smallest tremor through her nerves (as the voice of Bruno did) she was lost. Fortunate for her that the trombone was a caricature of masculinity, that it was an inflated trombone, drowning the sound of the telephone. So she smiled one of her eerie smiles, pixen and vixen too, at the masculine pretensions. Fortunate for her that the flute persisted in its delicate undulations, and that not once in the concerto did they marry but played in constant opposition to each other throughout.

The telephone rang again, with a dead, mechanical persistence and no charm, while the music seemed to be pleading for a subtlety and emotional strength which Bruno was incapable of rivaling. The music alone was capable of climbing those stairways of detachment, of breaking like the waves of disturbed ocean at her feet, breaking there and foaming but without the power to suck her back into the life with Bruno and into the undertows of suffering.

She lay in the darkness of her white satin bedroom, the mirrors throwing aureoles of false moonlight, the rows of perfume bottles creating false suspended gardens.

The mattress, the blankets, the sheets had a lightness like her own. They were made of the invisible material which had once been pawned off on a gullible king. They were made of air, or else she had selected them out of familiar, weighty materials and then touched them with her aerial hands. (So many moments when her reality was questionable—the time she leaped out of her immense automobile, and there on the vast leather seat lay such a diminutive pocketbook as no woman could actually use, the pocketbook of a midget. Or the time she turned the wheel with two fingers. There is a lightness which belongs to other races, the race of ballet dancers.)

Whoever touched Stella was left with the tactile memory of down and bonelessness, as after touching the most delicate of Persian cats.

Now lying in the dark, neither the softness of the room nor its whiteness could exorcise the pain she felt.

Some word was trying to come to the surface of her being. Some word had sought all day to pierce through like an arrow the formless, inchoate mass of incidents of her life. The geological layers of her experience, the accumulated faces, scenes, words and dreams. One word was being churned to the surface of all this torment. It was as if she were going to name her greatest enemy. But she was struggling with the fear we have of naming that enemy. For what crystallized simultaneously with the name of the enemy was an emotion of helplessness against him! What good was naming it if one could not destroy it and free one's self? This feeling, stronger than the desire to see the face of the enemy, almost drowned the insistent word into oblivion again.

What Stella whispered in the dark with her foreign accent enhancing strongly, markedly the cruelty of the sound was:

ma soch ism

Soch! Och! It was the och which stood out, not ma or ism but the och! which was like some primitive exclamation of pain. Am, am I, am I, am I, am I, whispered Stella, am I a masochist?

She knew nothing about the word except its current meaning: "voluntary seeking of pain." She could go no further into her exploration of the confused pattern of her life and detect the origin of the suffering. She could not, alone, catch the inception of the pattern, and therefore gain power over this enemy. The night could not bring her one step nearer to freedom...

A few hours later she watched on the screen the story of the Atlantis accompanied by the music of Stravinski.

First came a scene like a Paul Klee, wavering and humid, delicate and full of vibrations. The blue, the green, the violet were fused in tonalities which resembled her feeling, all fused together and so difficult to unravel. She responded with her answering blood rhythms, and with the same sense she always had of herself possessing a very small sea, something which received and moved responsively in rhythm. As if every tiny cell were not separated by membranes, as if she were not made of separate nerves, sinews, blood vessels, but one total fluid component which could flow into others, divine their feelings, and flow back again into itself, a component which could be easily moved and penetrated by others like water, like the sea.

When she saw the Paul Klee scene on the screen she instantly dissolved. There was no more Stella, but a fluid component participating at the birth of the world. The paradise of water and softness.

But upon this scene came the most unexpected and terrifying explosion, the explosion of the earth being formed, broken, reformed and broken anew into its familiar shape.

This explosion Stella was familiar with and had expected. It reverberated in her with unexpected violence. As if she had already lived it.

Where had she experienced before this total annihilation of a blue, green and violet paradise, a paradise of welded cells in a perpetual flow and motion, that this should seem like the second one, and bring about such a painful, physical memory of disruption?

As the explosions came, once, twice, thrice, the peace was shattered and blackened, the colors vanished, the earth muddied the water, the annihilation seemed total.

The earth reformed itself. The water cleared. The colors returned. A continent was born above.

In Stella the echo touched a very old, forgotten region. Through layers and layers of time she gazed at an image made small by the distance: a small figure. It is her childhood, with its small scenery, small climate, small atmosphere. Stella was born during the war. But for the diminutive figure of the child the war between parents—all division and separation—was as great as the world war. The being, small and helpless, was torn asunder by the giant figures of mythical parents striving and dividing. Then it was nations striving and dividing. The sorrow was transferred, enlarged. But it was the same sorrow: it was the discovery of hatred, violence, hostility. It was the dark face of the world, which no childhood was ever prepared to receive. In the diminutive and fragile vessel of childhood lies the paradise that must be destroyed by explosions, so that the earth may be created anew. But the first impact of hatred and destruction upon the child is sometimes too great a burden on its innocence. The being is sundered as the earth is by earthquakes, as the soul cracks under violence and hatred. Paradise (the scene of Paul Klee) was from the first intended to be swallowed by the darkness.

As Stella felt the explosions, through the microscope of her emotions carried backwards, she saw the fragments of the dispersed and sundered being. Every little piece now with a separate life. Occasionally, like mercury, they fused, but they remained elusive and unstable. Corroding in the separateness.

Faith and love united her to human beings as a child. She was known to have walked the streets at the age of six inviting all the passersby to a party at her home. She hailed carriages and asked the driver to drive "to where there were many people."

The first explosion. The beginning of the world. The beginning of a pattern, the beginning of a form, a destiny, a character. Something which always eludes the scientists, the tabulators, the detectives. We catch a glimpse of it, like this, through the turmoil of the blood which remembers the seismographic shocks.

Stella could not remember what she saw in the mirror as a child. Perhaps a child never looks at the mirror. Perhaps a child, like a cat, is so much inside of itself it does not see itself in the mirror. She sees a child. The child does not remember what he looks like.

Later she remembered what she looked like. But when she looked at photographs of herself at one, two, three, four, five years, she did not recognize herself. The child is one. At one with himself. Never outside of himself.

She could remember what she did, but not the reflection of what she did. No reflections. Six years old. Seven years old. Eight years old. Eleven. No image. No reflection. But feeling.

In the mirror there never appeared a child. The first mirror had a frame of white wood. In it there was no Stella. A girl of fourteen portraying Joan of Arc, La Dame Aux Camélias, Peri Banu, Carlota, Electra.

No Stella, but a disguised actress multiplied into many personages. Was it in these games that she had lost her vision of her true self? Could she only win it again by acting? Was that why now she refused every role—every role that did not contain at least one aspect of herself? But because they contained only one aspect of herself they only emphasized the dismemberment. She would get hold of one aspect, and not of the rest. The rest remained unlived.

The first mirror in which the self appears is very large, inlaid in a brown wood wall. Next to it a window pours down so strong a light that the rest of the room is in complete darkness, and the image of the girl who approaches the mirror is brought into luminous relief. It is the first spotlight, actually, the first aureole of lighting, bringing her into relief, but in a state of humiliation. She is looking at her dress, a dress of shiny, worn, dark blue serge which has been fixed up for her out of an old one belonging to a cousin. It does not fit her. It is meager, it looks poor and shrunk. The girl looks at the blue dress with shame.

It is the day she has been told at school that she is gifted for acting. They had come purposely into the class to tell her. She who was always quiet and did not wish to be noticed, was told to come and speak to the Drama teacher before everyone, and to hear the compliment on her first performance. And the joy, the dazzling joy which first struck her was instantly killed by the awareness of the dress. She did not want to get up, to be noticed. She was ashamed of the meager dress, its worn, its orphan air.

She can only step out of this image, this dress, this humiliation by becoming someone else. She becomes Melisande, Sarah Bernhardt, Faust's Marguerite, La Dame Aux Camélias, Thais. She is decomposed before the mirror into a hundred personages, and recomposed into paleness, immobility and silence.

She will never wear again the shrunken worn serge cast-off dress, but she will often wear again this mood, this feeling of being misrepresented, misunderstood, of a false appearance, of an ugly disguise. She was called and made visible to all, out of her shyness and withdrawal, and what was made visible was a girl dressed like an orphan and not in the costume of wonder which befitted her.

She rejects all the plays. Because they cannot contain her. She wants to walk into her own self, truly presented, truly revealed. She wants to act only herself. She is no longer an actress willing to disguise herself. She is a woman who has lost herself and feels she can recover it by acting this self. But who knows her? What playwright knows her? Not the men who loved her. She cannot tell them. She is lost herself. All that she says about herself is false. She is misleading and misled. No one will admit blindness.

No one who does not have a white cane, or a seeing eye dog will admit blindness. Yet there is no blindness or deafness as strong as that which takes place within the emotional self.

Seeing has to do with awareness, the clarity of the senses is linked to the spiritual vision, to understanding. One can look back upon a certain scene of life and see only a part of the truth. The characters of those we live with appear with entire aspects missing, like the missing arms or legs of unearthed statues. Later, a deeper insight, a deeper experience will add the missing aspects to the past scene, to the lost character only partially seen and felt. Still later another will appear. So that with time, and with time and awareness only, the scene and the person become complete, fully heard and fully seen.

Inside of the being there is a defective mirror, a mirror distorted by the fog of solitude, of shyness, by the climate inside of this particular being. It is a personal mirror, lodged in every subjective, interiorized form of life.

Stella received a letter from Laura, her father's second wife. "Come immediately. I am divorcing your father."

Her father was an actor. In Warsaw he had achieved fame and adulation. He had remained youthful and the lover of all women. Stella's mother, whose love for him had encompassed more than the man, permitted him great freedom. It was not his extravagant use of this freedom which had killed her feeling for him, but his inability to make her feel at the center of his life, feel that no matter what his peripheries she remained at the center. In exchange for her self-forgetfulness he had not been able to give anything, only to take. He had exploited the goodness, the largeness, the voluntary blindness. He had dipped into the immense reservoir of her love without returning to it an equal flow of tenderness, and so it had dried. The boundlessness of her love was to him merely an encouragement of his irresponsibility. He thought it could be used infinitely, not knowing that even an infinite love needed nourishment and fecundation; that no love was ever self-sustaining, self-propelling, self-renewing.

And then one day her love died. For twenty years she had nourished it out of her own substance, and then it died. His selfishness withered it. And he was surprised. Immensely surprised, as if she had betrayed him.

She had left with Stella. And another woman had come, younger, a disciple of his, who had taken up the burden of being the lover alone. Stella knew the generosity of the second wife, the devotion. She knew how deeply her father must have used this reservoir to empty it. How deeply set his pattern of taking without giving. Again the woman's love was emptied, burnt out.

"He threatens to commit suicide," wrote Laura, "but I do not believe it." Stella did not believe it either. He loved himself too well.

Stella's father met her at the station. In his physical appearance there was clearly manifested the fact that he was not a man related to others but an island. In his impeccable dress there was a touch of finite contours. His clothes were of an insulating material. Whatever they were made of, they gave the impression of being different materials from other people's, that the well pressed lines were not intended to be disturbed by human hands. It was sterilized elegance conveying his uniqueness, and his perfectionism. If his clothes had not carried this water-repellent, feeling-repellent quality of perfection, his eyes would have accomplished this with their expression of the island. Distinctly, the person who moved toward him was an invader, the ship which entered this harbor was an enemy, the human being who approached him was violating the desire of islands to remain islands. His eyes were isolated. They created no warm bridges between them and other eyes. They flashed no signal of welcome, no light of response, and above all they remained as closed as a glass door.

He wanted Stella to plead with Laura. "Laura suspects me of having an affair with a singer. She has never minded before. And this time it happens not to be true. I dislike being...exiled unjustly. I cannot bear false accusations. Why does she mind now? I can't understand. Please go and tell her I will spend the rest of my life making her happy. Tell her I am heartbroken." (As he said these words he took out his silver cigarette case and noticing a small clouded spot on it he carefully polished it with his handkerchief.) "I've been unconscious. I didn't know she minded. Tell Laura I had nothing to do with this woman. She is too fat."

"But if you had," said Stella, "wouldn't it be better to be truthful this time? She is angry. She will hate a lie now more than anything. Why aren't you sincere with her? She may have proofs."

At the word proof his neat, alert head perked, cool, collected, cautious, and he said: "What proofs? She can't have proofs. I was careful..."

He is still lying, thought Stella. He is incurable.

She visited Laura, who was small and childlike. She was like a child who had taken on a maternal role in a game, and found it beyond her strength. Yet she had played this role for ten years. Almost like a saint, the way she had closed her eyes to all his adventures, the way she had sought to preserve their life together. Her eyes always believing, diminishing the importance of his escapades, disregarding gossip, blaming the women more often than him.

Today as she received Stella, for whom she had always had a strong affection, these same believing eyes were changed. There is nothing clearer than the mark of a wound in believing eyes. It shows clear and sharp, the eyes are lacerated, they seem about to dissolve with pain. The soft faith was gone. And Stella knew instantly that her pleading was doomed.

"My father's unfaithfulness meant nothing. He always loved you above all others. He was light, but his deep love was for you. He was irresponsible, and you were too good to him, you never rebelled."

But Laura defended her attitude: "I am that kind of person. I have great faith, great indulgence, great love. For that reason if someone takes advantage of this I feel betrayed and I cannot forgive. I have warned him gently. I was not ill over his infidelities, but over his indelicacies. I wanted to die. I hoped he would be less obvious, less insolent. But now it is irrevocable. When I added up all his selfish remarks, his reckless gestures, the expression of annoyance on his face when I was ill, his indifferences to my sadness, I cannot believe he ever loved me. He told me such impossible stories that he must have had a very poor idea of my judgment. Until now my love was strong enough to blind me...but now, understand me, Stella, I see everything. I remember words of his he uttered the very first day. The kind of unfaithfulness women can forgive is not the kind your father was guilty of. He was not unfaithful by his interest in other women, but he betrayed what we had together: he abandoned me spiritually and emotionally. He did not feel for me. Another thing I cannot forgive him. He was not a natural man, but he was posing as an ideal being. He covered acts which were completely selfish under a coat of altruism. He even embroidered so much on this role of ideal being that I had all the time the deep instinct that I was being cheated, that I was living with a man who was acting. This I can't forgive. Even today he continues to lie. I have definite proofs. They fell into my hands. I didn't want them. And then he was not content with having his mistress live near me, he still wanted me to invite her to my house, he even taunted me for not liking her, not fraternizing with her. Let him cry now. I have cried for ten years. I know he won't kill himself. He is acting. He loves himself too much. Let him now measure the strength of this love he destroyed. I feel nothing. Nothing. He has killed my love so completely I do not even suffer. I never saw a man who could kill a love so completely. I say a man! I often think he was a child, he was as irresponsible as a child. He was a child and I became a mother and that is why I forgave him everything. Only a mother forgives everything. The child, of course, doesn't know when he is hurting the mother. He does not know when she is tired, sick; he does nothing for her. He takes it for granted that she is willing to die for him. The child is passive, yielding, and accepts everything, giving nothing in return but affection. If the mother weeps he will throw his arms around her and then he will go out and do exactly what caused her to weep. The child never thinks of the mother except as the all-giver, the all-forgiving, the indefatigable love. So I let my husband be the child... But he, Stella, he was not even tender like a child, he did not give me even the kind of love a child has for the mother. There was no tenderness in him!" And she wept. (He had not wept.)

As Stella watched her she knew the suffering had been too great and that Laura's love was absolutely broken.

When she returned to her father carrying the word "irrevocable" to him, her father exclaimed: "What happened to Laura? Such a meek, resigned, patient, angelical woman. A little girl, full of innocence and indulgence. And then this madness..."

He did not ask himself, he had never asked himself, what he must have done to destroy such resignation, such innocence, such indulgence. He said: "Let's look at our house for the last time."

Until now it had been their house. But in reality the house belonged to Laura and she asked her husband not to enter it again, to make a list of his belongings and she would have them sent to him.

They stood together before the house and looked up at the window of his room: "I will never see my room again. It's incredible. My books are still in there, my photographs, my clothes, my scrap books, and I..."

At the very moment they stood there a slight earthquake had been registered in Warsaw. At that very moment when her father's life was shaken by the earthquake of a woman's rebellion, when he was losing love, protection, faithfulness, luxury, faith. His whole life disrupted in a moment of feminine rebellion. Earth and the woman, and this sudden rebellion. On the insensitive instrument of his egoism no sign had been registered of this coming disruption.

As he stood there looking at his house for the last time the bowels of the earth shook. Laura was quietly weeping while his life cracked open and all the lovingly collected possessions fell into an abysm. The earth opened under his perpetually dancing feet, his waltzes of courtship, his contrapuntal love scenes.

In one instant it swallowed the colorful ballet of his lies, his pointed foot evasions, his vaporous escapes, the stage lights and halos with which he surrounded and disguised his conquests and appetites. Everything was destroyed in the tumult. The earth's anger at his lightness, his audacities, his leaps over reality, his escapes. His house cracked open and through the fissures fell his rare books, his collection of paintings, his press notices, the gifts from his admirers.

But before this happened the earth had given him so many warnings. How many times had he not seen the glances of pain in Laura's eyes, how many times had he overlooked her loneliness, how many times had he pretended not to hear the quiet weeping from her room, how many times had he failed in ordinary tenderness...before the revolt.

"And if I get sick," he said, walking away from his house, "who will take care of me? If only I could keep the maid Lucille. She was wonderful. There never was anyone like her. She was the only one who knew how to press my summer suits. With her all my problems would be solved. She was silent and never disturbed me and she never left the house. Now I don't know if I will be able to afford her. Because if I have her it will mean I will have to have two maids. Yes, two, because Lucille is not a good enough cook."

Sadly he walked down the street with Stella's arm under his. And then he added; "Now that I won't have the car any more, I will miss the Fête des Narcisses at Montreux, and I am sure I would have got the prize this year."

While he balanced himself on the tight rope of his delusions, Stella had no fear for him. He could see no connection between his behavior and Laura's rebellion. He could not see how the most trivial remarks and incidents could accumulate and form a web to trap him. He did not remember the trivial remark he made to the maid who was devotedly embroidering a nightgown for Laura during one of her illnesses. He had stood on the threshold watching and then said with one of his characteristic pirouettes: "I know someone on whom this nightgown would look more beautiful..." This had angered the loyalty of the maid and later influenced her to crystallize the proofs against him. Everyone around him had taken the side of the human being he overlooked because they could see so obviously the enormous disproportion between her behavior towards him and his towards her. The greater her love, almost, the greater had grown his irresponsibility and devaluation of this love.

What Stella feared was a moment of lucidity, when he might see that it was not the superficial aspect of his life which had destroyed its basic foundation, but his disregard of and undermining of the foundation.

For the moment he kept himself balanced on his tight-rope.

In fact he was intently busy placing himself back on a pedestal. He was now the victim of an unreasonable woman. Think of a woman who bears up with a man for ten years, and then when he is about to grow old, about to grow wise and sedentary, about to resign from his lover's career, then she revolts and leaves him alone. What absolute illogicality!

"For now," he said, "I am becoming a little tired of my love affairs. I do not have the same enthusiasms."

After a moment of walking in silence he added: "But I have you, Stella."

The three loves of his life. And Stella could not say what she felt: "You killed my love too."

Yet at this very moment she remembered when it happened. She was then a little girl of twelve. Her father and mother were separated and lived in opposite sections of the city. Once a week Stella's mother allowed her to visit her father. Once a week she was plunged from an atmosphere of poverty and struggle to one of luxury and indolence. Such a violent contrast that it came with a shock of pain.

Once when she was calling on her father she saw Laura there for the first time. She heard Laura laugh. She saw her tiny figure submerged in furs and smelled her perfume. She could not see her, as a woman. She seemed to her another little girl. A little girl dressed and hairdressed like a woman, but laughing, and believing and natural. She felt warmly towards her, did not remember that she was the one replacing her mother, that her mother would expect her to hate the intruder. Even to this child of twelve it was clear that it was Laura who needed the protection, that she was not the conqueror. That in the suave, charming, enchanting manners of her actor father there lurked many dangers for human beings, for the vulnerable ones especially. The same danger as had struck her mother and herself: danger of abandon and loneliness.

Laura too was looking at Stella with affection. Then she whispered to her father and Stella with her abnormally sensitive hearing caught the last words, "buy her stockings."

(From then on it was Laura who assumed all her father's sentimental obligations, it was Laura who sent gifts to his mother, to her later.)

The father and daughter went off together through the most beautiful shopping streets of Warsaw. She had become acutely aware of her mended stockings now that Laura had noticed them. Her father would be ashamed of walking with her. But he did not seem concerned. He was walking now with the famous grace that the stage had so much enhanced, a grace which made it appear that when he bowed, or kissed a hand, or spoke a compliment, he was doing it with his whole soul. It gave to his courtships such a romantic totality that a mere bow over a woman's hand took on the air of a ceremony in which he laid his life at her feet.

He entered a luxurious cane shop. He had the finest canes spread before him. He selected the most precious of all woods, and the most delicately carved. He asked Stella for her approval. He emptied his pocketbook, saying: "I can still take you home in a cab." And he took her home in a cab. With his new, burnished cane he pointed out Stella's drab house to the cabman. With a gesture of romantic devotion, as if he were laying a red carpet under her feet, he delivered her to her poverty, to the aggressions of creditors, to the anxieties, the humiliations, the corroding pain of everyday want.

Today she was not walking with her father in mended stockings. But she was riding in taxis like an ambassador between Laura and her father. Laura sent her father an intricate Venetian vase on an incredibly slender stem which could not be entrusted to the moving van. Stella was holding it in one hand, her muff in the other, and at her feet lay packages of old love letters. And her father sent her back in the same taxi with a locket, a ring, photographs, letters.

Stella attended the thousandth performance of a play called *The Orphan* in which her father starred.

"*The Orphan*," he said, "that suits me well now, that is how I feel, abandoned by Laura." And speaking of the orphan, he the orphan, the abandoned one, the victim for the first time, he wept. (But not over Laura's pain, or broken faith.)

In the middle of the performance, when he was sitting in an armchair and speaking, suddenly his arms fell, and he sat stiffly back. It was so swift, so brusque, that he looked like a broken marionette. No man could break this way, so sharply, so absolutely.

People rushed on the stage. "It's a heart attack," said the doctor.

Stella accompanied him to his house. He lay rigid as in death.

She could not weep. For him, yes, for his sadness. Not for her father. All links were broken. But a man, yes, any man who suffered. The darling of women. White hair and elegance. Solitude. All the women around him and none near enough. Stella unable to move nearer, because none could move nearer to him. He barred the way with his self-love. His self-love isolated him. Self-love the watchman, barring all entrance, all communication. One could not console him. He was dying because with the end of luxury, protection, of his role, his life ends. He took all his sustenance from woman but he never knew it.

It was not Stella who killed him. She had not been the one to say: you killed my love.

Pity convulsed her, but she could do nothing. He was fulfilling his destiny. He had sought only his pleasure. He was dying alone on the stage of self-pity.

But when he was lying down on a bench in the dressing room, his collar for the first time carelessly open, the fat doctor listening to his heart (breaking with self-pity), so slender, so stylized, so meticulously chiseled, like an effigy, a burning pity choked her.

Someone whose every word she had hated, whose every act and thought she condemned, whose every mannerism was false, every gesture a role, yet because this figure lay on a couch dying of self-pity, lay with his eyes closed in a supreme comedian's act, Stella could love and pity again. Does the love of the father never die, even when it is buried a million times under stronger loves, even when she had looked at him without illusion? The figure, the slenderness of the body, the fineness of its form, still escaped from the dark tomb of buried love and was alive, because he had so artfully lain down like a victim, fainted before a thousand people, because he had been an actor until the end; as for Laura, and Stella's mother—no one had seen or heard them weep.

A fragile Stella, lying in her ivory satin bed, amongst mirrors.

Her eloquent body can speak out all the feelings in the language of the dance. Now her hands lie tired on her knees, tired and defeated.

Her dance is perpetually broken by the wounds of love.

In her white nightgown she does not look like an enchantress but like an orphan.

In her white nightgown she runs out of her room downstairs to spare the servants an added fatigue, she the exhausted one.

Her body and face so animated that they do not seem made of flesh, but like antennae, breath, nerve.

Delicate, she lies back like a tired child, but so knowing. Bright, she speaks as she feels, always.

Unreal—her voice vanishes to a whisper, as if she herself were going to vanish and one must hold one's breath to hear her.

Oriental, she takes the pose of the Bali dancers. Her head always free from her body like the bird's head so free from its fragile stem.

The language of her hands. As they curve, leap, circle, trepidate, one fears they will always end clasped in a prayer that no one should hurt her.

No role could contain her intensity.

She gave off such a brilliance in acting it was unbearable. Too great an exaltation for the role, which breaks like too small a vessel. Too great a warmth. The role was dwarfed, was twisted and lost. When she begged for the roles which could contain this intensity they were denied her.

Off the stage she continued the same mischievous wrinkling of her little nose, the same entranced eyes, the child's ease and grace and impulsiveness (in the most pompous restaurant of the city she reached out towards a passing silver tray carried by a pompous waiter and stole a fried potato).

The intensity made the incidents she portrayed seem inadequate and small. There was a glow from so deep a source of feeling that it drowned the mediocre personages of the Hollywood gallery.

She ate like a child, avidly, as if in fear that it would be taken away from her, forbidden her by some parent. Like the child, she had no coquetry. She was unconscious of her tangled hair and liked her face washed of make-up. If someone made love to her while she still carried the weight of the wax on her eyelashes, if someone made love to her artificially exaggerated eyelashes, she was offended, as if by a betrayal.

She was a child carrying a very old soul and burdened with it, and wishing to deposit it in some great and passionate role. In Joan of Arc, or Marie Bashkirtseff...or Rejane, or Eleonora Duse.

There are those who disguise themselves, like Stella's father, who disguised himself and acted what he was not. But Stella only wanted to transform and enlarge herself and wanted to act only what she felt she was, or could be. And Hollywood would not let her. Hollywood had its sizes and standards of characters. One could not transgress certain limited standard sizes.

Philip. When Stella first saw him she laughed at him. He was too handsome. She laughed: "Such a wonderful Don Juan plumage," she said, and turned away. The Don Juan plumage had never charmed her.

But the next morning she saw him walking before her, holding himself as in a state of euphoria. She was still mocking his magnificence. But as he passed her, with a free, large, lyrical walk, he smiled at his companion so brilliant a smile, so wild, so sensual that she felt a pang. It was the smile of joy, a joy unknown to her.

At the same time she took a deeper breath into her lungs, as if the air had changed, become free of suffocating fogs, noxious poisons.

He was at first impenetrable to her, because the climate of lightness was anew to her.

She glided on the wings of his smile and his humor.

When she left him she heard the wind through the leaves like the very breath of life and again she breathed the large free altitudes where anguish cannot reach to suffocate.

She followed with him the capricious outlines of pure desire, trusting his smile.

The pursuit of joy. She possessed his smile, his eyes, his assurance. There are beings who come to one to the tune of music. She always expected him to appear in a sleigh, to the tune of sleigh bells. As a child she had heard sleigh bells and thought: they have the sound of joy. When she opened his cigarette case she expected the tinkling, light, joyous music of music boxes.

The absence of pain must mean it was not love but an enchantment. He came bringing joy and when he left she felt it was to go to his mysterious source and fetch some more. She waited without impatience and without fear. He was replenishing his supply. And every object he came in contact with was charged with the music that causes gayety to flower.

The knowledge that he was coming held her in a suspense of pleasure, that of a high, perilous trapeze leap. The long intervals between their meetings, the absence of love, made it like some brilliant trapeze incident, spangled, accompanied by music. She could admire their deftness and accuracy in keeping themselves outside of the circle of pain. The little seed of anguish to which she was so susceptible could not germinate in this atmosphere.

She laughed when he confessed to her his Don Juan fatigues, the exigencies of the role women imposed upon him. "Women keep such strict accounts and compare notes to see if you are always at the same level!" A weary Don Juan resting his head upon her knees. As if he knew that for her, awake or asleep, he was always the magician of joy.

He bore no resemblance to any other person or moment of her life. She felt as if she had escaped from a fatal, repetitive pattern.

One evening Stella entered a restaurant alone and was seated at the side of Bruno. So much time had passed and she felt herself in another world, yet the sight of Bruno caused her pain. He was deeply disturbed.

They sat together and lingered over the dinner.

At midnight Stella was to meet Philip. At eleven-thirty when she began to gather her coat, Bruno said: "Let me see you home."

Thinking of the possibility of an encounter between him and Philip (at midnight Philip was coming to her place), she showed hesitation. This hesitation caused Bruno such acute pain that he began to tremble. At all cost, she felt, he must not know... So she said quickly: "I'm not going home. I'm expected at some friends'. I forgot them when I saw you. But I promised to drop in."

"Can I take you there?"

She thought: if I mention friends he knows, he will come with me. She said: "Just put me in a taxi."

This reawakened his doubts. Again a look of pain crossed his face, and Stella was hurt by it, so she said hastily and spontaneously: "You can take me there. It's on East Eighty-ninth."

While he talked tenderly in the taxi, she thought desperately that she must find a house with two entrances, of which there are many on Fifth Avenue, but as she had never been on East Eighty-ninth Street, she wondered what she would find on the corner, perhaps a club, or a private house, or a Vanderbilt mansion.

From the taxi window she looked anxiously at the big, empty lot on the right and the private house on the left. Bruno's voice so vulnerable, her fear of hurting him. Time pressing, and Philip waiting for her before the door of her apartment. Then she signaled the driver to stop before an apartment house on the corner of Eighty-ninth Street and Madison Avenue.

Then she kissed Bruno lightly but was startled when he stepped out with her and dismissed the taxi. "I need a walk," he said.

First of all the front door was locked and she had to ring for the doorman whom she had not expected to see quite so soon. As she continued to walk into the hallway, he asked, "Who do you want to see? Where are you going?"

She could only say: "There is a door on Madison Avenue?" This aroused his suspicion and he answered roughly: "Why do you want to know? Who do you want to see?"

"Nobody," said Stella. "I just came in here because there was a man following me and annoying me. I thought I might walk through and slip out of the other entrance and get a cab and go home."

"That door is locked for the night. You can't go through there."

"Very well, then, I'll wait here for a while until that man leaves."

The doorman could see through the door the figure of Bruno walking back and forth. What had happened? Was he considering trying to find her? Did he believe she had no friends in this house and that he would catch her coming out again? Was he intuitively jealous and wondering if his intuition was right? Waiting. He waited there, smoking, walking in the snowy night. She was sitting in the red-carpeted hall, in a red plush chair, while the doorman paced up and down, and Bruno paced up and down before the house.

Thinking of Philip waiting for her, sitting there, heart beating and pounding, mind whirling.

She stood up and walked cautiously to the door and saw Bruno still walking in the cold.

Pain and laughter, pain out of the old love for Bruno, laughter from some inner, secret sense of playing with difficulties.

She said to the doorman: "That man is still there. Listen, I must get away somehow. You must do something for me."

Not too gallantly, he called the elevator boy. The elevator boy took her down the cellar, through a labyrinth of grey hallways. Another elevator boy joined them. She told them about the man who followed her, adding details to the story.

Passing trunks, valises, piles of newspapers, and rows and rows of garbage cans, then bowing their heads, they passed through one more alleyway, up some stairs and unlocked the back door.

One of the boys went for a taxi. She thanked them, with the gayety of a child in a game. They said it was a great pleasure and that New York was a hell of a place for a lady.

In the taxi she lay low on the seat so that Bruno could not see her as they passed Madison Avenue.

Philip was in a state of anxiety over her lateness.

She wanted to say: you are not the one who should be anxious! It is you I came back to! I struggled to get to you. But I'm here. And Bruno it is who is standing outside, waiting in the cold.

One day Philip asked her to wait for him in his apartment because his train had been delayed. (Before that he had always come to her.) For the first time he wanted to find her there, in his own home.

She had never entered his bedroom.

It was the first time she stepped out of the ambience he created for her by his words, stories, actions. The missing dimensions of Philip she knew must exist but he had known how to keep them invisible.

And now late at night, out of idleness, out of restlessness, fumbling very much like a blind person left for the first time to himself, she began to caress the objects he lived with, at first with a tenderness, because they were his, because she still expected them to emit a melody for her, to open up with playful surprises, to yield to her finger an immediate proof of love. But none of them emitted any sound resembling him... And slowly her fingers grew less caressing, grew awkward. Her fingers recognized objects made for or given by women. Her fingers recognized the hairpins of the wife, the powder box of the wife, the books with dedications by women, the photographs of women. The fingerprints on every object were women's fingerprints.

Then in the bedroom she stared at his dressing table. She stared at an immaculate and "familiar" set of silver toilet articles. It was not that Philip had a wife, and mistresses, and belonged to the public which awakened her. It was the silver toilet set on the dressing table, a replica of the aristocratic one which had charmed her childhood. Equally polished, equally symmetrically arranged. She was certain that if she lifted the hair brush it would be fragrant. Of course, it was fragrant.

The silver toilet set of her father had reappeared. And then of course, it made the analogy more possible. Everything else was there too—the wife, and the public, and the mistresses.

Her father receiving applause and the flowers of all women's tribute, the flowers of their femininity with the fern garnishings of multicolored hair given prodigally to the stage figures—the illusion needed for desire already artificially prepared for those too lazy to prepare their own. (In the love we have for those who are not on the stage the illusion has to be created by the love. The people who fall in love with the performers are like those who fall in love with magicians; they are the ones who cannot create the illusion or magic with the love—the mise-en-scène, the producer, the music, the role, which surrounds the personage with all that desire requires.)

In this love Philip will receive bouquets from women, and Stella will find again the familiar pain her father had given her, which she didn't want.

Because they had touched the ring around the planet of love, the outer ring of desire, had taken graceful leaps across visitless weeks, she had believed these to be marvelous demonstrations of their agility to escape the prisons of deep love's pains.

There were days when she felt: the core of this drama of mine is that at an early age I lost the element of joy. (In childhood we glimpse paradise, its possibility, we exist in it.) At what moment was it lost and replaced by anguish? Could she remember?

Standing before the silver brushes, combs and boxes on Philip's dressing table she remembered that just as other people watch the sun and rain for barometers to their moods, she had run every day to watch these silver objects. When her father was in stormy periods and ready to leave the house, they were disarranged and clouded. When he was in full bloom of success, harmony and pleasure they were symmetrically placed, and highly polished. The initials shone with exquisite iridescence. And on days of great discord and tragedy they disappeared altogether and were placed in their niches in his valise. So she consulted them like the barometers of her emotional climate.

When he left the house altogether it seemed as if none of the objects that remained possessed this power to gleam, to shed a brilliance. It was a transition from phosphorescence to continuous greyness.

It was when he left that her life changed color. Because he took only the pleasure, he also shed this pleasure around him. When she was thrust out of this effulgence and away from the gleam of beautiful objects, she was thrust into sadness.

How could joy have vanished with the father?

A person could walk away without carrying everything away with him. He might have left a little casket from which she could draw joy at will! He could have left the silver toilet set. But no, he took everything away with him because he took away the faith, her faith in love, and left her the prey of doubts and fears.

Human beings have a million little doorways of communication. When they feel threatened they close them, barricade themselves. Stella closed them all. Suffocation set in. Asphyxiation of the feelings.

She appeared in a new story on the screen. Her face was immobile like a mask. It was not Stella. It was the outer shell of Stella.

People sent her enormous bouquets of rare flowers. Continued to send them. She signed the receipts, she even signed notes of thanks. Flowers for the dead, she murmured. With only a little wire, and a round frame, they would do as well.

Notes

Text: *Winter of Artifice* (Denver: Alan Swallow, 1961), 7-54.

∝ *DIARY 4* ∞

Context

Because no commercial publisher was interested in her work, in the early 1940s Nin established the Gemor Press to publish her fiction and books by other writers. At mid decade, Gore Vidal secured her a contract with E. P. Dutton, where he worked as editor. To him, Nin dedicated *Ladders to Fire* (1946), her first novel and her initial book published by Dutton.

◆ ◆ ◆

December 1945. Gore came.

We slide easily into a sincere, warm talk. He dropped his armor, his defenses. "I don't like women. They are either silly, giggly, like the girls in my set I'm expected to marry, or they are harsh and strident masculine intellectuals. You are neither."

Intellectually he knows everything. Psychologically he knows the meaning of his mother abandoning him when he was ten, to remarry and have other children. The insecurity which followed the second break he made, at nineteen, after a quarrel with his mother. His admiration, attachment, hatred, and criticalness. Nor is it pity, he says. He is proud that she is beautiful and loved, yet he condemns her possessiveness, her chaos, her willfulness, and revolts against it. He knows this. But he does not know why he cannot love.

His face, as the afternoon light changed, became clearer. The frown between his eyes disappeared. He was a child thrust out too soon, into a world of very famous, assertive, successful, power personalities. His mother confesses her life to him. He moves among men and women of achievement. He was cheated of a carefree childhood, of a happy adolescence. He was rushed into sophistication and into experience with the surface of himself, but the deeper self was secret and lonely.

"My demon is pride and arrogance," he said. "One you will never see."

I receive from him gentleness and trust. He first asked me not to write down what he would say. He carries his father's diplomatic brief case with his own poems and novel in it. He carries his responsibilities seriously, is careful not to let his one-night encounters know his name, his family. As future president of the United States, he protects his reputation, entrusts me with state secrets to lighten his solitude. Later he wants to write it all down, as we want to explore his secret labyrinth together, to find the secret of his ambivalence. To explore. Yet life has taken charge to alter the situation again. He, the lonely one, has trusted woman for the first time, and we start the journey of our friendship, as badly loved children who raised themselves, both stronger and weaker by it.

He suffers the consequences of his wartime frostbite, great malaises and neuritis. He suffers from black depressions. He is nearsighted. A boy without age, who talks like an old man. My other children do not accept him, understand him.

While all the society mothers are looking for him for their cocktails, dances, we may be talking quietly somewhere in a restaurant, a night club. A debutante wrote him: "Why are you so detached?" Gore attends the functions, bows, dances, leaves. Dear mothers and debutantes, can you give this boy back his childhood, his mother, his security, the warmth and understanding he needed then? Can you answer his thoughts, dialogue with his brightness, keep pace with his intelligence?

He came at four and left at midnight. He made me laugh with the most amazingly well acted pastiches of Roosevelt, Churchill, a southern senator, a petition at the House of Commons. He has a sense of satire.

He is very much concerned with establishing a contrast between Pablo, Marshall, and Charles, as adolescents not yet successful, not yet matured, and himself, already mature in his roles as writer, editor, etc.

"I give you the true Gore."

And then: "I'm coming Wednesday. Send the children away."

Wednesday I met Gore at a restaurant. He had news for me. Dutton had had an editorial conference, was offering an advance of one thousand dollars, and a contract for all the novels. We celebrated. He tells me I must finish the new book, *Ladders to Fire*, in two months. I am not sure I can do it, with the work at the press, the visitors.

Gore thinks I live a fantasy, that I see things that are not there, that I am inventing a world.

Gore's visits on Sunday now a habit. He brings his dreams written out, his early novel to show me: the one he wrote at seventeen, *Williwaw*.

I enjoy his quick responses. He never eludes. He holds his ground, answers, responds. He is firm and quick-witted. He has an intelligent awareness, is attentive and alert, and observant.

Part of the great fascination of Gore's age, and the children's, is the mystery of what they will become. One is watching growth. Unlike Wilson, who sits determined and formed, with opinions, judgments.

Already set, in these young men one sees the ambivalences and conflicts. Is the illumination which surrounds them that of hope? They are still tender, still vulnerable, still struggling.

Gore said: "I belong nowhere. I do not feel American. I do not feel at home in any world. I pass casually through all of them. I take no sides."

The writing I do has created a world which draws into it the people I want to live with, who want to live in my world. One can make a world out of paper and ink and words. They make good constructions, habitable refuges, with overdoses of oxygen.

"I think, dear Gore, that you choose to write about ordinary people in an ordinary world to mask the extraordinary you and the out-of-the-ordinary world in which you live, which is like mine. I feel in you imagination, poetry, intuition of worlds you do not trust because they are linked with your emotions and sensibilities. And you have to work far removed from that territory of feeling where danger lies."

To find the poet in Gore was more difficult. Leonard looked like a poet and a dreamer. Gore looks warm, near and realistic. But there it is, another inarticulate poet, a secret dreamer.

The direction of Gore's writing distresses me. But at twenty did I know my direction? At twenty I imitated D. H. Lawrence.

My never glorifying the famous, the achieved, powerful figures restores to Gore a sense of his individual value. I am not awed by success.

I do respond when he tells me about his worship of Amelia Earhart, and how shocked he was by her death. She was a friend of the family. Gore's father financed her fatal trip.

Gore has a feeling of power. He feels he can accomplish whatever he wishes. He has clarity and decisiveness. He is capable of leadership. This on the conscious, willful level. In the emotional realm, imagination and intuition are there, but not trusted. It may be that he associates them with softer and more feminine qualities he does not wish to develop in himself.

Gore's three evenings. One with a writer: a drinking bout. One escorting a debutante to the Victory Ball, and feeling stifled and bored. The third evening with me. He brings me a poem, two pages of childhood recollections, the fourth chapter of his novel, his physical troubles from the war, talks about his mother, his father, his childhood. Complains of a feeling of split, of unreality. Talks of death. Reveals the mystic. Obsessed, as Leonard was, by the circles.

Sunday. Midnight. Gore is sitting at the foot of the couch writing his play on the werewolf.

He said: "We met just at the right moment."

He reads my new book and likes it. He tells me his father read *This Hunger* and saw himself in Jay.

"But I won't let you meet him. He would like you too well, and you might like him too well. You might get along too well."

"Not better than you and I."

"It is so good to be oneself without poses," he said.

Why do I not have this trust in Wilson? Why did I never talk with Wilson like this? Because Wilson is the critic, and would pass judgment on me as he did on my work? Because he would not understand? Why did I never trust him, and yet trust Gore?

In the world of Wilson there was no magic and no poetry. No sweet delights of intimacy, admission of doubts. The mystifications and surprises of the young. The mysteries. Always a shadowy labyrinth. There was in Wilson a harsh absolutism and literalness. A spade is a spade is a spade. Oh no, a spade can be a symbol of something other than what it was built for, can carry a message, represent a hundred other things.

Gore says about my continuation of *This Hunger* into *Ladders to Fire*: "You have expanded in depth, now expand in width."

He finished his play and brought it as a Christmas present. It was intense and strong. "I've never written this way, impulsively, directly, and without plan." He was pale. Worn. I let him read my pages on adolescence and snow and the timidities of adolescent love.

Gore wanted to know when I would make his portrait. "I made it in the diary when you gave me permission."

"I gave you permission because I knew you would do it anyway."

He asked if he could read it.

I let him.

I was uneasy, anxious about unmasking him.

"I didn't mind being unmasked by you," said Gore.

The end of *Ladders to Fire* brings two worlds into opposition: nature and neurosis. The external world, the salon, the garden, the mirrors, and the reflections of them in the mirror. The sense of unreality in the neurotic comes when he is looking at the reflections of his life, when he is not at one with it.

Gore says his feeling about writing is changing. He wants color, magic. He is aware of the conventional mask of his first novel.

His hidden self is emerging. His imagination is manifesting itself in the play. He is no longer dying. There is a warm flush on his cheeks, and warmth in his voice. The frown has vanished.

He mocks his world, but draws strength from being in the *Social Register*, from his friends' high positions, from the power of his father and mother. He needs his class privileges. I was saddened by his vanity, his display of position. He was partly dependent on worldly attributes. Terribly in need of glorification. I saw his persona in the world. It was another Gore.

Notes

Text: *The Diary of Anaïs Nin, 1944-1947* (New York: Harcourt Brace Jovanovich, 1971), 112-17.

Gore is Gore Vidal (1925-2012), the son of Eugene L. Vidal (1895-1969) and Nina S. Gore Vidal (1903-1978). Vidal performed pastiches of president Franklin Delano Roosevelt (1882-1945) and Winston Churchill (1874-1965); in 1945, Churchill was defeated for re-election as British prime minister. Pablo is Pablo Mendez; Marshall, Marshall Barer (1923-1998); Charles, Charles Duits (1925-1991). Dutton published Vidal's *Williwaw* in 1946. In referring to the children's age, Nin means men around age twenty with whom she associated in the mid 1940s. She wrote about them in *Children of the Albatross* (1947). Wilson is Edmund Wilson. Leonard is a pseudonym for William Pinckard (1927-1989), to whom Nin dedicated *Realism and Reality* (1946). The chapter Vidal brings Nin is probably from the manuscript that was published as *In a Yellow Wood* (1947), which he dedicated to her. Amelia Earhart (1897-1937), famous aviator, disappeared while attempting to fly around the world. Jay, based on Henry Miller, appears in many of Nin's fictions. Nin refers to Jay's presence in "Lillian and Djuna" (later "This Hunger") in *This Hunger* (1945). Vidal's novel *A Search for the King* (1950) includes werewolves.

ℭ REALISM AND REALITY ℬ

(1946)

Context

Nin wrote unconventional, non-commercial fiction. In the mid 1940s, she attempted to explain it in two brief essays published as pamphlets. In the first, *Realism and Reality*, she characterizes her fiction as poetic and symbolic, as focused on reality and not on what is generally considered realism.

◆ ◆ ◆

I want to clarify some misunderstandings that have occasionally blocked the response to my work. They arise mostly from the fact that I write as a poet in the framework of prose and appear to claim the rights of a novelist.

I deal with characters, it is true, but the best way to approach my way of dealing with them is as one regards modern painting. I intend the greater part of my writing to be received directly through the senses, as one receives painting and music. The moment you begin to look at my writing in terms of modern painting you will be in possession of one key to its meaning and will understand why I have left out so much that you are accustomed to find in character novels.

There is a purpose and form behind my partial, impressionistic, truncated characters. The whole house, or the whole body, the entire environment, may not be there, but we know from modern painting that a column can signify more than a whole house, and that one eye can convey more than two at times. We know that in Brancusi's sculpture he achieved the closest expression of the flight of a bird by eliminating the wings.

As my books take place in the unconscious, and hardly ever outside of it, they differ from poetry not in tone, language or rhythm, but merely by the fact that they contain both the symbol and the interpretation of the symbol. The process of distillation, of reduction to the barest essentials is voluntary because dealing with the chaotic content of the unconscious in the form of the poet is natural, but to poeticize and analyze simultaneously is too elusive and swift to include much upholstery.

If the writing has a dream-like quality it is not because the dramas I present are dreams, but because they are the dramas as the unconscious lives them. I never include the concrete object or fact unless it has a symbolical role to play. As in the dream, when a chair appears in my book it is because this chair has something portentous to reveal about the drama that is taking place. Thus alone I can achieve the intensification and vividness of a kind of drama which we know to be highly elusive and fragmentary and which takes place only in psychoanalysis.

These dramas of the unconscious to gain a form and validity of their own must temporarily displace the over-obtrusive, dense, deceptive settings of our outer world which usually serve as concealment, so that we may become as familiar with its inner properties and developments as we are with the workings of our conscious external worlds.

As in Miro's painting, the circus is indicated by a line, a red ball, and space. This conforms to my concept that modern writing must have the swift rhythm of our time, and can be as lightly cargoed as the airplane to permit flight and speed. It is my belief that emotionally as well as scientifically, we are going to travel more lightly and that writing will not belong to our time if it does not learn to travel faster than sound!

And how are we going to fly with novels which begin: "She was sitting under a 40 Watt Mazda lamp" (the author I will not quote for fear of libel).

The new investigations of the unconscious have brought people nearer to poetry, for every man now knows that he is continuously constructing a dream duplicate of his life in the same symbolical terms used familiarly by the poets and that he too possesses a very subtle and intricate way of dramatizing the concealed meaning of his life.

At night every man dreams in the imagery of the poets, but in the daytime he denies and rejects the world of the artist as if it were not his world, even to the length of classifying such dream activity as symptomatic of neurosis when it is actually a symptom of the creativity latent in every man.

These investigations will also make us more impatient with the opaque quality of our external world which is used in most novels as defenses against a disturbing deeper world, as an obstacle in reaching it, as an obstruction created by fear; and a greater impatience even with meaningless acts, with all evasions of the essential inner drama practiced by the so-called realistic novel in which we are actually being constantly cheated of reality and experience.

The occasional resistance I have encountered has been due, I believe, to my use of the symbolical, my use of daily objects not as they stand around us as reassuring, consoling solidities, like a cup of coffee, or an alarm clock, but that I come like a magician of doubtful authenticity and transform this cup of coffee and this alarm clock into stage property for a story which then seems like a dream and not reality.

Yet everyone does this, as we know, every night, whenever he begins to interpret or dramatize the deeper significance of his acts.

Now I place you in a world which is like the world of the dream, sparingly furnished only with the objects which have proved their symbolical value, and not their familiar value as objects which give us our daily gravitational security. It is because I assume that the world of the dream like the world of my books is actually the way we re-experience our life, and I expect people to recognize its contours or its lack of contours without fear (the most disturbing element of the dream is that it has no frames, no walls, no doors and no boundaries...like my novels). Whatever anxiety my writing may create, can only be the anxiety people feel in the presence of an incomplete but highly significant dream.

I cannot claim the privileges granted to the poet (he is allowed his mystery and praised for what he does not reveal) because the poet is content with bringing forth the flow of images but does not set about to interpret them as characters. All mysteries become explicit when they are personified and dramatized, and I tend towards a greater explicitness, but not before the reality of the inner drama is made completely valid in itself.

The conventionalities of the novel can no longer communicate what we know. That is why James Joyce exploded the form of the novel and let his writing erupt in a veritable flow. As Edmund Wilson put it: "Just as Joyce in *Ulysses* laid the *Odyssey* under requisition to help provide a structure for his material—a material which, once it had begun to gush forth from the rock of Joyce's sealed personality at the blow of Aaron's rod of free associations, threatened to rise and submerge the artist like the floods which the sorceress's apprentice let loose by his bedeviled broom."

But there is no need to seek a structure from the old myths. In the human unconscious itself, once unraveled, there is an indigenous structure and pattern. If we are able to detect and seize and use it we have the conflicts and the forms of the novel of the future.

The pattern of the new novel will be one in which everything will be produced only as it is discovered by the emotions: by associations and repetitions, by associative memory as in Proust, by repetitious experiences out of which the meaning finally becomes clear as it does in life, making it possible to seize the inner pattern and not the false exterior ones. The pattern of the deeper life covered and disguised will be uncovered and demasked by the writer's process of interpretation of the symbolical meaning of people's acts, not a mere reporting of them or of their words. The incoherence of such a way of writing, often practiced by D. H. Lawrence is only apparent and ceases as soon as the writer strikes the deepest level of all, for the unconscious creates the most consistent patterns and plots of all.

Many novels today include the psychoanalytical experience. That is only a crude makeshift. The novelist knows that psychoanalysis has uncovered layers not uncovered in the narrative novel (particularly in a society where people's acts no longer correspond to their inner impulses; this does not apply, for instance, to the Dostoevskian novels in which people act by the impulses of their unconscious, as we do not). But so far he has granted this uncovering power only to the professional analyst, not realizing that this power must become an integral part of his novelist's equipment.

Historical knowledge as it was used by a Joyce or a Proust was never introduced into the novel as pure history but as an integrated part of the novelist's total vision. Thus the new perspective of character as it can be created by the novelist familiar with the unconscious will be slowly integrated within the novel and will not need to be voiced through a doctor. The novelist has allowed the doctor to do what he felt impotent to do himself, shifting the responsibilities of breaking through false patterns, disguises, thus increasing the reader's feelings that neurosis in a character made it a "case" and not an experience very common in our world today, which it is. The novelist himself has not yet accepted the unconscious activity, the unconscious dramas as an integral part of all characters.

A woman was complaining of her bad health to a friend, and this friend said: "With you I'm sure it's not a neurotic complaint."

"Of course not," said the sick woman, "it's not neurotic. It's just human."

If we can accept neurosis as a part of our humanity it will cease to be a case in literature and become one of the richest sources of fiction writing.

There is no denying that we are suffering from a collective neurosis and the novel which does not face this is not a novel of our time. Collective neurosis can no longer be dismissed as exceptional, pathological or decadent. It is a direct result of our social system. As soon as we accept this we are ready to face the causes and to reach into deeper relations to history.

While we refuse to organize the confusions within us we will never have an objective understanding of what is happening outside. We will not be able to relate to it, to choose sides, to evaluate historically and consequently we will be incapacitated for action. The novelist's preoccupation with inner distortions is not morbid or a love of illness but it comes as a truthful mirror of today's drama. In order to take action full experience is required. All novels which contribute to our emotional atrophy only deepen our blindness. The novels today do not reflect our life but people's fear of life, of experience, of the deeper layers of self knowledge by which we alone can defeat tragedy.

Reportage, the other extreme from unconscious writing, is not reality either, because facts stated objectively, scientifically, statistically without the artist's power to communicate their meaning do not give us an emotional experience. And nothing that we do not discover emotionally will have the power to alter our vision. In reportage we are once more cheated of experience, and realism is substituted for reality.

As soon as I say experience there are some who grow afraid again, who think that experience means to be first of all everything one writes about.

But by experience I do not always mean to act, but to feel. A young writer said to me one day: "I saw a workman who had had his hand torn off by a machine. I didn't feel anything." Such a person is not only schizophrenic; he is no doubt a bad writer. To experience this one does not have to be the workman to whom this happened.

The richest source of creation is feeling, followed by a vision of its meaning. The medium of the writer is not ink and paper but his body: the sensitivity of his eyes, ears and heart. If these are atrophied let him give up writing.

Notes

Text: *Realism and Reality* (Yonkers: Alicat Book Shop, 1946).

Nin refers either to the "Maiastra" or less abstract "Bird in Space" sculptures of Constantin Brancusi (1876-1957) and to *Le Cirque* (1937), by Joan Miró (1893-1983). Edmund Wilson comments about James Joyce in "H. C. Earwicker and Family," *The New Republic* 99 (28 June 1939): 203-6 (the quotation is from p. 205). Wilson included this essay, revised, as "The Dream of H. C. Earwicker" in *The Wound and the Bow: Seven Studies in Literature* (New York: Oxford University Press, 1947), 243-71 (the quotation is from p. 251). Joyce's *Ulysses* (1922) is possibly the most important modernist novel. Proust is Marcel Proust. In *À la recherche du temps perdu (In Search of Lost Time)* (1913-1927), he uses associative memory in order to avoid chronological structure and traditional plot. Incoherence in the novels of

D. H. Lawrence may be observed in the characters Clara Dawes and Miriam Leivers in *Sons and Lovers* (1913).

⌘ *ON WRITING* ⌘

(1947)

Context

Nin continued commenting about the nature of writing in *On Writing*. In this essay, she expands on ideas expressed in *Realism and Reality*, as well as in the prologue to *Ladders to Fire* (1946).

◆ ◆ ◆ ◆

There has been an attempt to categorize my work as a mere depiction of neurosis, and therefore as dealing with an exceptional rather than a general theme.

But on the contrary, I *not* only believe that we are suffering from a collective neurosis, but that this is precisely one of the most *urgent* themes for the novel today: the struggle between the forces of nature in us and our repressive and consequently destructive treatment of these forces.

This struggle has, for the moment at least, resulted in neurosis, which is simply a form of protest against an unnatural life.

That is why I want to speak about writing not in formal terms, but mainly of *naturalness* in writing, because in the presence of a collective neurosis it is all the more essential for the novelist not to share with the neurotic this paralyzing fear of nature which has been the cause of so much sterility in life and in the writing of today.

I chose to write about neurotic women because woman being closer to nature has made a more vehement protest against repressions.

Man has faced boldly the forces of nature outside of himself, has investigated them, mastered and harnessed many of them. But this conquest deprived him at the same time of his primitive, intimate contact with nature, resulting in a partial loss of his power and vitality.

Woman has retained her communication with nature (even in its negative form of destruction) and could have remained the symbol of nature for man, because her language and her means of perception are more unconscious and non-rational. But she has failed to fulfill that role, partly because of her tendency to imitate man and adopt his goals, and partly because of man's fear of complete contact with the nature of woman.

Perhaps this fear in man arose from his being not quite so certain that the forces of nature manifested through woman could be as easily mastered or harnessed!

This has led to the absence, or failure of relationship between men and women so prevalent today, and it is a dramatic proof of the absence of relationship between man and nature.

While we refuse to organize the confusions *within* us we will never have an objective understanding of what is happening *outside*.

We will not be able to relate to it, to choose sides, to evaluate historically, and consequently we will be incapacitated for *action*.

Today a novelist's preoccupation with inner psychological distortions does not stem from a morbid love of illness but from a knowledge that this is the *theme* of our new reality.

Like the modern physicist the novelist of today should face the fact that this new psychological reality can be explored and dealt with only under conditions of tremendously high atmospheric pressures, temperatures and speed, as well as in terms of new time-space dimensions for which the old containers represented by the traditional forms and conventions of the novel are completely inadequate and inappropriate.

That is why James Joyce shattered the old form of the novel and let his writing erupt in a veritable flow of associations.

Most novels today are inadequate because they reflect *not our experience*, but people's fear of experience. They portray all the *evasions*.

I believe that the experience of war might have been less disastrous to the mental and emotional life of young Americans if they had been prepared by an honest literature for all the deep primitive experience with birth, sex and death.

In order to take action full maturity in experience is required. Novels which contribute to our emotional atrophy only deepen our blindness.

And nothing that we do not discover *emotionally* will have the power to alter our vision.

The constant evasion of emotional experience has created an immaturity which turns all experience into traumatic shocks from which the human being derives no strength or development, but neurosis.

Frederick Hoffman writing about D. H. Lawrence says: "Lawrence sensed a definite danger that the novel might deaden the senses and simply present dead matter persisting in a dead world. But if it is handled as a live portrait it is at once the artist's most fluid medium and his best opportunity to convey to the world the *meaning* of the world, 'the changing rainbow of our living relationships.' How can creative art accomplish this? Life is so fluid that one can only hope to capture the living moment, to capture it alive and fresh—not the ordinary moment of an ordinary day but the critical moment of human relationships. How to capture this oscillation within the prison of cold print, without destroying that movement?"

It was while writing a Diary that I discovered how to capture the living moments.

Keeping a Diary all my life helped me to discover some basic elements essential to the vitality of writing.

When I speak of the relationship between my diary and writing I do not intend to generalize as to the value of keeping a diary, or to advise anyone to do so, but merely to extract from this habit certain discoveries which can be easily transposed to other kinds of writing.

Of these the most important is naturalness and spontaneity: These elements sprung, I observed, from my freedom of selection: in the Diary I only wrote of what interested me genuinely, what I felt most *strongly* at the moment, and I found that this fervor, this enthusiasm produced a vividness which often withered in the formal work. Improvisation, free association, obedience to mood, impulse, brought forth countless images, portraits, descriptions, impressionistic sketches, symphonic experiments, from which I could dip at any time for material.

The Diary dealing always with the immediate present, the warm, the near, being written at white heat, developed a love of the living moment, of the immediate emotional reaction to experience, which revealed the power of recreation to lie in the sensibilities rather than in memory or critical intellectual perception.

The Diary, creating a vast tapestry, a web, exposing constantly the relation between the past and present, weaving meticulously the invisible interaction, noting the repetitions of themes, developed the sense of the totality of personality, this tale without beginning or end which encloses all things, and relates all things, as a strong antidote to the unrelatedness, incoherence and disintegration of the modern man. I could follow the inevitable pattern and obtain a large, panoramic view of character.

This personal relationship to all things, which is condemned as subjective, limiting, I found to be the core of individuality, personality, and originality. The idea that subjectivity is an impasse is as false as the idea that objectivity leads to a larger form of life.

A deep personal relationship reaches far beyond the personal into the general. Again it is a matter of depths.

The Diary also taught me that it is in the moments of emotional crisis that human beings reveal themselves most accurately. I learned to choose the heightened moments because they are the moments of revelation. It is the moment when the real self rises to the surface, shatters its false roles, erupts and assumes reality and identity. The fiery moments of passionate experience are the moments of wholeness and totality of the personality.

By this emphasis on the fiery moments, the explosions, I reached the reality of feeling and the senses.

The split from reality, fragmentation, the dismemberment of modern man has been the theme of modern literature beginning with Proust's microscopic analysis, through the dissolutions of Joyce's undifferentiated flow of associations, but neither of these processes needed to prove fatal. The discovery of the collective richness flowing underground below our consciousness need not have led to a loss of the total self. But what remains to be done is a new synthesis to include the new dimensions discovered.

The new dimension in character and reality requires a fusion of two extremes which have been handled separately, on the one side by the poets, and on the other by the so called realists.

I am not saying that I have done it.

I actually think it will be accomplished by the younger unpublished writers I have been reading.

The Diary writing also taught me that to achieve perfection in writing while retaining naturalness it was important to write a great deal, to write fluently, as the pianist practices the piano, rather than to correct constantly one page until it withers. To write continuously, to try over and over again to capture a certain mood, a certain experience. Intensive correcting may lead to monotony, to working on dead matter, whereas continuing to write and to write until perfection is achieved through repetition is a way to elude this monotony, to avoid performing an autopsy. Sheer playing of scales, practice, repetition—then by the time one is ready to write a story or a novel a great deal of natural distillation and softing has been accomplished.

There is another great danger for the writer, perhaps the greatest one of all: his consciousness of the multiple taboos society has imposed on literature, and his inner censor. In the Diary I found a devious (a woman's) way to evade this outer and inner censor. It is surprising how well one writes if one thinks no one will read you.

This honesty, this absence of posturing, is a most fecund source of material. The writer's task is to overthrow the taboos rather than accept them.

With all my insistence on the overthrow of outworn taboos, I nevertheless respected the power of art.

Naked truth is unbearable to most, and art is our most effective means of overcoming human resistance to truth. The writer has the same role as the surgeon and his handling of anaesthesia is as important as his skill with the knife.

Human beings, in their resistance to truth, erect fortresses and some of these fortresses can only be demolished by the dynamic power of the symbol, which reaches the emotions directly.

D. H. Lawrence says: "Symbols don't MEAN something, they ARE units of human experience. A complex of emotional experience IS a symbol. And the power of the symbol is to arouse the deep, emotional, dynamic, primitive self."

The fact that man persists in dreaming in terms of symbols shows how he clings to this primitive emotional perception.

It is even more interesting to talk about what has not yet been done.

For instance, I believe a rich fund of symbolism lies in science. The old romantic symbols no longer correspond to our reality.

Modern science is giving birth to symbols which parallel the new psychological realities, and could make their tenuous patterns more concrete.

I can't do it because I know too little about science!

My studies led me rather towards language and art.

Having come to America as a foreigner and not knowing English I caught a new perspective of the language.

But whatever marvelous word I unearthed from the dictionary with the enthusiasm of an explorer was always condemned to disuse by my English teacher as obsolete or affected. When I asked: who proclaimed them so? she could not answer me. It was prim evasiveness which led me to suspect that of this mysterious censorship of expansiveness in language had been caused by puritanism: a puritanical disapprobation of richness, a puritanical fear of color, a puritanical shame of the senses and suspicion of charm.

Coming from Spain it struck me that we had forgotten in America how masterfully the ancients used charms to encourage salvation.

Whoever has smelled incense in a church will admit that religion made a wise use of *olfactory enchantments*.

Are we going to discard all these forms of communication and persuasion because they were sometimes mishandled?

Whoever has read the Arabian nights knows how much art has to do here with enlivening the energies!

Art is our relation to the senses.

The great potency of ancient tales, legends, ballads, lay in their power to prepare the senses for the magic effect of the tale.

This sounds as if I were recommending hypnotism. If the sound of Joyce's voice reading the chanting quality of his rhythms is hypnotic then I say better be hypnotized than to die in the deserts of bare and barren writing.

The inciting to naturalness immediately brings up the problem of form.

By following rigorously and exclusively the patterns made by the emotions I found that in the human unconscious itself there is an indigenous structure and if we are able to detect and grasp it we have the plot, the form and style of the novel of the future.

In this apparently chaotic world of the unconscious there is an inevitability as logical, as coherent, as final as any to be found in classical drama.

In this new dimension of character the form is created by the meaning, it is born of the theme. It is created very much as the earth itself is created, by a series of inner convulsions and eruptions, dictated by inner geological tensions.

It is an organic development.

For instance, when I began the portrait of Stella I had no premeditated plan, but the character of Stella being a summation of the feminine spirit—labyrinthean, elusive, and mobile, this gave to the writing itself its contours, its rhythms. The writing was determined by the form of her nature, it reflected the tonalities of her voice. I instinctively chose light weight words to match the volatility of her gestures, words of the same substance as her moods and mannerisms.

I would like to give now an example of how creative the unconscious can be if one allows it to work spontaneously.

In *Ladders to Fire* I had written the section called This Hunger up to the description of an impasse in the relationship between Jay and Lillian: because she has to mother the child in him, she cannot have a real child. She surrenders the human child and accepts her role.

And there I stopped for a few days.

One morning I awakened to remember a concert I had heard in Paris years ago. The memory came up with great vividness and persistence. I was a little annoyed for it had no apparent connection with what I was writing and I looked on it as an irrelevant interruption.

But it confronted me with the clarity and precision of a painting and to rid myself of its hauntingness I decided to write it down. The concert itself was not what had made a lasting impression on me but the strange sight I had caught as I looked out through a big bay window into a garden: three large mirrors had been placed in the center of the garden. The incongruity of mirrors in a garden was striking, but such a scene only stirs a deep response when it touches off some primitive recognition of a symbolical drama.

As I wrote on, about the woman pianist, about the real garden, and its reflection in the mirror I still wondered why the impression had been deep enough to last for years, and why it should have come to the surface of my memory at this particular moment. It was only when I was finished writing that I realized I had continued the story of This Hunger and completed it by giving the key to the book: the woman pianist playing with such intensity was trying to divert a natural instinct (the need of a human child) into music.

But the transmutation was not being made.

The real garden represented nature, relaxed, fulfilled. The mirrors— neurosis, reflection, artifice.

The mirrors in the garden were the perfect symbol of unreality and refraction, a miniature reproduction of the drama I had been portraying of a conflict between nature and neurosis.

Notes

Text: *On Writing* (Yonkers: Alicat Bookshop, 1947).

Nin refers to *Ulysses* (1922), by James Joyce. Frederick J. Hoffman (1909-1967) writes about D. H. Lawrence in "Lawrence's Quarrel with Freud," *Freudianism and the Literary Mind* (Baton Rouge: Louisiana State University Press, 1945), 149-80 (the quotation is from p. 176). Proust is Marcel Proust. Lawrence comments about symbols in "Introduction," *The London Mercury* 22 (July 1930): 217-26 (the quotation is from p. 220). By "Arabian nights," Nin means *One Thousand and One Nights* (also known as *Arabian Nights*), a collection of ancient tales.

♥ *DIARY 5* ♥

(August 1954)
On mother's death

Context

Rosa Culmell de Nin, Joaquín Nin-Culmell, Anaïs Nin, and Hugh Guiler lived together in France more-or-less continuously from 1924 or 1925 until 1939. Then, mother and son lived together, with brief interruptions, until her death.

◆ ◆ ◆

August, 1954. Every time I went to visit my mother at Oakland, I felt it might be for the last time. She was over eighty and although not ill, she had one light stroke some years ago. I was always preparing myself for the separation. I would have liked to be able to sense when I should be there. I would have liked to know, but then it might have been more terrible. I would have liked to know so that I could express my love, which something in her prevented me from expressing fully. I would have liked her to die when we felt the closest (during her last illness).

But it did not happen like this. I had no premonition. It was an ordinary visit. I arrived when Joaquin had just finished his summer job. I arrived at night. Mother was already in bed, at midnight. She got up to kiss me and to drink a glass of milk. The next morning Joaquin made breakfast. The maid had not come for a week and they were looking for a new one. Mother read her newspaper sitting in her favorite chair by the window. On the sofa was her bobbin lace, on which she had been working. I worked on my rug and we talked. I teased her about the rug, saying: "Would you like to finish it? I don't work on it enough." Mother answered: "I don't like rug-making."

"But you like the rug, I hope, as I am making it for you."

Then I asked her if she would tell me her life story and that I would write it in the diary. She laughed at that, made fun of the idea, and I gave it up while Joaquin said to her: "*Tu n'est pas gentille.*" But this did not change our good-humored mood. Joaquin worked at his music, copying a page, and then asked me to play canasta. Mother did not like canasta. She preferred solitaire. She quietly played solitaire while Joaquin and I played canasta, clowning to amuse her. At times she closed her eyes as if tired.

After dinner Joaquin and I went to a movie. I wish I had stayed with her, but as she always went to bed at eight or nine, I did not feel it mattered. But before dinner, to please me, Joaquin made martinis. We became very gay and clowned for mother. I always tell *Marius and Olive* stories with a real southern French accent. Mother would smile but she disapproved of the cocktail. Mother's expression of anger, like my father's expression of severity, was reserved for our actions. The laughter, exuberance, was given to strangers. I missed the in-between moods: tenderness and gentleness.

Before we took the cocktail, Joaquin took us for a ride, the "long drive," as they call it, over the mountains of Oakland. Why did I not notice mother was more subdued than usual? Why can't we know those we love are about to die, so as to give them the words of love they need, the last praise or reassurance? We could not bear to know, but that is not true, for it is in the not knowing that is prepared all the sources of our suffering later. We are still like animals; we do not tell our thoughts or our feelings. Mother must have had a million thoughts that day. She may not have sensed death approaching. She did not sense it because her last words to me were: "When you come next time will you stay more than two days?"

That afternoon passed quickly. When we returned from the movie, mother was asleep. The next morning we rose early to go to Mass together. Mother wore the fur coat Joaquin gave her and her black mantilla. She and Joaquin received communion. On the way out of church we were stopped by Arthur Schnitzler's widow, a converted Jewess. Joaquin stayed to talk with her while mother sat in the car. Mother complained that Joaquin had squeezed her arm too tightly when he was leading her up to the altar. Joaquin explained he could not find her arm in the big sleeve of her coat.

We had lunch. We ate a sponge cake mother had baked. Joaquin scolded her for not eating. We should have been alarmed, but we weren't. We took another drive together, the "short drive." I saw my mother's small eyes looking at the hills and fields, which were sepia colored. I should have known she was looking at them for the last time. And I could have been tender and said: "Mother, I love you." After death, that is what you weep over, but after death the one you love is not there to place an obstacle before your tenderness. Mother inhibited my tenderness. She had a generous, valiant, rough-hewn, cheerful, combative, aggressive temperament.

After our drive Joaquin and I played cards. My mother had refused to get a hearing aid. She could hear concerts but not the voices at the movies. She did not like the detective story she was reading. I left her the one I was reading. I apologized for having leaned over her bobbin-lace cushion and bent the pins (the piece of lace she was never to finish).

Then at seven thirty I left.

At the airport I did not let Joaquin stay until I left. Noise, crowds make intimate talk impossible and the separation begins really as soon as one arrives at the airport, so it is better not to delay it, to hang on, to talk like the deaf and mute in the deafening roar of the propellers. "Go home," I said, and Joaquin agreed. Stations and airports are rehearsals for separations by death.

In the plane I took a martini and a sleeping pill. Anxiety awakened me at midnight. I did not know that when Joaquin returned home Mother was ill with what she thought was stomach trouble. She had vomited and felt pain. She had a heart attack.

Joaquin called me. Mother was rallying under oxygen and drugs, and had talked with Joaquin. In the afternoon she talked with a young priest she asked for. But the next day she was semiconscious, and did not recognize Joaquin, answered feebly when she was called. That evening she died, unconscious, painlessly. Joaquin called me at midnight.

The pain of irrevocable loss. A greater and deeper pain because there was no sense of unity, of fusion, of closeness and I had hoped to achieve this. The loss is greater and more terrible when closeness is not attained. All my life I had struggled to come closer to her, and now she was lost to me. It eluded me. Pain of remembrance. The lace unfinished. Her game of solitaire unfinished. That ordinary family last day, nothing to lift it from an ordinary family day, with family disharmonies stemming from childhood. Pain, her shrunken body in part dying, withering, but when she was very ill and I rubbed her body with alcohol her back was white, smooth, unwrinkled, shockingly smooth and not ready to die. Pain. I could not look at my bathing suit she sewed a few stitches on, without a pain as great as the stab of a knife. Pain not to have been there, to see her, to help her and Joaquin. Joaquin having to live alone through all the horrors, the loss itself, and all the details attending death. Once I called him. He had been fixing her room. I heard him weep.

"Joaquin, remember, you made Mother's life very happy for many years. She had a happy life. You were the best of sons."

But I tormented myself with regrets and guilts. Why did it happen the night I left? Why did Joaquin and I drink a martini? It displeased her. Not only my mother had died, but my hope of fulfillment, of union with her, of an understanding, penetrating love.

I rebelled against death. I wept quietly. Every now and then the sorrow pierced me again, in the street, in a movie, at dawn, any time. The guilt came from my rebellions against her. The anguishing compassion for her life.

She started at fifteen to be a mother to her six brothers and sisters (because her own mother ran away with a lover, to a life with many lovers), and to give them the same fierce protectiveness, fierce courage she gave us. Her brothers and sisters speak of her as children do: "A tyrant with a heart of gold." Perhaps, then, marrying my father when he was only twenty-two years old and she thirty, another motherhood, and sacrificing her life to her three children may have been what gave her so much anger. She loved to sing. She had a very beautiful voice, she was sociable, natural, very cheerful.

But for the last ten years I had no discord with my mother. Her buoyancy and gaiety made her beloved. Her frankness was total, her honesty absolute, as was her generosity and her spontaneity.

I am now awaiting Joaquin, who took her body to Cuba where she wanted to be buried beside her father.

Why do people carry away with them so great a part of our knowledge of them, of their thoughts and feelings which would make us love them better.

We are still like animals. We think we understand intuitively. We do not. My mother closed the door on me the day I sought an independent life from her, and after that I spent endless effort and time returning to her, being a good daughter.

What a burden of guilt when a mother serves you, does all the menial tasks, feeds you, works for you, but then does not approve what you become. Do we all withhold our feelings and our thoughts because of this fear of condemnation?

A confession Mother made to me once, but she made it with pride.

Her father, whom she adored, was dying of cancer of the liver. He was suffering agony. His death was long, drawn out. The doctor consulted the family. Grandfather was asking for an end to his misery. Mother, as head of the family, had to decide if the doctor should continue with injections of morphine in an increased dose because the present dose no longer relieved him. In increasing the dose there was danger of hastening the death. It was my mother who had to take the responsibility of consenting to the increased dose.

Caring for their children physically but not approving their final development, is this an epitaph for all mothers?

Her courage and her generosity were immense.

It hurt me to remember that even when we gave her new dresses, she still wore her rich sister's castoff clothes. Until the end she hated perfume and gave me whatever perfume or cologne was given to her. Whenever anyone admired an object in her home she would say: "Do you want it?"

Once she stayed with me in New York. An Irish carpenter was building bookcases and singing Irish songs. My mother sang with him, laughed and talked with him. I want to remember always the image of her at that moment, carefree, happy that her voice at seventy was clear and beautiful, happy to be singing. I asked myself then whether she would always have been happy and carefree if she had followed her first passion, singing. Music brought her and father together. She had dreams of concert life. At the beginning he tutored her to sing the most difficult songs, and she was praised by Gabriele d'Annunzio for her rendering of old Italian songs. When she sang *O Cessate di Piagarmi* I wept. I do not remember her singing very often until she went to Spain and there Enrique Granados made her a singing teacher at the Granados Academy. She was happy then.

In New York she tried to make a career again. She gave a concert at Aeolian Hall. She sang old Italian songs, Catalan folk songs, and Granados' *tonadillas*. But nothing came of it.

Was this a secret wound? When I was a girl of sixteen, she sang for the young men who came courting me and I was wistful to be so thoroughly outshone.

Her singing moved me. What would her life have been without children, concertizing, traveling, as pampered by the public as my father was?

This is the image I want to preserve, of my mother at seventy with the crystal-clear voice of a young girl, singing for and with the Irish carpenter.

On the way to New York I stopped at San Francisco to see Joaquin. He had been at the opera and stood far away at the end of the gleaming airport terminal. Small, in black and white, with, even at that distance, a tragic way of standing. It is the way of standing of those pierced by an arrow. I felt I was right to have come. The basic, fundamental Nin sadness, or is it the Spanish tragic sense of life? We are doomed. But gallant. Gallantly creative, active, even gay.

He talked more than usual on the drive to his home, about his plans, his desire to go to Europe for a year, his musical projects, his practical problems at the University, his tiredness after fifteen years of teaching. It is strange, when my mother died, the contact between Joaquin and me was re-established. It had been interrupted. When? I do not remember. Perhaps in Paris, when my mother felt I might be a bad influence on Joaquin. As children we were very close. Now this contact was open again. He talked. This new intimacy began when he came to New York after Mother's death.

When we arrived at the house, I was silent. I missed my mother's face at the window, or her standing at the door, or, what was more often true lately, she would be asleep when I arrived and would turn on her light to greet me. Perhaps even rise to have a glass of milk with us. Her bedspread was of crochet, made by her own hands. The room was bare and simple. There was a crucifix over her bed.

When I entered the bedroom I broke down. I slipped to the floor and sobbed. Joaquin wept. I kept saying: "I am sorry, I am sorry" to Joaquin, because I had come to cheer him, not to heighten his sorrow.

I was to sleep in my mother's bed. It was utterly painful. But my concern over Joaquin was so strong I forgot what I felt. He was in bed and weeping. I sat on the edge of his bed and said: "Mother is resting. She would not want you to hurt yourself. Don't hurt yourself." He went to sleep, and I too.

I awakened resigned to the ordeal of helping Joaquin dispose of her belongings. She owned so little! A box of holy medals, rosaries, and a prayer book for the Society of Saint Vincent de Paul. A box of lace remnants, those we carried all through our lives and travels, from Europe to America, my mother always saying: "Someday we will make a whole tablecloth out of all those pieces of real lace."

Some came from the dresses she wore as a debutante in Cuba. A box of sewing threads and needles which I wanted, as well as her gold thimble, in hope of inheriting my mother's ability to sew. I accepted mending and sewing now, and asked for the sewing machine, the knitting needles.

My mother's jewelry were gifts from me, gold earrings from Mexico, trinkets from Italy, pins and a few rings from her sisters. I wanted her unfinished bobbin lace, the pale-blue pillow with a pattern pinned to it, and the white thread on bobbins which her hands wove in and out, changing the pins. There was an unfinished piece of lace on it, and Joaquin preferred to give it to a nun who makes bobbin lace and would finish it. The unfinished bit of lace would have caused me sadness.

Her bookbinding press and bookbinding material Joaquin sent to a pupil of hers in Williamstown. The pain was deeper which came from the handling of small objects, her bobby pins, her comb, her face powder. I never saw anyone who possessed so little. A few dresses her sisters gave her, a fur coat from my brother, a half-empty closet. The stark simplicity of her taste, her stripping away of possessions. She took nothing, possessed nothing but what was given to her by her children. But she kept all mementos, our childhood teeth, our first locks of hair, my first piece of embroidery, our first notes to her, all our letters. Three enormous boxes of my letters to her. *I had expressed my devotion.*

It was a comfort to give her clothes to the sisters of Saint Vincent de Paul for the poor, because that is what she would have wanted; it seemed a more sacred way of dispersing them.

Then came the sharing of photographs in three piles: two for the sons and one for me. Still we felt like criminals dispersing parts of her, the coat which had warmed her, her modest handbag. I can now understand those who lock the door upon everything and never enter again. And yet, was it not better that those objects should continue to live. The final casting off of objects which belong to the dead is full of taboos and full of the pains of the ritual of separation.

The final dispersion. Separating from my mother, separating from my mother. As you disperse these objects which hold a terrifying life, you feel the separation is now final.

But each one has his way of remembering. Mine is to enclose her in the diary. And for days after her death I felt possessed by the spirit of my mother. I wanted to express love by cooking, sewing, mending, lacemaking, bookbinding.

We worked all afternoon. Some of our decisions were dictated by an austere mourning. We cast off Christmas-tree ornaments as if Christmas were no longer possible to celebrate without her, we cast off the playing cards with which she played solitaire, as if we would never play cards again. We cast off the detective stories she liked to read in those days when I had the feeling that she was waiting for death. But we kept the black lace fan, the one she waved with a Latin rhythm in church, which seemed irreverent to the American priest.

Joaquin looks mortally wounded. When he cooked he talked about his discovery of the monotony of woman's work and the endless rounds and repetition.

I hide myself to throw away my mother's toothbrush because I know the sight of it will hurt him, yet he won't be able to throw it away. I did it for him, and hurt myself.

The black lace mantilla I brought her from Spain she was buried in.

I knew that Joaquin wanted me to go to church with him, and that he was embarrassed to ask me, knowing my estrangement from formal religion. He was happy when I suggested it. I waited for him, but refused to pray as I had as a child. I watched the little blue lights wavering in their glasses, some freshly lit by penitents, some already burned out, and I could not bear it, my mother's life burning out, so I went and lit a new one, and Joaquin thought I was offering a renewal of my faith.

Every Saturday evening Joaquin and my mother went to church. When he left me to go to confession, he said with one of his half smiles: "It won't take long," alluding to the brevity of the list of his sins.

Joaquin's sadness, the austerity of his life, which I spent a lifetime running away from, rebelling against austerity, and my mother's humble, sacrificed life.

But some bonds are never broken. I inherited from my mother not only her gold thimble, a sewing machine, but the maternal passion and care for others.

The pain deeper than at my father's death. I didn't love her well enough.

Except from the age of eleven until twenty, when I was completely and utterly devoted to her, thinking only of helping her.

But later when I began to grow in a different direction, when I left her house, became independent, then conceding my love and admiration of her would have meant an acceptance of beliefs and attitudes which I considered a threat to my existence. Her belief in motherhood, so strong that in Paris when my life was in danger, she felt the child should have been saved even at the cost of my life, and would not listen to medical explanations that a child would always be strangled by old adhesions. My mother wanted me to be someone other than the woman I was. She was shocked when I defended D. H. Lawrence. She disliked my artist friends. She wanted me to be as she had been, essentially maternal. While she was alive, she threatened my aspiration to escape the servitudes of women. Very early I was determined not to be like her but like the women who had enchanted and seduced my father, the mistresses who lured him away from us.

When did I first feel this? When did I repudiate the model of my mother and decide not to be a wife or a mother but a mistress? In spite of this I did inherit from her a strong protective instinct toward human beings. But I also cultivated what would give men not only their down-to-earth needs, but euphoria, ecstasy, pleasure, delight.

When she died I remembered only her courage. Her beautiful voice which was a balm, her care.

During her life she condemned my freedom. She often harked back to the lovely, submissive child I once was, and frowned upon what I had become.

It was not the loss of my mother which reawakened my love for her, it was because my mother's disappearance removed the stigma of her judgments, the dangers and guilt brought about by her influence, and left me a simple human being no longer concerned with my own survival, but able to recognize her qualities.

During her life I fought her influence, and she fought in me the kind of women who had displaced her.

When she died I could recognize our similarities. She did not recognize a form of maternity in my protection of the weak and helpless.

As soon as she died my rebellion collapsed. She left me a sewing machine, a gold thimble, the diaries she had bound by hand in France. I became "possessed" by the spirit of my mother. It was my only way to maintain her alive within myself.

How wise the primitives were who retained their ritual of possession so they would know when it took place and also know how to exorcise it.

My aunt Antolina telephoned me today. She censured the entire family for not being present at the burial of my mother; but during her life they caused her much unhappiness by interfering with her, censured one aunt for being a Christian Scientist, censured all of us for going to live in other countries and not keeping the family together, praised Joaquin only for his goodness, not his music, me for my devotion to my mother, not for my work, upholding the family as a sacred unity which should never be broken, and ending with the reproach I have suffered since childhood, when I rebelled against the succession of family rituals, feast days, birthdays, arrivals and departures, weddings and baptisms, funerals and hospital visits, this huge Cuban clan, proliferating children and endless duties; as soon as I could I freed myself of all of them and became the "indifferent" one in the family.

Joaquin so pale, and this reawakened in me my past role as a substitute mother while my mother was working. I had to control my impulse to enclose, hold, and protect him, had to control acting as my mother. Had to remind myself he is forty-five years old, mature, and fully able to make his own decisions. Do parents never change their vision of us as helpless and inadequate? When I took care of my mother during her illness, and found so many ways to make her comfortable, when I massaged her, she turned to me naively and said: "I did not know you knew so much about caring for others."

Joaquin successfully reversed the roles as my mother grew older and dependent. He imposed his will on the household and assumed great responsibilities as Chairman of the Music Department at Berkeley. He handled her death, the problems of her funeral, his relationship to the whole family, his trip to Cuba, exceedingly well. He respected the taboos, the family customs, the religious rituals with perfect grace.

Joaquin has no anger. He has become a saint, a human and tolerant saint. He is returning to the house two weeks after mother's death. I would have delayed that. Death of a loved one is like a mutilation, a part of your body is torn from you, you die a little. And then following that, the spirit of the dead one enters into you, as if in this way you sustain his life, assure his continuity. I who had refused to iron and wash clothes long ago, washed and ironed Joaquin's shirts and felt myself becoming my mother. I took on her maternal virtues. But I also carry within me her defect, anger, and all my life I had to struggle against this anger.

Better than the cult of objects, better than the keeping of physical reminders is this moment when we cease to struggle against the parent's own image of us and accept our resemblances as part of our being.

In ancient mystic beliefs, the spirit of the dead entered a newborn child. Surely our parents give birth to us twice, the second time when they die, and as they die, in rebellion against death, we accept the legacy of their character traits.

Joaquin inherited my mother's wholeness, I my father's dualities. But Joaquin also proved that the only way to remain close to the parent is to become this ideal figure they desire: the respectful and devoted son, religious, who never loved anyone more than his mother. I tried this when I was eleven, twelve, thirteen, fourteen, fifteen, and almost up to my eighteenth year. I was the perfect daughter; I submerged my personality into the personality of my mother. She chose my dresses, and kept me at home when other young women were out working. I was lost in my submission to her. But my first rebellion came when I decided I could not bear the passive suffering of poverty and I insisted on going to work. My mother opposed that. A friend helped me to find work I could do (being untrained in any profession). I became an artist's model, joined the Model's Club, and began to earn money to help the family. I may have lost her love before that, when at sixteen I rebelled against Catholicism.

Notes

Text: *The Diary of Anaïs Nin, 1947-1955* (New York: Harcourt Brace Jovanovich, 1976), 174-84.

At the time of her death, Rosa Culmell de Nin lived with Joaquín Nin-Culmell at 5830 Clover Drive, Oakland, CA. He taught at the University of California, Berkeley. "*Tu n'est pas gentille*" means "You are not nice." Marius and Olive stories are jokes set in Marseilles, France. Arthur Schnitzler (also Schnizler) (1862-1931) was an Austrian novelist whose widow was Olga Gussmann (1882-1970), though they divorced in 1921. Gabriele d'Annunzio (1863-1938) was an Italian man of letters and politician. Enrique Granados's *Tonadillas al Estilo Antiguo* (1910) consists of compositions for voice and piano. Nin-Culmell and his mother lived in Williamstown, MA, from 1940 to 1950, while he taught at Williams College. In stating that her mother believed that Nin's fetus should be born even if Anaïs died, Nin refers to the 1934 pregnancy that she aborted in Paris. Antolina, Nin's aunt, is Antolina Culmell de Cárdenas, sister of Rosa Culmell de Nin. Juana Culmell, Nin's aunt and godmother, became a Christian Scientist.

‹§ *DIARY 6* ℥

(Summer 1965)
On publishing the diary

Context

This selection documents Nin's concerns about selling the diary, editing it in such a manner that Nin remains true to herself while not injuring others, and publishing it. The following year, the first volume of her diary was published.

◆ ◆ ◆ ◆

Summer, 1965. Having done the editing of the diary for the Kinsey Institute and then been faced with the disintegration of the Institute, the impulse to continue editing "for the future" kept me at work. Gradually I began to see how I could edit it for the present. I let others read the pages I had done, first hoping to find a home for the original diaries, then confiding in Swallow and Gunther. One activity would lead to another. The reactions encouraged me. But before I let Gunther show it to publishers there was a crisis.

It began with a nightmare: I opened my front door and was struck by mortal radiation.

I grew fearful, anxious. I went to talk with Dr. Bogner. We discussed each fear separately. The main fear was my concern with hurting others through my revelations. Having written the diary always with the conviction that no one would read it, I never censored myself. I wrote spontaneously. The only fragments I showed others were selected (I let Henry read his and June's portraits because he was anxious about what I was writing). So, there was the problem of the frankness of the portraits.

There was another dream: My mother (no longer alive) was reading the diary and was as shocked as she was when I wrote a book about D. H. Lawrence.

Another fear. As most critics had treated my novels so maliciously, what would they do with the diary?

Bogner pointed out that most of my fears were related to *past* experiences.

There was also the old guilt about sensual experiences. This taboo was my own.

Meanwhile, as if to confirm the old fears, several publishers wrote negative letters.

Joaquin was tolerant and understanding, noting only the different versions of the past which arise in every family. He reacted against my father's tendency to enhance and color his past. I employed legends and rumors which I never sought to confirm; Joaquin was cautious: "This was neither proved nor disproved." I, the fiction writer, opted for my father's embellishments. We reached a compromise.

Bogner stressed how all of us were deeply marked by events in the past in which parents or teachers appeared as *judges*. Childhood sexual games punished left a deep scar.

Suddenly it seemed to me I was exposing myself to the maliciousness of the world.

No. I would not publish it.

But another force, far stronger, was pushing me on—I had faith in the diary. I had put my most natural, most truthful writing in it. I was weary of secrecy, of showing only a small portion of my work. I felt the strongest and best of my work was there. I felt a maturity in the editing. I felt able to solve the problems. There was plenty of material so that what I could not publish would not be missed. I could avoid the blank spaces.

A driving faith urged me on. It was the vulnerable human being who trembled. But had I not always made these audacious leaps in spite of my fears? When I wrote the preface to *Tropic of Cancer* I risked losing everything, everyone who loved or protected me. It was an act of defiance and rebellion against the very world which sheltered me.

Dr. Bogner watched the struggle. She took the fears one by one and we considered them. What would be left if I took out the few phrases which distressed Henry? So much more! Those who asked not to be in the diary. I could not violate their wish. Some people have a horror of exposure. One by one we struggled with the human problems, the ethical problems. For example, I could not write about what was confessed to me during the five months that I acted as a therapist under Rank's supervision. Henry had never considered all this when he was working in Paris. His life was the theme of his work. He mocked my concerns. Yet today he is concerned about June and about his first wife. And in his letter to me, he protected his first daughter.

After each talk, the fact remained that there was so much richness of experience that the excisions did not matter. And people would read between the lines. It was not in my nature to be explicit in sexual matters because for me they were welded to feeling, to love, to all other intimacies. Explicitness destroyed the atmosphere, the secret beauty, the moonlight in which sensuality took place.

The ambivalent condition was painful. I wanted to give, to share. I could give and share myself, but as my life was entangled with others, I could not *give* their lives. They did not belong to me.

One main theme emerged: I had to act according to my own nature or else the diary itself would be destroyed. Others trusted me with their intimate life. If I betrayed this, I would no longer be Anaïs and the diary would end. It was in my nature anyway to bypass the destructive aspect of others and to relate to their creative or numinous aspects. That was my world.

Soon I began to see the fears as born out of the past—the eye over your shoulder, parent, teacher, therapist—as, for example, when Allendy forgot the therapist does not judge and he judged my artist life from the point of view of a bourgeois and a Marxist—I may not have listened to him but the judgment left its mark. America's puritanism, even though I did not believe in it, was expressed in all its criticism of writers. And the standard applied to women was truly a double standard, twice as strong!

So, Dr. Bogner, the world appears as a vast jungle full of dangers to one's vulnerability. I have to venture, not with a work of art separate from myself, but with myself, my body, my voice, my thoughts, all exposed.

Already, I had had to suffer from the concept that all diaries are narcissistic, that introspection is neurotic, when I knew that I overflowed with love of others and that introspection was the only way to accomplish the inner journey of self-creation.

Help me, Dr. Bogner. She is aware that I am reverting to the Catholic confession. Give me absolution. That would give me peace.

But she is too wise to re-enact a childhood conditioning. Her role is to show me there is no sin, no wrongdoing, just an artist obsessed with her portrayal of experience. Ever since I left Europe and the marvelous confessional talks (such as Henry and I had in Louveciennes), I felt the loneliness of Americans locked in their fear of intimacy with their secret self and therefore with others. I felt the need to publish the diary as strongly as the snake pushing out of its old skin, the crab desperately pushing out of his old shell grown too tight, too small. All evolution had this impulse. The impulse to give and the impulse to hide fought a mighty battle in this quiet office overlooking a garden. I would call it a battle between the woman and the creator. The woman, protective, secretive, placing the needs of others before her own, accustomed to her mysteries which man has feared; and the creator, no longer able to contain her discoveries, her knowledge, her experiences, her lucidities, her compiling of the hidden aspects of people so ardently pursued. Dr. Bogner, you won't just give me absolution in the old way and tell me that I have committed no crime. You want me to see that the fears are created by the past, that there is a possibility that this work is beyond such petty judgments, that it is beyond the personal. You, Anaïs, have to be as courageous now as you were while writing it. While writing it, no one looked over your shoulder; while writing it, your mother did not read it; or your father, who said D. H. Lawrence was all chaos and clumsy writing; the Irish priest who forbade your reading Zola and Gide was not reading it. You admired Henry for not having such concerns about the family reunion in Brooklyn he depicted so savagely. Your diary is mostly a work of love. You were primarily a lover. Let the woman lose her small personal fears. Let her dare to offer her creation and if necessary suffer the consequences. After all, the fear of being judged is a very minor one. Every artist had taken that risk.

Dr. Bogner sits so calm, so serene, so wise. The small, timorous concerns fall away. The main, mature objective becomes clear. I believed every word I wrote. They were written by another self. So let this self, the creator, face the world.

As I worked to bring all the fears to the surface, the mature writer accepted the challenge. I solved the problems of editing according to my own standards, my own ethics.

Notes

Text: *The Diary of Anaïs Nin, 1955-1966* (New York: Harcourt Brace Jovanovich, 1976), 378-81.

The Institute for Sex Research (Kinsey Institute) was interested in purchasing Nin's diary. Because the Institute did not buy it, Nin began reducing its size. Swallow is Alan Swallow; Gunther, Gunther Stuhlmann. Dr. Bogner is Inge Bogner (1910-1987), Nin's analyst. Henry is Henry Miller; June, June Miller. Joaquin is Joaquín Nin-Culmell. *Tropic of Cancer* (1934) is a novel by Henry Miller. Rank is Otto Rank. Henry Miller and his first wife, Beatrice Miller, had a daughter, Barbara Miller. Allendy is René Allendy. Zola is Émile Zola; Gide is the French author André Gide, who won the 1947 Nobel Prize in literature. Nin probably refers to Miller's reunion with family as depicted in his "Reunion in Brooklyn" (1944).

❧ *AN INTERVIEW WITH ANAÏS NIN* ☙

(March 1969)

Context

In this interview with Duane Schneider, Nin comments about writing, both fiction and non-fiction.

♦ ♦ ♦ ♦

INTERVIEWER: Does it bother you to discuss writing as it does some authors?

NIN: No. I do a great deal of talking about writing because the majority of my readers are students and writers.

INTERVIEWER: It is well known that one of your first pieces of sustained writing was the diary that you kept as a girl, since age eleven, I believe. And now, years later, you are seeing the diary through the press, coming back to them after writing short stories and novels. Do you have a sense of coming full circle, of returning where you began?

NIN: I feel that I am fusing two seemingly contradictory trends. I thought the fiction and diary were in opposition to each other; I thought they were split activities, and that one was even bad for the other, because, as Miller said, for fiction you have to wait until time lapses and go through a transformation with the material. And I was doing both. Now I feel at last they are unified and at peace with each other. They have influenced each other instead of being opposite activities. The fact that I write fiction helps me to write the diary better; the fact that I write the diary helps me to stay closer to reality.

INTERVIEWER: Did writing the diary lead you to write fiction?

NIN: No, I think the only thing that led me to writing fiction was what leads almost every novelist, the necessity for disguise. The problem of how to write about one's friends or one's self or one's relatives, I think, has driven people into the novel, don't you?

INTERVIEWER: Yes, I think so, and this is interesting in your case because there seem to be some clear connections between the published diaries and your fiction. There are characters in the diary who seem to correspond to those in the fiction. Is this true?

NIN: Yes, it is true. Some of them were even untransformed. For instance, the story "Birth" is taken literally from out of the diary. I made hardly any changes in it. Some of the characters usually go through some kind of composite transformation. For example, the portrait of my father is recognizable in "Winter of Artifice" but it is not altogether my father and the incidents are not written according to the diary. Some are and some are not.

INTERVIEWER: Do you find any contradiction in writing something as fact in the diary and then publishing it as a story, as fiction?

NIN: No. It seems like development in music. You might say that the diary plays on a theme very quietly and then the art of fiction develops it further; I expand, I try to see how far the imagination will carry me. The documentary is not enough. For example with the "Ragpickers" I did go and see the ragpickers, but what I say in the diary is not as interesting as the story.

INTERVIEWER: Do you still keep your diary?

NIN: Yes. It's very different now. It's almost a dialogue with other people. There are some people I am writing the diary to. More goes into letter writing than into the diary.

INTERVIEWER: You wrote once, "Under great pressure sometimes I dream a letter instead of writing." Does anything like that happen with the diary?

NIN: Yes. I think so. There are experiences I had intended to write, and I wrote in my head while I was walking in the streets. I kept writing as I walk the streets and never did the actual writing. One can never catch up.

INTERVIEWER: Do you have a standard, some way of determining what will and what will not be included in the published versions of the diary?

NIN: Yes, the standard is purely a human and personal one; there are things that I cannot publish until the death of certain people involved. The standard is not a literary one, whether I have written it well. I will go as far as I can without breaking certain reservations and taboos.

INTERVIEWER: It seems to me that I read some place that the published versions of the diary comprise about 10% of the real diary. Is that estimate correct?

NIN: I think that would be about it, yes.

INTERVIEWER: I suppose readers would be interested in those portions of the diary you feel you cannot publish now. Do you anticipate publishing them in the future?

NIN: I feel that what I left out was not essential. I did try to give all the richness of the relationships without certain personal revelations or intimacies. I feel that I've left out very little that will be important, that is really important.

INTERVIEWER: Do you feel that the critical reception to the published diaries was just?

NIN: Yes, very just. It was just as just as the reception of the novels was not, which led me for a while to think that I had failed as a novelist because I couldn't get the same critical estimate. Until the diaries came out for some reason the novels never received serious attention, what I call serious criticism—but now they have.

INTERVIEWER: How do you account for that?

NIN: I think I came too soon, I published too soon. I published in '46, which was a very bad period for my kind of writing, which was international and took its key from surrealism and psychoanalysis and poetry and French literature, in great part, although my first influence was D. H. Lawrence. I was typed as a very special coterie writer, and as you know these typings are sometimes fatal, and they continued to pursue me, so that the publishers always felt I had only a very small following. Then suddenly when the diaries came out, people were able to write to me and find me, and I connected with the young, through their interest in Eastern religions, in Hesse, and poetry and more imaginative literature. '46 was a very bad year for American literature. Today Professor [Wayne] McEvilly is making a study of the works from a Zen point of view.

INTERVIEWER: Would you call the published diaries art?

NIN: [Pause] Well, we would have to define art. I never thought of it as art, let me put it that way.

INTERVIEWER: Don't you believe that your diary is popular partly because of its literary value?

NIN: It's not enough, you mean, to have had interesting experiences, you have to be an artist? I agree with you because if I had not written fiction, and had not become a stylist, and had not studied writing, certainly the diary wouldn't have been as well written.

INTERVIEWER: Do you and Gunther Stuhlmann, through your editing, produce something radically different from the original?

NIN: No, because usually I wrote well the first time or not at all. In the diary I seem to have been so much at ease, so relaxed, that I never wrote badly really. There were some times when in editing I did leave out things that were a little diffuse, a little vague, or repetitious...usually what I left out was not the most important. In the diary you repeat a great deal.

INTERVIEWER: What do you think of Miller's statement that your diary will rank with those of Petronious, Abelard, St. Augustine, and others?

NIN: I can't answer that because the ones he mentions I never read.

INTERVIEWER: I believe you had plans long ago to publish the diary. What happened?

NIN: We talked once about doing the child diary in France. That's probably what you heard. And every now and then I would have a wish to see it out. I showed 600 pages to Maxwell Perkins. Is that what you were referring to?

INTERVIEWER: No. In Henry Miller's letters to you published by Putnam's he says that he is happy you have your own press because you will be able to publish your diary, which he admired so much.

NIN: He was always urging me to publish it.

INTERVIEWER: He was urging you to publish it more than you actually wished it to be published?

NIN: Yes, and I found myself always in a conflict—I was not ready to do the editing at that time. It requires objectivity, and perspective of time. Now I know what is important. But—could I give enough to be of interest while not being able to do the whole thing? That was the question in my mind which was answered when the first volume came.

INTERVIEWER: You felt once that the diary was a necessary and beneficial opiate for you during the 1930's. What happened during the '40's, and '50's, and '60's? Did your relationship to the diary stay the same?

NIN: No, I think the relationship to the diary changed. In the early diaries there is a distinct feeling of the ivory tower, the escape, the place where I could be truthful. And later on it changed in character. It became the diary of other people, the diary of others. More and more characters came into the diary and I painted them more fully, in a more rounded way, not only, say, in relation to myself, but I tried to go around the way that a fiction writer does, to go around a character. So the character of the diary did change.

INTERVIEWER: Why has the diary attracted so much attention? It is clearly more popular than anything you have written before.

NIN: Perhaps because our culture had put a taboo on what they call introspection and the growth of the self. And I broke this taboo. There was a great deal of writing about others and leading a collective life, but any attention you gave to your own world was sinful. And I think what I get mostly in the letters people write me is that this is a study of growth. And in very serious terms they can watch themselves. I always get letters from very young women or very interesting men. It is always the relation of the younger woman to the interesting man, the same as in the diary. And they are growing as women; they are trying to be women also in relation to the rest of the world.

INTERVIEWER: Do you describe an evolution in the diary, a development in your self that you believe is universal?

NIN: Yes, it is a record of growth, my growth, other people's growth, and the growth of the artists around me, but I did maintain always that if you yourself were not a sensitive instrument and aware, you couldn't record anything. First of all I had to be a person who could receive all these impressions. Some accuse me of narcissism and subjectivity. And I always answer, a narcissist does not relate to a thousand characters! I've written about a thousand characters; once I counted them in the diary! So this self is purely a way of relating to others and receiving what others have to tell you.

INTERVIEWER: What has been Gunther Stuhlmann's role in editing the diary?

NIN: He has been a wonderful editor for me because he is ultimately more objective than I can ever be. So when I have done the small editing, you might say, he has an over-all image—he helps me with the balance, with what is missing, with what is lacking. He has a great sense of structure and he has more objectivity. His criticism is very valuable and helps me a great deal, whereas I might get lost in the detailed work.

INTERVIEWER: Maybe we could change direction a bit. Could you describe your methods of composition? How does a story begin?

NIN: A story with me is very much like a poem; it's a line, one line, like a line of poem, or one image, or a theme, or a character. I can compare it almost to a musical theme. I develop it without knowing where I'm going, without knowing what incidents I'm going to bring in. It's almost like casting out a net. When I told the story of the *Collages*, for example, I had only the first line, that "Vienna was the city of statues." And I didn't know where I was going from there, any more than if one were writing a poem. And I began to collect all kinds of stories that this Viennese friend of mine had told me about herself. The theme is what attracts the characters and the incidents—the other way around from the real storyteller who first of all has a framework, a structure. It's a quest for meaning.

INTERVIEWER: Do you employ this kind of approach in writing your diary also?

NIN: Yes, I do, but sometimes it turns out more successfully in a story. For example, the "Ragpickers." When I went to visit the ragpickers I didn't think of them as having symbolic meaning. Then in the story—because you have a story only when you have a meaning—I suddenly realized "The Ragpickers" was really a story about trying to discard our past selves and past belongings, and we couldn't because the ragpickers picked them up and put them back there for sale. So in the story sometimes you can push a symbol further than you would in the diary. In the diary I wouldn't do that. You are satisfied with the recording of the facts in the diary. You cannot develop the symbolism.

INTERVIEWER: Why do you consistently place so much value on the unconscious in your writing?

NIN: Because I think that our social structure and our external world have created false selves, have made us behave according to certain configurations, and that the secret self very often hid itself below consciousness. We became social beings; we were regulated by certain mores, we became part of a group or a family or a situation, and this created a conventional self which sometimes was very far from our sincere self. And this is what attracted me to it. In the first place I always noticed about people how they felt rather than what they said, or what they did, or what they were in the world. I was very sensitive to how they were feeling.

INTERVIEWER: "Feeling" in what way, in what sense?

NIN: How their emotional life sometimes was a different thing from what they were representing from the mask, or the profession, or their behavior in the world, or the social behavior, or the class behavior. Have you read R. D. Laing who works in England? He speaks of the real relationship beginning only when we peel all these layers which society forces us to grow.

INTERVIEWER: But can't you find out a good deal about what a person is or how he feels by observing what he does in his leisure, what he does when he doesn't have to do anything? Doesn't this give an accurate indication of where his real interests lie?

NIN: No, I don't think it's enough because sometimes we're not aware of what our real interests are. They are varied. Some people do express themselves that way—something different from their profession, from their role in the world. But that is not enough. There is a great deal more going on. I think there is more going on in the subconscious than in our conscious self. That's why I became so interested in it. And the key—even the key to what the scientists are doing today is part of that legend, has another meaning.

INTERVIEWER: Have you consciously tried to explore and investigate the feminine point of view in your writing, or has this been exaggerated?

NIN: No, I think that was there. But I do feel that today with the knowledge of this non-rational self, which man has now, the distinctions between masculine and feminine are not to be so sharp. But woman, I think, because of her role in society, did not develop what I call a rationalization, philosophical rationalization, of her feelings. So she remained a little closer to nature, a little closer to her non-rational self, to her impulses in general. And she wasn't so susceptible to be taken into abstract ideas or to play a role: she remained much closer to nature, and in that sense that's the feminine part of the diary that everybody stresses, the one that is non-verbal, really, that has not acquired a historical, philosophical or ideological explanation of everything. And woman did remain closer to how she felt. Even in analysis the woman would say "I felt" and the man would say "I think."

INTERVIEWER: How has analysis affected your career?

NIN: First of all I submitted to it, and then I studied it, and then I practiced it, and I have retained an interest in it up to the present time. I'm interested now in R. D. Laing who has created such a sensation in London with his methods. The interest has remained, and I think I made that the basis of my work, the philosophical basis of my work. It was my touchstone.

INTERVIEWER: That seems to be quite explicit in all your writing.

NIN: I often judge writing as to whether it is psychologically true or untrue.

INTERVIEWER: Does that explain the appeal that writers like D. H. Lawrence and Proust have held for you, that they were psychologically oriented?

NIN: Yes, they were so concerned with awareness. I am more concerned with awareness. The Zens claim now that awareness is what one reaches by meditation. I was concerned with that in psychological terms—awareness of people's true feelings, which are masked by their talk.

INTERVIEWER: Do you consciously label yourself or your techniques as being surrealistic or belonging to some other particular school?

NIN: No, I really don't. I think I've used surrealism for flights, as I call them, as so many writers do. First I have what I call the real character and then I have what I call taking flights into the waking dream, the dream, or fantasy; that requires a different style and is not the simple telling of the factual story. I don't consider any particular label appropriate.

INTERVIEWER: What other writers have influenced you? Who have you learned from?

NIN: D. H. Lawrence, I think, was the first one, because he was always trying to express the language of the emotions, instinct, and intuition. He was always trying to tell us what intuition was, which was very difficult to describe. A young woman recently wrote a Master's thesis in social work and used my writing for the first time as an example of nonverbal communication. She meant that because of reading me she had become more observant of how people dress, of what they didn't say, how they felt about what they said, and the meaning of listening to their words, but watching everything else.

INTERVIEWER: What about Rimbaud?

NIN: I was very influenced by Rimbaud at the time when I was trying to write something outside of the diary, and I had only done the book on Lawrence. I read the *Illuminations* and then I saw a way of putting together the dream material I had been collecting; I had collected dreams. And I thought the imagery of dreams was wonderful and could be used, but before Rimbaud I was worried about the connecting links. When I read Rimbaud I felt suddenly free, and I could just have the images, and finally by accumulation they would acquire meaning.

INTERVIEWER: Many contemporary critics hold your writing in high esteem. Do you feel that your work has directly influenced other writers?

NIN: [Pause] No, I don't think I can trace a direct influence, sometimes it doesn't come out right away. It may come out a little later. Don't you think? It takes, sometimes, a whole generation.

INTERVIEWER: Yes, I think so, and sometimes influences are too subtle to be detected with assurance, stylistically or otherwise. Were there distinct stages of development in your writing?

NIN: That's a difficult question. I can think of various stages; one, of course, was the terrible struggle and the great difficulties of not knowing English, which makes one grapple with the language and work harder, and not take it for granted. It's a real learning of the language. That was one stage. And it was a very awkward stage, when I imitated everybody and couldn't find my own English. This was the problem. I had to find my own kind of English. The second step was that I wrote English resembling everyone; it didn't have any particular personality. And then the third stage was when I began to say things in my own way. At the beginning I used to be told, "Well, you can't say that in English." And that was always my defeat; "You can't say that in English," and I would say, "But why can't you say it?"

INTERVIEWER: Did you find out why? Or wasn't it true?

NIN: Well, there were conventional rules which I broke. And then there were some grammatical errors which I had to learn to avoid. But then there was also the creation of my own language, which ultimately I think I've reached. I was trying to use English to express how I felt and thought.

INTERVIEWER: Some say that your diction is exotic; do you have a theory of diction?

NIN: Diction! I will say about that that I am not conscious of any exoticism; I try to write the way I think. I wasn't born here and therefore I never picked up colloquial English, which Oliver Evans reproaches me with. When you're not born to use colloquial English, it would be very artificial to try. So I used my own English, and of course there may be a preference for the Latin origin of words rather than the Anglo-Saxon because of the knowledge of French and Spanish preceding that of English.

INTERVIEWER: What are the physical circumstances when you write?

NIN: Everything except the diary I write during the day. I write very long hours. Usually what doesn't come out well the first time I don't revise. I have great faith in that first spontaneous attempt. Usually what I write best I write in a few minutes. And then at night I write the diary. So the day is divided really into three parts, which consist of writing in the morning, fiction, editing the diary, and other work; then the correspondence during the afternoon; and then at night, when I'm relaxed and not controlled at all, I handwrite the diary.

INTERVIEWER: And you never write the diary during the daytime?

NIN: No.

INTERVIEWER: Do you write the diary in a ledger book or some other kind of bound volume?

NIN: I used to have notebooks, but now I have loose leaves because I can slip in the letters I receive, so that it's all a uniform looseleaf book, and I can put in letters, photographs, programs, and the whole story together with the pages of my diary.

INTERVIEWER: Are these pages eventually typed?

NIN: Yes, when I edit the diary I have to type them.

INTERVIEWER: But if you're not preparing a portion of the diary for publication?

NIN: Then it stays in hand-writing.

INTERVIEWER: Your prose is often poetic. Do you write poems?

NIN: No, I never did. I only wrote the prose poem *House of Incest*, which was really not a poem.

INTERVIEWER: How do you stay fresh and productive?

NIN: I guess by enthusiasm, by fervor. I'm terribly interested in whatever is happening. For example, now I'm going through a phase of interest in science. And it started with an astronomer, one of the most brilliant young astronomers out West, Eugene Epstein, inviting me to visit the radar station where they receive the messages from the stars. And then a scientist from Stanford, Dr. [Robert] Newcomb, is giving next fall a seminar on integrated circuits and my work. I've always thought there was a great deal of imagination in science but that it required some special knowledge, and I was a little shy of it; but now I've become very interested, in both the poetic and the metaphoric quality of it.

INTERVIEWER: As a person you've had a powerful effect on many people, Lawrence Durrell, Henry Miller, and others. When I once inquired about this you simply said that you were a good listener. But it must be something more than that. What is it that you provide that has interested and sustained other writers?

NIN: I can't analyze that. I know that it may have to do with what I call being in contact with myself, and this may put others in contact with themselves, which is the source of creation. And I know that after a few letters from me, they want to write, they want to work, and I don't know exactly why.

INTERVIEWER: Is this the awareness you were speaking of earlier?

NIN: It may be that, I don't know. I do know that I have that effect even on writers I've never met who begin a correspondence with me. They begin their book. They begin to flow, as they say. What unleashes that, I don't know. Do you remember D. H. Lawrence always talking about "flow?" You see, I have this flow, and I think it communicates itself to others, and then, I think, they're set in motion.

INTERVIEWER: And is there something that keeps you active, keeps you in motion?

NIN: Love of life.

INTERVIEWER: Much of this sounds like Blake. Do you read Blake?

NIN: I haven't read him for a long time, but you rediscover these things. I never read Zen, for example, until a friend of mine began to send me material, and then I find that in Zen awareness has to be shared. I had always thought that, that my secret for writing has to be shared, my flow has to be shared, whatever I discover has to be shared. And, of course, this is an influence; it would be like a teacher's influence. I was born of a family of teachers.

INTERVIEWER: Which do you think is your best work of fiction?

NIN: The two I think of that I couldn't change a word in are *Under a Glass Bell* and *House of Incest*. And shorter works, like *Collages*. I think I could have improved the novels.

INTERVIEWER: You did revise *Winter of Artifice* rather radically, didn't you?

NIN: Yes, I did, because that was my first novel.

INTERVIEWER: What was the problem with it?

NIN: Well, I didn't touch the first part of "Winter of Artifice" but the second part was my first novel which I later recast into *Ladders to Fire*. It was really my first novel, and came before "Winter of Artifice." I felt it was very badly done. The transitions were difficult for me. Because I didn't want to fill in as a novel is usually done, the transitions were very brusque. So I recast that for *Ladders to Fire* and it is all in that novel, recast and rewritten. The section titled "Winter of Artifice" and "The Voice" remained very much the same. The only one that was weak was the one in the middle, which became *Ladders to Fire*.

INTERVIEWER: Do you still write fiction?

NIN: Not at the moment.

INTERVIEWER: Why not?

NIN: Because I've too much to do on the diary. That's a fulltime job, editing. It's a tremendous job. It's a harder job than writing a book.

INTERVIEWER: Do you know how much of the diaries will be published?

NIN: That I don't know. I'll go as far as I can go.

INTERVIEWER: Volume III is to be published in fall of 1969. Are you working on a fourth volume now?

NIN: Yes.

INTERVIEWER: And what will it cover?

NIN: From 1944 to...I never know. When I reach a reasonable length I stop. If there is an especially good place, I stop.

INTERVIEWER: Do you have any plans for fiction in the future? Do you have any surprises for us?

NIN: I think that the diary is going to get better and be inclusive—the whole thing will be all-inclusive. There may be a third form born, of a diary that will also take flights. Do you think such a thing could be possible?

INTERVIEWER: I thought Volume I of the diary contained something like that.

NIN: I think someday there may not be a distinction made between them. I think we're awfully tired of the novel, as such. We're getting so close to what I call psychological reality that we're not going to want the fiction unless it enhances something that we know is genuine. A documentary.

INTERVIEWER: Do you plan to experiment with other genres?

NIN: My main interest now is the filming of the work. I'm enormously interested in films.

INTERVIEWER: What hand will you have in the filming of your novel, *A Spy in the House of Love*?

NIN: They let me write the script with the director. I would love to do *Collages* as a Fellini film, a very impromptu happening type of thing. I really could go into film-making. I love it so much.

INTERVIEWER: You have done something in mixed-media recently, haven't you?

NIN: No, but I wanted to. Are you referring to the light show?

INTERVIEWER: Yes.

NIN: I had put together a light show with costumes by a friend of mine, Rachel Chodorov. But then UCLA didn't have the funds to carry it out.

INTERVIEWER: You seem to be sensitive to contemporary literature, both in this country and in Europe. Are there particular developments in modern fiction that you find especially interesting?

NIN: Yes, for example Marguerite Young's *Miss MacIntosh, My Darling*. I think it ushered in—or strengthened—the imaginative trend in American literature, which had been somewhat subdued by the journalistic trend. And I think it showed how close the imaginative work is to surrealism. I think there is a great deal of surrealism in American literature in its widest sense. That's why I wrote about so many of the writers. She is my favorite. So is Julio Cortazar. His story was used by Antonioni in "Blow-up." He also wrote *Hop Scotch*, and *The Winner*.

INTERVIEWER: Do you like everything that's happening in France?

NIN: I think they are very experimental and they have always had the cult of the original. I don't care for Le Clezio, Butor, Sarraute, or Robbe-Grillet. I do love Marguerite Duras. But on the American scene there is a great deal happening. All the writers I have written about—in *The Novel of the Future* and the expanded-consciousness writers, as I call them, such as Daniel Stern, William Goyen and others.

INTERVIEWER: What do you think you will be remembered for? What would you like to be remembered for?

NIN: [Laughing] I can't answer that!

INTERVIEWER: In your literary career what have been your greatest disappointments and your greatest satisfactions?

NIN: My greatest disappointment—my only disappointment—has been time, that it took so long, from '46 to now. Now I am really enjoying a sense of connection with other writers. But I can't tell you what exactly I'm going to be remembered for, if at all.

INTERVIEWER: I suppose your popularity has brought with it some things you wish it hadn't.

NIN: Yes, the problem I have now is which letters to answer and which not to answer, which correspondents are going to be very important friends and which are not; it's interesting; it's very difficult to tell, from a letter. I try to understand whether this is someone I want to answer, and I try to answer all the letters.

INTERVIEWER: So what do you do?

NIN: I make mistakes! And I also make great friendships.

INTERVIEWER: Do you mind talking about the Paris coterie, the group that included yourself, Miller, Durrell and others?

NIN: I've written so much about it! It's in the past.

INTERVIEWER: Perhaps I bring up Miller too frequently. It was his enthusiasm for your work that led me to read you. But this coterie is interesting because three major writers evolved from it.

NIN: We certainly had no intimation whatever of being meaningful except to each other. Also, at the same time, we were a very disparate group. You can't say that we were alike. I think there are tremendous differences between Durrell and Miller and myself.

INTERVIEWER: And there were others in the group who did not become well-known writers at all.

NIN: That's true. The strange thing is that we did come together, but not on the basis of sameness; we had a respect for each other. And if you remember, in the diary I speak of the three directions we're going to take—I took one direction, Durrell took a different direction, and so did Miller. And I know that we had no feeling at all about the future. The attraction was the friendship, which encouraged us through very difficult moments. Certainly I was not a good writer at the time. When I met Miller I had just written the book on Lawrence. He had written two novels which were very different from *Tropic of Cancer*, which you would never believe were written by him. We had not found our voices. Miller was the oldest and he began quite late to find what he wanted to do, how he wanted to write, his own voice, his own tone. And Durrell was much younger. At that time we sustained, inspired, encouraged and helped each other. But after a while we went in very different directions. After we left Paris, that was the end of the close-knit relationship. Very soon after that Henry went to live out West. He couldn't take New York. I stayed in New York. Durrell was in England, or Greece, I think. And I didn't correspond with Durrell.

INTERVIEWER: Did you read each other's material critically?

NIN: Oh yes, we were critical. Durrell sent *The Black Book* to Miller, and we both read it and commented on it. I commented on Henry's work, but not to flatter him; we were not kind to each other, not just saying, "Yes, it's wonderful." Henry was very critical, and helped me. We really were very honest and helpful. I had a difficult time when I first came to New York City because I didn't find that same thing with the writers. I don't know why, whether it was geographical, whether we didn't have the café life, or whatever the reason. I didn't find that kind of fraternity.

INTERVIEWER: But it didn't take you long to get into activity in this country. How long were you here before you bought your own press and started to publish?

NIN: Three years. The first year here I noticed there was a sort of lull in the diary; the transplanting didn't take. And that period of American history was so insular, shut off from Europe, closed off voluntarily, as if to say, "Now we can attend to our own growth," which was natural. It was a necessary period.

INTERVIEWER: So the psychology of the country was different from France.

NIN: Yes, it was the predominance of the political economic preoccupation. The European preoccupation was always the individual—the center is the individual, and then he acts upon the world. The American culture stated: "Forget yourself, you have no self." Part of that was English false modesty tradition, I think. You don't talk about yourself; you belong to a group. It is the group, a collective thing and this has many admirable elements, but I feel it was the cause of alienation later. We often talk about this with students— they are alienated from themselves. So we have that whole period of no relationship, no friendship, no closeness. How could you get close if you didn't know what you were getting close to? No intimacy. And that was the difference between the two cultures. Together in France we talked about our writing, our problems—everything was out, everything was open, everything was shared. It was intimate. And here there was this great impersonality. I went to parties with the writers and they talked mostly about politics and social questions, which was another kind of activity.

INTERVIEWER: So then you began printing your own work.

NIN: Yes, I wanted to be part of the literary life; I had no other way of being a part of it except by creating something of my own.

INTERVIEWER: If we might change direction, I'd like to ask you about a few other topics. Did you ever know Joyce?

NIN: I saw Joyce twice when he sang at the house of Stuart Gilbert; he had a beautiful voice, and he sang Welsh or Irish songs, I'm not sure which. I still remember the voice, a wonderful voice.

INTERVIEWER: Could you tell us a little more about those evenings?

NIN: Yes—there were just two evenings, both at the house of Stuart Gilbert who was a very important commentator on Joyce and his lifelong friend. Joyce came in, and instead of talking about literature—which he really did not like to do very much—he liked to sing. So he sang for us. I imagine they were Irish songs—very beautiful. And he had a beautiful voice. We talked very little; we were just having music; the two evenings were mostly music.

INTERVIEWER: What place in your life did some other writers hold? Is Pound anything to you?

NIN: No, I never felt close to Pound. There were some writers I would liked to have known. I wanted to be a friend of Djuna Barnes. *Nightwood* exerted a strong influence on me. I have had some enduring friendships with writers, but it seems to have been more kaleidoscopic. It's more like *la ronde*!

INTERVIEWER: Do the ancient classical writers have any place in your work?

NIN: Now we come to a very delicate subject. You know that I had no formal schooling, formal education. That may have been for better or for worse because it threw me into contemporary writing and reading only contemporary writers. I made use of that in focusing and concentrating on the present. Every few decades we have to rewrite certain books which we need. So that's a lack in me, but it's a lack that I made use of, like a painter who doesn't know academic drawing and becomes a modern painter. I have very little tie with the classical.

INTERVIEWER: Have you belonged to political organizations?

NIN: With regard to the question of politics, I felt that most of it was power politics and manipulation, and I never joined anything. There were activities that I felt sincerely I wanted to be a part of. Whatever was done for the Negroes, for example, I did participate in, and I worked for Eugene McCarthy, and even though I realized that power politics was stronger than all these movements, such as the movement for peace, I still have never given up struggling for them. But my philosophy is that if we have an individual integrity then somehow it will influence total history.

INTERVIEWER: Is this what you think Eugene McCarthy was trying to do?

NIN: Yes, and I think if the people had been mature enough, they would certainly have preferred that kind of leader.

INTERVIEWER: Let me clarify a question I asked earlier. When you and Gunther Stuhlmann edit the diary, do you re-structure or re-organize material? Do you alter it to make it cohere better?

NIN: No, I think I was very careful to keep the attitudes, the philosophy, the feelings, and the atmosphere of that time. The temptation, of course, is that one changes one's opinions. I was very true to everything. The cutting I did was really mostly repetitious passages; they were the weaker parts of the diary. There were not important ones. In a diary you repeat the way you sketch a person over and over again; if you were a painter you might sketch the same person over until you get a satisfactory sketch. Most of what we eliminated was unimportant—I never eliminated anything important.

INTERVIEWER: Let me cite a specific example of the kind of editing I was thinking of. Miller once wrote you a letter in 1938 that dealt in some detail with the early years of his life. But through your editing the letter was included in the typescript of the diary that covered the year 1931.

NIN: I think I know what happened then. Later I wanted to give the background of Henry's childhood, and I felt that he had done it better than I did, and I think that is why I placed that letter there. So I let him speak for himself, feeling that he told it better and that it was more factual than the way I had told it in the diary. When I looked at it again—we did this together, Miller and I—we looked at it and mine was as good as memory will record it, but it didn't have the authenticity of this letter, I found.

INTERVIEWER: And when it came to editing the diary, and there are portions that deal with Miller along with you, he looks at these portions too?

NIN: Yes.

INTERVIEWER: This seems like a good explanation. Putting the letter ahead seven years helped to establish the childhood of Miller.

NIN: Right. You see, in the diary occasionally that kind of thing happens, and that's where the editing comes in. In the diary if you begin anywhere you assume that people know what comes before; but I found that some of the things were not explained. I placed the description of the house at the beginning also, although it came later. Because in the diary you are not worrying about setting up anything. Those are things of editing that were important.

INTERVIEWER: In yesterday's portion of the interview you referred to yourself as an international writer—what did you mean by that?

NIN: We speak of folk music as against classical music. I meant that there is a kind of writer that is not local or regional doesn't belong to any particular country. His work transcends nationality. And I think because I straddled two cultures and was made up of different trends—just as American literature is made up of various trends and not all Anglo-Saxon—that is a sort of writer that I would call international, that goes beyond the national characteristics.

INTERVIEWER: In what way?

NIN: Well, there are some American writers that you say definitely belong to regional America and have never been out of it and could never write about anything but the American scene. And then there are some writers who go beyond that, who go into a bigger world, such as Nabokov, or Marguerite Young, who goes into a metaphysical world which is universal. There are universal writers and then there are strictly American writers, native and typical American writers. Do you agree?

INTERVIEWER: I was wondering how this manifests itself, how you tell. It couldn't be just subject matter because Marguerite Young and others deal with American subjects. Yet you call her international.

NIN: Yes. I think the metaphysical quality makes it universal. This I will define the way Jung did: that there is an individual unconscious and then there is a universal unconscious. When a writer is great enough, like Dostoyevsky, he becomes a universal writer. But there has to be the metaphysical quality. If he is very local, I am thinking of a Sinclair Lewis or some very strictly American writer, then he doesn't have this meaning for the entire world.

INTERVIEWER: What other writers have you been closely associated with besides your friends in Paris?

NIN: Well, I tried very hard when I came to have very close associations with writers here, but the whole life in America doesn't lend itself to that. There isn't any leisure, and there were no cafés at the time. And there was no meeting place, and very little time for this kind of association. I found that people were moving and shifting, and they were not very good letter writers. They were not even very good conversationalists; they didn't really enjoy sitting and talking. I miss certain things about the period in Paris. I miss the fraternity and the friendships which the life in Paris made important. And the opportunities for meeting in Paris were easier. You see, it's different if all the writers are living in one city; here they are scattered all over the United States. And I miss the friendships and the talent for friendships, and the time, the devotion to it.

INTERVIEWER: Did you find these problems to exist generally in the United States?

NIN: The writers I know are scattered all over the United States and we can become friends and meet perhaps once a year, and correspond. The only person I've had a very close association with as a writer is Marguerite Young, who was reading me entire sections of *MacIntosh* over the telephone when she was finishing it. And she reads everything I write and I read everything of hers. And very often I speak to her students and they think that there is a collusion between us because we teach the same thing. She teaches exactly the same way that I would.

INTERVIEWER: Do you have a sense of humor?

NIN: [Laughs, obviously surprised at the question] That's something that you have to answer. Oliver Evans didn't understand what I call my own kind of humor. That's something that I can't answer; you'll have to answer that. I think that the *Diary* is humorous; I think *Collages* is humorous, and I think Oliver Evans didn't get any of it. Critics who say you have no humor are usually the ones who show no humor in their appreciation of it. Isn't that true?

INTERVIEWER: Possibly.

NIN: He didn't understand any of the playful parts of the *Diary* at all. I don't think I have what is called humor in the American sense. I have playfulness, and fantasy. But my humor is quieter—it's more like the Japanese. I don't like farce, broad humor.

INTERVIEWER: I was going to ask you this earlier, but it didn't seem to fit. Can you explain why the Japanese are fond of your writing?

NIN: Oh yes, I can explain it very well. I realized that when I went there, when they invited me over, and I began to study Japanese literature, I could see the affinities because I began to read everything that has been translated. They stress the same things I stress; they stress atmosphere and mood, and they stop, they meditate, they give aesthetics and the surroundings, and they're more interested in that than they are in action; they are more interested in what they call states, states of mind, moods, feelings, much more introspective than the American novelist, so it was obvious that there was an affinity. And their humor is very subdued, speaking of humor—like mine, and they understood that. Little things, little details, not broad and farcical, not the big comic spirit, say, of Miller, or the comic spirit of Marguerite Young. Quite different from mine.

INTERVIEWER: You travel a great deal. Is your traveling connected to your writing?

NIN: I was always very curious about places that I haven't seen. It was in connection with my writing, that I was invited to go to Japan, and that I am invited now to go to the Book Fair in Germany because they like the diary. But I've always loved traveling. I remember when I was in an airplane that caught fire once, all I could think of was, "I haven't seen Bangkok yet."

INTERVIEWER: How did Alan Swallow come to publish you?

NIN: This happened when Dutton and Duell, Sloan and Pearce gave me up, and the books were going out of print. I was getting letters requesting the books, saying they couldn't find the books. I began first of all by offsetting the books and answering the demand for them, just privately. I just kept them alive. All I wanted to do was to keep them available for the people who wanted them. But then that didn't work because it took a great deal of my time, so I once wrote to Swallow. I had heard that he had his own printing press in his garage, that he was an independent, and that he published only what he liked—that he was one of the last idealists in publishing. And he not only answered that he would distribute the books that I had, but said that he would take them all up, all of them, unquestionably, and he kept them in print until he died. I owe him everything, and I have said so in an anthology soon to be edited by William Claire. I have never met any publisher like Swallow. He was self-educated. He read books while he was working. A wonderful man.

INTERVIEWER: Has Frances Steloff of the Gotham Book Mart been a close friend of yours?

NIN: Yes, a very good friend over many years. She became a friend when I first wrote to her—when we thought war was coming I wrote to her—that I had copies of *House of Incest* and I would like to send them to her so they would be safe. And she immediately said yes, without knowing, I think, what the book was. She was really very friendly and hospitable to writers in a very far-out way, without knowing exactly who they were. She gambled. So I sent the books to her—she already had my book on Lawrence—and I was very grateful, and she was one of the first persons I went to see in New York when I came. I always went to her bookshop; I was always welcome. And she loaned me the money for the printing press; she took the first books; she introduced the books to Edmund Wilson; she played a very important role.

Notes

Text: *An Interview with Anais Nin* (Athens, OH: Duane Schneider, 1970). Miller is Henry Miller. By "Ragpickers," Nin means the story "Ragtime." Hesse is Hermann Hesse (1877-1962), a German-Swiss writer whose novels include *Siddhartha* (1922) and *Steppenwolf* (1927). McEvilly is Wayne McEvilly (1937-), who wrote an essay about *Seduction of the Minotaur* that Nin used as an afterword to the novel, beginning with the fourth printing of the Swallow edition. Petronius (ca. 27-ca. 66), advisor to the Roman emperor Nero (37-68), is best known as the author of *Satyricon*. Peter Abélard (1079-1142), lover of Héloïse, was a significant logician and theologian; Miller probably refers to Abélard's *Historia Calamitatum*. St. Augustine of Hippo (354-430) was a major theologian who is known for his *Confessiones*. Maxwell Perkins (1884-1947) was the foremost American literary editor of the twentieth century. R. D. Laing (1927-1989) was a Scottish psychiatrist who thought that feelings are descriptions of real experiences. Proust is Marcel Proust. Rimbaud is the poet Arthur Rimbaud (1854-1891), a founder of the French symbolist movement and author of prose poems published as *Les Illuminations* (1886). As a radio astronomer for the Aerospace Corporation, Eugene Epstein (1934-) studied, among other things, radio emissions from quasars. At Stanford University in 1969, Robert W. Newcomb (1933-) taught a course titled "Anaïs Nin, Integrated Circuits, and the Poetics of Science." In *The Diary of Anaïs Nin, 1966-1974*, Nin writes about visiting the class. Blake is William Blake (1757-1827), English poet and artist perhaps best known for his *Songs of Innocence* (1789) and *Songs of Experience* (1794). The planned movie of *A Spy in the House of Love* was not made, nor was one made of *Collages*. Fellini is the Italian film director Federico Fellini (1920-1993), whose movies include *La Dolce Vita* (1960), *8½* (1963), and *Juliet of the Spirits* (1965). Rachel Chodorov (1934-) is an artist who paints figuratively. Marguerite Young (1908-1995) was an American author of poetry and prose; Nin championed her novel *Miss MacIntosh, My Darling* (1965). Julio Cortázar (1914-1984), from Argentina (though born in Belgium), wrote influential fiction. Antonioni is Michelangelo Antonioni (1912-2007), an Italian film director who based *Blow-Up* (1966) on Cortázar's "Las Babas del Diablo" (1959). A French author of novels, stories, essays, children's books, and more, Jean-Marie Gustave Le Clézio (1940-) was awarded the 2008 Nobel Prize in literature. Michel Butor (1926-) is a French writer known for his criticism, essays, and novels, including *La Modification* (1957). Born in Russia, Nathalie Sarraute (1900-1999) was a French literary critic and novelist; her works include *Portrait d'un inconnu* (1948) and *L'Ère du soupçon* (1956). Alain Robbe-Grillet (1922-2008) and Marguerite Duras (1914-1996) were French writers and filmmakers; he is perhaps best known for the novel *Le Voyer* (1955), while her novel *L'Amant* (1984) gained considerable popularity. Butor, Sarraute, and Robbe-Grillet were among the major figures in the nouveau roman movement of the 1950s; Duras was associated with the group. Among other works of fiction, Daniel Stern (1928-2007) wrote *The Suicide Academy* (1968), the 1985 reprint of which includes Nin's review of the novel as an introduction. William Goyen (1915-1983) was a novelist and short-story writer admired by Nin; he reviewed her *Collages* in *The New York Times Book Review* (29 November 1964). Durrell is Lawrence Durrell. Joyce is James Joyce. Stuart Gilbert (1883-1969) was a translator and scholar whose books include *James Joyce's "Ulysses"* (1930); he was the first person to review Nin's fiction (1936). Pound is Ezra Pound (1885-1972), one of the most important figures in literary modernism. Djuna Barnes (1892-1982) was a modernist writer whose major work is *Nightwood* (1936); Nin used Barnes's first name for one of the recurring figures in her fiction. Eugene McCarthy (1916-2005) was a senator from Minnesota who sought the Democratic nomination for president in 1968, but lost it to Hubert Humphrey. Nabokov is Vladimir Nabokov (1899-1977), a Russian-born fiction writer who lived in the United States from 1940 to 1961, and then in Switzerland; his most famous novel is *Lolita* (1955). Jung is Carl Jung (1875-1961), a Swiss psychiatrist who formulated several concepts, including that of the collective unconscious. Dostoyevsky is Fyodor Dostoyevsky (1821-1881), Russian author of such novels as *Crime and Punishment* (1866), *The Idiot* (1869), and *The Brothers Karamazov* (1881). Sinclair Lewis (1885-1951) wrote, among other novels, *Main Street* (1920), *Babbitt* (1922), and *Elmer Gantry* (1927); he was awarded the 1930 Nobel Prize in literature. William F. Claire (1935-) edited *Publishing in the West: Alan Swallow* (1974), which includes Nin's "Alan Swallow." Frances Steloff (1887-1989) established the Gotham Book Mart in 1920 and owned it until 1967, though she remained involved with it.

&#x3; *DIARY 7*

Context

Here, Nin offers specific information about her writing and editing processes.

♦ ♦ ♦ ♦

Fall, 1969. My publisher asked me to write a few pages on the problems of editing the Diary:

When I began editing the Diary, I was faced with problems which are not solved by ambiguous legal definitions. An editor must ultimately set his own rules.

The law speaks of damage, but how do you tell the truth without injuring the lives of others, and how do you define injury when this damage varies with each person portrayed, with each situation, with each period of time? We had to study each case separately. If the person was alive we consulted with him. The law entitles a living person to excise himself completely from the Diary or to erase damaging lines. We had remarkably few characters bowing out and very few erasures. I believe this was due to the basic motivation of my portraits. I am concerned with *understanding*, with knowing, exploring, rather than with judgments. I made the portraits very full, in depth as well as in range, allowed everyone to speak for himself by way of letters and conversations. In the end, all the elements are there and a balance is achieved, which is an approximation of justice. If a man is big enough he can support his frailties. I was faithful to motivations. I never began with an intent to caricature, to mock, to judge or to distort. But I did not glamorize or retouch either. It was the basic intent to understand which guided the selections and made the ultimate portrait acceptable.

When I dramatized Dr. [Rene] Allendy's limitations as a psychoanalyst, I also made it clear that this limitation was only in relation to me, as an artist. I included his own revelations about his personal difficulties, a description of his positive achievements, his pioneer work in the French courts (he was the first one to bring psychoanalysis as a factor in the trial of a criminal), his role in the exploration of new ideas. It shocked me when someone said I should have turned in anger against Dr. Allendy. What right had I to judge him only because of his error in my case when I understood his personal traumas, the origin of his fallacies, and I knew his contribution in other fields?

A personality only emerges truthfully when all aspects are included. Everyone has an image of himself which conflicts with the image held by others. People have been shocked to hear their voices on tape; it is never the voice they imagined they had. They have been shocked to see their faces for the first time on film. How much more shocked they are by others' portraits. But if these are made without intent to damage, they are usually not damaging. It is possible to tell the truth without committing character assassination if one's motive is not to ridicule or disparage. The desire to be faithful has to be stronger than the desire to expose faults.

Truth remains relative, but a knowledge of psychoanalysis helps to reveal motivations. A listing of incidents and anecdotes does not add up to a faithful portrait, but familiarity with the inner man gives the key to his acts, which is more important. To study a person in depth is more important than to catalogue his actions. If one is deaf to the vulnerabilities of a human being, one also has no ear for the more subtle recording of his sensitive wavelengths. Giving all the facts, all the incidents, all the anecdotes, rather than a meaningful selection of them in order of their importance and accompanied by clarification, very often leads to a petty, shrunken portrait. If a full psychological portrait is given, and if it is accurate enough, one can infer the rest, fill in, read between the lines, as with a close friend, or a member of one's family. To seize upon the basic, essential lines of a character is more important than details. Nothing essential to a portrait was left out of the Diary.

Sacking and invading privacy belongs to war, not peace. Anyone filled with aggression, hostility and venom makes a very poor portraitist and reveals more about himself than about others, for people intuitively rarely disclose themselves to the enemy. Insensitivity usually causes a human being to lock up his secrets.

The portrait of the diarist has to be included as well, to balance as indicator, receptor, barometer. "I am a camera." You, the reader, have the right to know the brand, range, quality of the diarist-camera. For the Diary's truth is ultimately an alchemy of portrayer and portrayed. People relate to a presence. Many manifestations of the personality only bloom in the presence of love or friendship. More is revealed by interrelation than by so-called objectivity.

By objectivity I never meant impersonality. We learn more about others from relationships than from objective scrutiny. People only unmask themselves in the privacy of love or friendship. But such revelations impose noblesse oblige. One has to treat them with care to keep them alive and warm. A human being who reveals himself should be treated with the same care we accord to a unique discovery in science or nature. He is unique, and we may never see another like him. We must protect him from injury if we are to share his life. Only a long-lasting friendship will give a continuous portrait. To offend, insult, humiliate as some diarists do, is simply to cut all lines of communication with human beings.

I am not claiming that I have avoided all the pitfalls: I may have offended certain susceptibilities, because one cannot always know what they are. I have not changed anything in the Diary, only omitted, and the greater part of what was left out was repetition. Repetitions are inevitable in a diary, but they have to be eliminated. The very process of the diary resembles that of a painter making series of sketches each day in preparation for a final portrait. This portrait is made only by cumulative effect because the diary never ends. As the diarist does not know the future, he reaches no conclusion, no synthesis, which is an artificial product of the intellect. The Diary is true to becoming and to continuum. I could not make conclusions which even death does not make. The portrait of Dr. Otto Rank did not end with his death. I am making new discoveries about him, revising some of my opinions because of new information.

If the diarist has no humanity, no psychological insight, no ethics, the portrait will lack these dimensions too. It will read like a vivisection. Many portraits have been acts of hatred or revenge, others are so shallow that the characters pass like shadows with names pinned to their lapels. Some resemble the voodoo hexing ceremonies during which a vengeful native sticks pins in a doll as a substitute for the original.

I remind myself that as a diarist I can create a prejudiced view of my model. I once introduced a letter thus: "His war letter from a safe place was a monument of egotism." This statement was prejudicial to the defendant. I crossed it out and quoted the letter itself allowing the person to make his own portrait.

The solution to the negative consequences of truth lies in the fullness and richness of the portrait so that all sides are heard, all aspects considered, and in such organic development lies a possibility of balance.

The writer is not limited to painting one aspect of the personality. He is able to include all of them. The sum is achieved by completeness. A selection of the major traits takes the place of a petty accumulation of anecdotes, which may resemble snapshots taken by an unprofessional photographer when they are told without their proper interpretation or out of *Context*.

The destructive element of truth is neutralized by a deep probing into motivation which makes you understand a character beyond appearances. What is understood is not judged. Psychoanalysis was my invaluable teacher in the study of motivation and interpretation. Understanding creates compassion and suspends judgment.

Today we live by a savage code: that the life of one man is always to be sacrificed for the benefit of the many, that a public figure belongs to history, that we have a right to know all. But we never stop to realize that a great part of this curiosity has nothing to do with history or psychological progress, that it is often on a par with the curiosity of gossipers, and we must draw a boundary line indicating where respect for the life of a human being is more important than the satisfaction of a sensation-seeker.

Writers have given an example of ruthless invasion instead of a lesson in the creative possibilities of intimate portraits. This becomes very crucial in an age which is repudiating the disguises of the novel because it lives through TV and films, closer to actuality and the reality of personalities.

If our age is noted for alienation, it is largely because we treat each other without tact or sensitivity, because we have lost our faith in our confidants and can trust no one to deal humanely with the truth. Diarists have given examples of sniping, if not outright murder. Respect for the vulnerability of human beings is a necessary part of telling the truth, because no truth will be wrested from a callous vision or callous handling.

Notes

Text: *The Diary of Anaïs Nin, 1966-1974* (New York: Harcourt Brace Jovanovich, 1980), 107-10.

In 1969, the publisher of Nin's diary was Harcourt, Brace & World.

❧ *DIARY 7* ❧

(1975-1976)
Facing death

Context

Near the end of her life, Nin kept two diaries: "The Book of Music" and "The Book of Pain," which were intended to chronicle, from different perspectives, her dying. The following paragraphs, which concern music, were probably written during 1975 and 1976.

◆ ◆ ◆ ◆

My friend designed a very beautiful diary book, handmade, with soft Japanese rice paper and in gold on the red leather cover, my handwritten diary signature: *"Mon Journal—Anaïs Nin."* I was determined that no illness would be recorded in this diary. So I decided to make it a diary of music. I will only write in it when the musicians come, when I hear music. And it will be a separate part of my life.

The quartet is playing late Beethoven. The most continuous, unbroken, life-giving thread of my life has been love and music. Over the years there were always the deep rich tones of the viola and cello contrasting with the soaring, ethereal violins. There were always the waves of music to lift the ship away from dangerous reefs, icebergs, to keep the nerves vibrating, the being resonating, never lulled but pierced with arrows of gold. The blood transfusion of love is music. As I watch the quartet sway gently, all sorrows and tensions are transposed. Love and music make of dissonant fragments a symphonic whole. It is as if the strings strain away the dross. Sharp ends soften. Dreams float to the surface. Memories pulsate, each note is a color, each note is a voice, a new cell awakened. It stills other sounds, drowns the harsh ones, it erects spirals and new planets. When the heart acquires rough edges, music is the mute. When the heart freezes, music liquifies it. When it is lonely, secret notes will escape and find their way to the pulse, restore its universal rhythms. It is remote and gentle.

It sobs for you. It cries for you. It laments, it rejoices, it explodes with vigor and life. It never allows our body to die because every wish, every fantasy, breathes and moves as if we were in the place of our first birth, the ocean. The notes fly so much farther than words. There is no other way to reach the infinite.

In music I feel most deeply the passing of things. A note strikes. It evokes an image. But with another note, this image is altered, it moves, it fades, it passes slowly, it melts into another image. Images of beauty and sorrow pass thus before me and are carried away in the forward movement of music. The note that was struck, and vanished, carried away with its sound the things that are precious. It left, with its echoes, an echo of things that are gone. Between it and the other note that is coming, there is a space that holds a loss and an emptiness. Music holds the movements of life, the chained incidents which compose it, the eternal melting of one note before another to create song. The notes must melt before one another; they must be lost after they have given their soul, for the sake of the whole. It may be a beautiful note, but it cannot strike alone forever. It must pass, as all things must pass, to make up the immense composition that is life.

Dick Stoltzman, clarinetist, and Bill Douglas, pianist-composer, came to play for me. They played Bill's compositions and improvised. The tenderest, most lyrical music. Incredible people—unspoiled. Their music undulates tenderly, the waves of feeling ebbing and flowing like gentle tides. No harshness, no dissonance, no savagery of rock and roll. The sweetness of tropical climate, and outburst of joy, playful, wistful, without diffusion.

The pool is steaming like those pools in the mountains of Japan, everything through glass, through prisms, the amethyst water acquires a different dimension, it enlarges itself, its colors; it is so beautiful.

The musicians are playing the Schubert cello quintet—the long sweetness, tender accents, the wistful, lingering plaint and bursts of joy. Joy wins out. Every note is set dancing, starting gently, ending vigorously. Then the plaint again, the repetition of the longing, the tenderness, the heartbeat and a burst of ecstasy. The lyrical tones mingle with soft shadowy secrets—feelings are suspended—then burst open, step step step toward intensity. Always a reverie, gentle and in unison, and then a tempestuous meeting of all the instruments. Peace, serenity, storm and undercurrent of intensity. The intensity wins in harmony and in moments of repose, reverie. The lullaby sets you dreaming, you float on the tenderness, but a storm awakens you. Gently now, the violins, the viola, the cellos lull you, repeating your most secret wish, lulling, caressing, swinging on a hammock of silk. Then the inner fires of the world burst and burn and spill over. All the reveries are forced to hide—one does not hear them anymore. Then the instruments seem to mourn the early reverie and seek it again. Drops of water from the trees, gold sparkle on the sea, words of passion, caressing notes, all light and sorrow.

The quartet played Debussy. It unleashed a flood of tears. I did not want to die. This music was a parting from the world. Music was always the music of exile. There existed another world I had been exiled from, the possibility that music was an expression of a better world. That is why I am moved by the Peruvian flute, the conch shell of the Tahitians, by the music of Satie and Debussy, who were the most aware of that other world. Satie's music is nothing but nostalgia.

My attitude toward music was always nostalgic. Emotional. I was never cold or detached or intellectual about music. I never tried to explain the feeling of exile. I accepted the weeping.

I talked with Joaquin. I said that the cry of music may have meant sorrow over exile from another world, a better world. Yes, he knew about the new world lost to us, about exile and a lost land. Yes, he knew the longing. My father felt this. Joaquin mentioned at what times he wept.

Today I asked a remarkable man, my healer, Dr. Brugh Joy. He feels the same way. Yes, music indicates another place, a better place. This was the place from which we were exiled for some great punishment which the Catholics call "sin" and other religions "evil." But what I do not understand is that some evil, sadistic, cruel people do not seem to remember having lost such a place. Perhaps to them music is an undiscovered realm. But for us it enters the body, it fills the body. Brugh explained that the tears come from remembrance of that place. And we cry because we sense at last the return home. One should think of this place joyfully. Then if it follows death, it is a beautiful place. A lovely thing to look forward to—a promised land. So I shall die in music, into music, with music.

Notes

Text: *The Diary of Anaïs Nin, 1966-1974* (New York: Harcourt Brace Jovanovich, 1980), 339-42.

Beethoven is Ludwig van Beethoven (1770-1827), one of the most important classical composers. Richard L. Stoltzman (1942-) is a classical and jazz clarinetist. In addition to playing the piano and composing, Bill Douglas (1944-) plays the bassoon. Stoltzman and Douglas have had a long-term professional relationship. Nin refers to the swimming pool at the home she shared with Rupert Pole (1919-2006) at Silver Lake, East Hollywood, CA. During their marriage (1955-1966), which was annulled, she remained married to Hugh Guiler, who resided in New York. (Nin dedicated *Collages* to R. P., who is probably Pole.) Schubert is Franz Schubert (1797-1828), noted Austrian composer. Debussy is Claude Debussy (1862-1918), French romantic and modernist composer. Erik Satie (1866-1925) was a French composer who influenced other composers, including Debussy. Joaquin is Joaquín Nin-Culmell. Brugh Joy (1939-2009) wrote *Joy's Way: A Map for the Transformational Journey* (1978) and *Avalanche: Heretical Reflections on the Dark and the Light* (1990).

✂ ABOUT THE AUTHORS ✂

After publishing an article about D. H. Lawrence in 1930 and a book about him in 1932, **Anaïs Nin** (1903-1977) wrote primarily fiction until 1964, when her last novel, *Collages*, was published. She wrote *The House of Incest*, a prose-poem (1936), stories collected mainly in *Under a Glass Bell* (1944; enlarged, 1947; enlarged, 1948), novellas collected in *This Hunger* (1945), and a five-volume continuous novel consisting of *Ladders to Fire* (1946), *Children of the Albatross* (1947), *The Four-Chambered Heart* (1950), *A Spy in the House of Love* (1954), and *Solar Barque* (1958; enlarged as *Seduction of the Minotaur* [1961]). These novels were collected as *Cities of the Interior* (1959; enlarged, 1974). She gained commercial and critical success with the publication of the first volume of her diary (1966); to date, sixteen diary volumes have been published. Her most commercially successful books were published posthumously: erotica published as *Delta of Venus* (1977) and *Little Birds* (1979).

Benjamin Franklin V has written about Nin since the 1960s. His books include *Anaïs Nin: A Bibliography* (1973), *Anaïs Nin: An Introduction* (with Duane Schneider, 1979), *Recollections of Anaïs Nin* (1996), and *Anaïs Nin Character Dictionary and Index to Diary Excerpts* (2009). He has written numerous articles about Nin, as well as the introduction to the facsimile edition of her *The Winter of Artifice* (2007).

Benjamin Franklin V and Anaïs Nin, 1973
Photo: Jeanne Rockwell

A Selected List of In-Print Works by Anaïs Nin

D. H. Lawrence: An Unprofessional Study—Swallow/Ohio University (OU) Press

House of Incest—Swallow/OU Press

The Winter of Artifice (original edition)—Sky Blue Press

Winter of Artifice (revised edition)—Swallow/OU Press

Under a Glass Bell—Swallow/OU Press

Cities of the Interior (consisting of 5 novels)—Swallow/OU Press

> *Ladders to Fire*
>
> *Children of the Albatross*
>
> *The Four-Chambered Heart*
>
> *A Spy in the House of Love*
>
> *Seduction of the Minotaur*

Collages—Swallow/OU Press

The Novel of the Future—Swallow/OU Press

The Diary of Anaïs Nin (7 volumes)—Houghton Mifflin Harcourt (HMH)

The Early Diary of Anaïs Nin (4 volumes)—HMH

Henry and June: From the Unexpurgated Diary of Anaïs Nin—HMH

Incest: From "A Journal of Love"—HMH

Fire: From "A Journal of Love"—HMH

Nearer the Moon: From "A Journal of Love"—HMH

Mirages: The Unexpurgated Diary of Anaïs Nin
—Swallow/OU Press/Sky Blue Press

Delta of Venus—HMH

Little Birds—HMH

A Selected List of In-Print Works about Anaïs Nin

ANAIS: An International Journal, ed. Gunther Stuhlmann—Anaïs Nin Foundation

Anaïs Nin's Narratives, ed. Anne T. Salvatore—University Press of Florida

A Café in Space: The Anaïs Nin Literary Journal, ed. Paul Herron—Sky Blue Press

Barbara Kraft, *Anaïs Nin: The Last Days*—Sky Blue Press; Pegasus Books

Benjamin Franklin V, *Anaïs Nin Character Dictionary and Index to Diary Excerpts*—Sky Blue Press

Suzanne Nalbantian, *Aesthetic Autobiography: From Life to Art in Marcel Proust, James Joyce, Virginia Woolf, and Anaïs Nin*—Palgrave Macmillan

Recollections of Anaïs Nin by her Contemporaries, ed. Benjamin Franklin V—Ohio University Press

Diane Richard-Allerdyce, *Anaïs Nin and the Remaking of Self: Gender, Modernism, and Narrative Identity*—Northern Illinois University Press

Anaïs Nin Blog

http://anaisninblog.skybluepress.com

Made in the USA
Columbia, SC
03 July 2018